Journeys to the
Underworld and Heavenly
Realm in Ancient and
Medieval Literature

Journeys to the Underworld and Heavenly Realm in Ancient and Medieval Literature

John C. Stephens

McFarland & Company, Inc., Publishers
Jefferson, North Carolina

ISBN (print) 978-1-4766-7451-3 ∞
ISBN (ebook) 978-1-4766-3497-5

LIBRARY OF CONGRESS CATALOGUING DATA ARE AVAILABLE

BRITISH LIBRARY CATALOGUING DATA ARE AVAILABLE

© 2019 John C. Stephens All rights reserved

No part of this book may be reproduced or transmitted in any form or by any means, electronic or mechanical, including photocopying or recording, or by any information storage and retrieval system, without permission in writing from the publisher.

The front cover image is a watercolor of Charon in a boat with a pole on the River Styx: © 2019 Koval Oleksandr/Shutterstock

Printed in the United States of America

*McFarland & Company, Inc., Publishers
Box 611, Jefferson, North Carolina 28640
www.mcfarlandpub.com*

To my children—
Danica, Elizabeth and Christopher

*I too have been in the underworld, like Odysseus,
and I shall yet return there often....*
—Friedrich Nietzsche,
Mixed Opinions and Maxims, 1879

Table of Contents

Preface 1

Introduction 3

One. Ancient Cosmology 17

Two. Numinous Otherworldly Journeys 27

Three. Mystical Otherworldly Journeys 48

Four. Journeys of Spiritual Transformation 68

Five. Courageous Journeys in the Face of Death 92

Six. The Journey to Philosophic Wisdom 107

Seven. The Journey to Moral Awareness 123

Conclusion 149

Chapter Notes 157

Bibliography 167

Index 171

Preface

The belief in heaven and hell is one of the oldest and most widely disseminated spiritual concepts of human civilization. In the history of Western literature, spiritual beliefs concerning the existence of heaven and hell have been featured in a variety of narratives and have appeared in countless historical and religious contexts. This book examines a group of narratives originating in medieval Europe and the ancient Mediterranean world which describe journeys to the underworld and heavenly realm undertaken by both gods and mortals. Like many other mythological and religious stories of this type, many of these otherworldly journey narratives address a variety of spiritual subjects ranging from the nature of the cosmos, life on earth and the existence of the gods.[1]

Stories about journeys to the underworld and heavenly realm first began to appear in the Western world in the epic literature and mythological writings of the ancient Near East and Greco-Roman world. Stories of this kind continued to grow and develop through the ages. In classical times, tales of otherworldly journeys began to crop up in a variety of new literary contexts including Greco-Roman philosophical writings and other types of religious literature and poetry. During medieval times, otherworldly journeys of gods and mortal heroes continued to be popular themes in the mythological tales of the Germanic, Celtic and Norse peoples. Despite the vast geographic and temporal differences existing between the cultures of the ancient Near East, the Greco-Roman world and medieval Europe, the mythology of each of these cultures shares similar concerns regarding the nature of the "sacred cosmos" and humanity's relationship to the gods. As a result, the content of many of these stories is, by definition, religious in the sense that attention is drawn to the supernatural world of

Preface

the gods rather than mundane earthly life. Otherworldly journey narratives situate human existence in the context of a preternatural realm where miraculous occurrences that defy the laws of time and space are regular occurrences.

By letting the stories speak for themselves and by providing analysis of their contents, this book explores these fascinating narratives. Although a number of books have been written about the literary aspects of religious narratives, few books have sought to clarify the ways in which these narratives give expression to religious experience, which is the goal of this book. Many years ago, when I was a graduate student in the Department of Religious Studies at the University of California, Santa Barbara, my research centered upon the study of religious individuals of the ancient past. The product of this research was my book, *The Dreams and Visions of Aelius Aristides*. The current enterprise examines the ways in which religious experience became articulated in otherworldly journey narratives originating in the ancient West and early medieval Europe. It follows up on some of the themes and persons discussed in my prior book, *Ancient Mediterranean Religions: Myth, Ritual and Religious Experience*.[2] In the current book, many of the same primary sources are mentioned but they are discussed and interpreted in terms of the kinds of religious experience to which they give expression.

Otherworldly journey narratives continued to evolve through the ages. One aspect of their development was the way in which they articulated certain aspects of religious experience. Six categories of religious experience have been identified including numinous experience, mystical experience, the experience of spiritual transformation, the experience of courage in the face of death, the intellectual apprehension of the sacred, and lastly the experience of moral judgment before God. Each category of religious experience finds expression in certain ancient and medieval stories of otherworldly journeys. A variety of stories have been carefully selected for the purposes of illustrating the fundamental characteristics of one or more of the six kinds of religious experience. Highlighting the underpinnings of religious experience in these literary narratives helps to explain why these stories have continued to capture the imagination of many people throughout the ages.

Introduction

Why Learn About the Religious Traditions of the Past?

At the outset, it is worth considering the reasons why anyone would be interested in looking at and examining the contents of religious texts from the distant past. One way to justify such an activity would be to argue that numerous religious beliefs from the distant past continue to be influential in modern times. Hence, an inquiry into these past ideas might throw light on certain aspects of current spiritual thinking. Religious beliefs about heaven and hell, as well as other spiritual ideas, including the concept of God and the immortal soul, have appeared through the ages and continue to play a significant role even the present age.[1] In today's world, just as in ancient times, many Christians hold firm to the idea that a final judgment awaits human beings at the end of time. Although many modern spiritual beliefs and practices have ancient parallels and can be traced back to similar beliefs and rituals circulating in antiquity, nevertheless the exact details concerning their actual origin remains shrouded in obscurity. One can only speculate, but never know with any certitude, regarding the origin of many fundamental supernatural beliefs and practices, including the belief in heaven and hell. However, even though the origin of these age-old religious ideas and practices remains unknown, there is still much to learn by examining them. Learning about the primordial religious past helps to clarify many of the motivations of people living in the present.

The thoughts and feelings of individuals have always been important in shaping the events of history, even though it may be difficult, if not impossible, to identify the exact historical circumstances in which individual

Introduction

persons were involved in influencing those events. Human beings act largely because of their emotions, beliefs and opinions. Undoubtedly, at any point in history, including both in modern and ancient times, the actions and experiences of individual human beings exerted a significant influence in the development of many social, political and religious institutions. Similarly, in certain instances, various types of religious writings from the past, including otherworldly journey narratives, provide a doorway for understanding how people of previous generations understood and perceived the sacred world of the gods.

Even prior to the dawn of civilization, as early as the Stone Age, many prehistoric burial sites included material that can provide us with clues regarding the culture of the deceased's religious beliefs concerning the hereafter.[2] For example, inside the caves of Lascaux, France, a prehistoric religious sanctuary containing a burial crypt was discovered. Archeologists have dated this site to between 50,000 to 100,000 years old. Paintings of various Paleolithic hunting rituals are drawn on the cave walls nearby. Many animals that were important sources of food for archaic peoples appear in these paintings, including deer and bison. In one cave painting located at Trois Frères at Ariège, a human figure appears to be disguised as an animal. Archeologists and historians have given various interpretations of this mysterious figure. One plausible interpretation is that the drawing depicts a sorcerer or shaman, since the figure possesses a human face with animal features including wolf ears, lion claws, a horse's tail and the antlers of a stag. It is likely that the image represents some type of priest or shaman who could travel between the human world and the world of totem spirits. Such an interpretation is consistent with the archaic worldview that divided the cosmos into three levels: heaven, earth and the underworld.

In general, the precise meaning of prehistoric cave paintings is difficult to determine, but an additional examination of Neolithic burial sites reveals that archaic people shared similar types of religious beliefs about the afterlife with modern people. Archeological evidence indicates that in Neolithic times, great care was taken in the burial of the dead. Archaic people frequently buried the dead with the head of the deceased person facing east, suggesting a belief for rebirth into a different realm. In addition, various items of the deceased person were placed inside the graves.

Introduction

In one prehistoric grave site located at Monte Circeo, Italy, a skull surrounded by a ring of stones was discovered. In Bavaria, a collection of skulls that had been immersed in red ochre, a color that also appears in many prehistoric cave paintings, was unearthed. Perhaps the archeological evidence at this ancient site indicates there was some type of cult of skulls or worship of the dead. Although it is impossible to determine exactly what was the nature of the religious beliefs associated with these burial practices, burial customs such as these makes it seem likely that these people had some type of belief in the afterlife.

At some point in prehistorical times, supernatural beliefs, especially those concerning the existence of the soul and the afterlife, came into existence, but the actual historical circumstances surrounding their birth is unknown. Some historians of religion have suggested that the appearance of supernatural beliefs arose from certain powerful emotions experienced by prehistoric people in response to the death of loved ones.[3] Others have suggested that when prehistoric people witnessed the inexplicable forces of nature, they may have begun to speculate about the mysterious forces of the cosmos. The incredible power and force of storms may have also played an important part in the development of supernatural beliefs about gods who were regarded as the agents of unusual weather events. Another possibility was that when archaic people saw the sun, the moon, the stars and planets move across the sky, they may have developed beliefs about heavenly deities existing in the world above who were responsible for these astronomical events. Observing the changing of the seasons may have inspired early humans to speculate about the existence of deities living under the earth who were responsible for producing the fertility of the land and the annual death of vegetation.[4] The significance of these speculations and life experiences is that they may have served as one of the underlying sources for the development of religious beliefs and stories, including stories of otherworldly journeys.[5]

The Search for Religious Origins

In the 19th and early 20th century, a number of scholars tried to establish a connection between the origin of religion and its essence. It

Introduction

was believed that if one could identify the origin of religion in the distant past, then one could safely assume that the fundamental nature of religious phenomena had been discovered.

The 19th-century German scholar Max Müller claimed that mythology was the byproduct of an illogical attempt on the part of archaic humans to explain natural phenomena existing within their environment. Müller's comparison of various myths throughout the world led him to argue that each of the divinities, demons and bizarre creatures populating these stories represented natural phenomena in the immediate environment, such as the sun, the moon, the wind, fire, frost and the darkness of the winter night. Thor was reduced to being essentially the god of thunder. Other gods of mythology were equated with other natural phenomena such as rain and earthquakes. It soon became apparent that a deity's nature could not be summed up in a single trait originating in the environment. As a result, Müller's theory regarding the origin of religion has been discarded.

Following the efforts of Müller, other attempts to locate the origin and essence of religion were made in the field of anthropology. In the early 20th century, an important contribution was made by the Scottish social anthropologist Sir James Frazer, in his multi-volume work *The Golden Bough*.[6] Frazer observed that in many myths from around the world, a common pattern existed that involved deities labeled as the "dying and rising gods." In these myths, a dying male god and a female deity of vegetation and the harvest are closely linked together. The death and rebirth of the male god symbolized the annual cycle of nature in which plant life comes to an end in the wintertime only to be reborn in the spring. For example, in Egyptian religious mythology, Osiris, the god of the dead functions as the male consort of the Great Mother goddess Isis; similarly, in the mythology of Asia Minor, the male god Attis is linked with the Great Mother goddess Cybele. In *The Golden Bough* Frazer also proposed his evolutionary theory regarding humanity's social development. In the early stages of human history, people saw the world primarily in terms of magic. Eventually religion evolved out of magic and then science emerged out of religion. According to Frazer, mythology and folklore are remnants of a bygone era wherein humanity tried to explain the world in a misguided childlike way. According to Frazer, the primitive magician is really a misguided scientist who seeks to know about how the universe operates and how the forces of nature can be con-

Introduction

trolled. However, due to a lack of knowledge, the magician makes an intellectual mistake by believing that similarities on the surface between two or more different things indicates that a real causal connection exists between the objects. A similar type of intellectual mistake is made by the religious person. Just as the magician believes that the forces of nature can be controlled using magical spells and incantations, the religious person believes that only the gods possess supernatural power and that humans need to communicate their wishes to the gods through prayer and sacrifice.

Viewing religion as the product of an intellectual mistake tends to ignore the emotional component of religious behavior. After Frazer's time, the origin and essence of religion was frequently explained in terms of the emotional dimension of religion. In the early part of the 20th century, continued efforts to uncover the origin and essence of religion were made in the field of psychology and sociology. In *Totem and Taboo*, Sigmund Freud developed a theory on the origins of religion and mythology that was largely based upon his ideas regarding the Oedipus Complex.[7] Freud speculated that in prehistoric times, religion arose in a tribal setting because of the guilt generated from the primal murder of the father by his sons. Freud's ideas on religion, especially his theory on the origins of religion, have been almost entirely rejected by the scholarly community because of their lack of evidence and their speculative nature.

In *The Elementary Forms of the Religious Life*, Émile Durkheim conducted an inquiry into the sociological function of religion.[8] He argued that the belief in totem spirits represented the earliest type of religious expression, out of which all the other forms of religion have evolved. Unfortunately, totemism is found only in certain locations and falls far short of being a universal phenomenon. Hence, Durkheim's attempt to locate the origin of religion in totemism has been largely discredited within the scholarly community.

The 20th century German theologian and historian of religion Rudolf Otto defined the fundamental constituents of religion in experiential terms. In his most famous book, *The Idea of the Holy*, Otto found the essence of religion in peoples' apprehension of the holy.[9] Otto noted that almost all members of the major religious traditions of the world, past and present, express feelings of awe and wonder in the presence of the sacred. Otto used some interesting terms in his characterization of "the

Introduction

holy." When confronting the holy, one typically feels *mysterium fascinans* (a sense of awe and fascination) in the presence of *mysterium tremendum* (the awe-inspiring mystery of the divine). Experiencing the sacred is categorically different from other forms of human experience. The numinous world of the sacred is "wholly other" from the profane world of everyday experience. The psychological experience of the numinous serves as the foundation of Otto's definition of religion. According to Otto, religion originated as an emotional response to feelings of awe and wonder in the presence of the sacred. Unfortunately, Otto's attempt to define religion as a psychological phenomenon poses problems. On the one hand, it is uncertain whether a distinct religious emotion, as Otto wanted to suggest, exists.[10] Further, Otto's approach ignored the fact that sociohistorical variables other than psychological factors are involved in religious phenomena and that many of these factors are shrouded in the vagaries of history.

In the final analysis, the complexities of religious phenomena and the lack of solid historical evidence closes the door to those seeking to uncover the origins of religion in human history. Undoubtedly, the life experiences of prehistoric people played a role in their view of the world, including the development of religion, but too many ambiguities and uncertainties surround these issues to be able to definitively assign a single type of experience or event as the essential one for explaining the origin of religion. None of these past efforts to uncover the origin and essence of religion were successful. Rather than engaging in a futile search for religious origins, a more fruitful approach for understanding religious phenomena begins with a careful description of their contents.

Defining Myth and Religion

Even though it is impossible to determine the origin of religion, people are still interested in learning more about the religious traditions of the past and present. One essential step in this process is to define some important terms. Before a person can describe something, first they need to know what it is that they are describing. It has already become apparent that a variety of different meanings have been assigned to the term "religion." Obviously, this is an ambiguous word that needs to be clarified and defined.

Introduction

Another confusing word is "myth." Both "religion" and "myth" have been defined in many different ways and so their meanings remain unclear. The modern philosopher Ludwig Wittgenstein once pointed out that when seeking to define a term, it makes more sense to ask about how the word is used rather than trying to determine its meaning in isolation from its use.[11] In other words, the best way to define a term is to examine how it is commonly used in speech and writing. As far as defining the terms "religion" and "myth," clarification needs to be offered regarding how these terms are used in this book.

In this book, the term "religion" is used in conjunction with an interpretation of otherworldly journey narratives. Since these narratives are filled with fantastic symbolism and imagery, it makes sense to seek a definition of "religion" which emphasizes its symbolic connotations. One definition which appreciates the complex interconnectedness of religious symbol systems is offered by the anthropologist Clifford Geertz. According to Geertz, religion is:

> a system of symbols which acts to establish powerful, persuasive, and long-lasting moods and motivations in men by formulating conceptions of a general order of existence and clothing these conceptions with such an aura of factuality that the moods and motivations seem uniquely realistic.[12]

Geertz' definition of religion recognizes the symbolic nature of religion and is especially useful for the understanding of religious mythology and other genres of religious literature closely aligned with it. Another suitable definition of religion is provided by Peter Berger who defines religion as "the human enterprise by which a sacred cosmos is established. Put differently, religion is cosmization in a sacred mode."[13] Similarly, the historian of religion Mircea Eliade states that early nomadic hunters of prehistoric times and the first sedentary cultivators shared a similar religious outlook about the cosmos. Eliade states that both groups of people lived in a sacred cosmos and shared in:

> A cosmic sacrality manifested equally in the animal world and in the vegetable world. We need only compare their existential situations with that of a man of the modern societies, living in a de-sacralized cosmos, and we shall immediately be aware of all that separates him from them. At the same time, we realize the validity of comparisons between religious facts pertaining to different cultures; all these facts arise from a single type of behavior, that of homo religiosus.[14]

Introduction

Rather than define religion purely in terms of its historical or psychological origins, the noted British religious scholar Ninian Smart defines religion descriptively by breaking it into six distinct dimensions: the mythic dimension, the doctrinal dimension, the ritual dimension, the social dimension, the ethical dimension and the experiential dimension.[15] The value of Smart's approach to the study of religion is that it recognizes the multifaceted nature of religious phenomena in that it consists of several strands.

In this book, the term religion is defined as *a system of symbols consisting of myths, doctrines, rites, ethical ideas, social institutions and inner experiences all of which are related to the realm of the sacred cosmos.* Such a definition combines valuable elements found in the definitions of religion provided by Geertz, Berger, Eliade and Smart. Even though religion is highly symbolic in nature, supernatural beings and gods may not always lie at the core of a religious tradition. In many religions, a belief in God or other kinds of supernatural beings is not necessarily an essential ingredient. For example, Theravada Buddhism denies the existence of gods and yet no one would deny that it is a valid religious tradition.

When examining otherworldly journey narratives, a useful way of defining religion is to see it as a system of symbols since these writings are richly filled with a variety of complex religious motifs and imagery. Many stories of otherworldly journeys belong primarily to the mythic strand of religion. Seen from the vantage point of their proper religious context, stories of otherworldly journeys symbolically articulate a people's relationship to the sacred cosmos. The essential message of these texts is that a spiritual connectedness exists between humanity and the three cosmic realms, that is, the heavens, the earth and the underworld. The details of the connection between humanity and the gods are spelled out in these stories and need to be understood against the background of the specific religious tradition from which the story arose. For example, those stories of otherworldly journeys of the ancient Near Eastern world should be interpreted in terms of ancient Near Eastern religious institutions. Otherworldly narratives appearing in Greco-Roman culture need to be viewed in the context of Greco-Roman religious institutions. Stories of otherworld journeys in Germanic mythology should be interpreted against the background of Germanic culture and religion. However, this should not lead

Introduction

to the erroneous conclusion that similarities and parallels do not exist between two or more narratives originating from widely different historical or religious contexts. Since the three-fold view of the cosmos was commonly shared by various groups of people living in the ancient Near East, the Greco-Roman world and the Germanic world, it is not surprising that many similarities exist between various otherworldly narratives originating from different times and places.

Besides, the term "religion," another ambiguous word that needs to be clarified is "myth." Many mythological narratives provide descriptions of otherworldly journeys of gods and mortals, and much confusion surrounds the meaning of the term "myth." The classical Greek word *mythos* means "story," and in those times, the word was used to refer to the stories about the Greek gods. Over time, the meaning of the term has changed largely due to the rejection of the mythological perspective of the cosmos as well as the traditional religious outlook of classical Greek society. Both in pagan and Christian religious circles, the truthfulness of popular myths of Greek and Roman religion was largely dismissed. As a result, for many the term myth has come to mean "a lie" or something that is not true. Such an understanding of the term originated in antiquity, a time when myths came to be seen as nothing more than fictitious tales whose fanciful content was intended to provide mindless entertainment for naïve listeners.

Toward the latter half of the 5th century BCE, several philosophers and sophists developed arguments designed to show that the traditional gods of Greek mythology did not exist. Protagoras (490–420 BCE) claimed that in a world where everything could be explained materialistically, there was no need to believe in the Olympian gods. Humanity was the measure of all things. The gods and the religious conventions connected to them were just one aspect of the many creations of human society. Critas, the 4th century BCE poet, thought the Olympians were created to scare people into obeying the moral and legal prohibitions of society. Euphemerus, the 4th century BCE sophist claimed that originally, the gods were really humans who had subsequently been transformed into divinities. The Pre-Socratic philosopher Xenophanes (565–470 BCE) proposed that the mythic tales of the *Iliad* and *Odyssey* were absurd and silly, and that surely, myths should not be taken seriously since they have little connection to the real

Introduction

world. Skeptical thinkers such as Xenophanes soundly rejected the existence of Olympian gods and discarded the idea that there was anything of value in these superstitious tales. The stories of gods and heroes were nothing more than fables imbued with ignorance and superstition. Ultimately, putting one's faith in the Homeric pantheon should be discarded in favor of a life of reason and contemplation. Along these same lines of thinking, members of the Christian Church condemned Greco-Roman mythology and ritual practices as a shameless reflection of the rampant immorality of pagan civilization. Largely because of these arguments against Greco-Roman paganism, the term "myth" has come to be associated with the idea of falsehood and lies. In the words of W.R. Comstock, "the word 'myth' has become associated in the West with a set of pejorative connotations and is in popular speech almost a synonym for 'untrue,' 'false,' or 'absurdly fantastic.'"[16]

In distinction to the derogatory connotations associated with the word "myth," a less disparaging view of mythology is essential for developing an objective perspective on the subject. Myths tell sacred stories about events transpiring in the archaic past that provide the model or paradigm for some custom or some aspect of the human existence. In the words of the historian of religion Mircea Eliade,

> Myth narrates a sacred history; it relates an event that took place in primordial time, the fabled time of "beginnings." In other words, myth tells how, through the deeds of supernatural beings, a reality came into existence, be it the whole of reality, the Cosmos, or only a fragment of reality—an island, a species of plant, a particular kind of human behavior, an institution. Myth then is always an account of a creation; it relates how something was produced, began to be.[17]

Accordingly, the historian of religions Gerald Larson describes myth as:

> a narrative or collection of narratives about the gods or supernatural beings used by people-clan, tribe, or ethnic community—for the purposes of interpreting the meaning of their experience and their world, both individually and collectively[18]

Myths focus upon topics such as the creation of the world, the birth of the gods, the origin of death and the noble quest of heroes. In comparison to other types of stories such as legends and fables, mythology has a distinct social function. Just as some religions, such as Buddhism, do not believe in gods and goddesses, likewise some myths tell stories about deities, but other myths do not. Myths reveal certain things about the

Introduction

social structure of a community and the relationship between the human world and the divine realm. In doing so, myth "articulates the basic self-understanding of a people and thereby operates as a kind of charter for the total cultural life."[19] Myths often play a significant role in the religious life of a people by giving a symbolic expression to various spiritual actions. Elements of this relationship can also be identified in a variety of other types of religious behavior such as prayer, sacrifice and funerary practices. Hence, the term "myth" is defined in this book as *a story that clarifies humanity's relationship to the sacred cosmos.*

If a myth is defined in simple terms as "stories of the gods," then many stories describing underworld journeys and heavenly ascents qualify as examples of myth because many gods and goddesses appear in these stories. Further, otherworldly narratives have mythic significance because they explain humanity's relationship with the world of the gods, i.e., the "sacred cosmos." The assignment of human traits is one important element in many mythological portrayals of the gods. Anthropomorphism appears frequently in many mythic narratives such as *The Epic of Gilgamesh* and *The Odyssey*. In the archaic way of thinking, the human world was structured in the same way as the world of the gods; just as human society was governed by earthly rulers, similarly, the cosmos was controlled by the gods. The world of the gods duplicated the social structure of the human world and thus served to underscore the reciprocal nature of the relationship between the gods and human beings. Just as humans traveled by foot or horseback to various places on earth, likewise the ancient gods of Mesopotamia, Greece and Rome had the supernatural ability to travel throughout the three cosmic realms. Just as gods could go on underworld journeys, similarly, archaic cultural heroes such as Gilgamesh and Odysseus could engage in otherworldly journeys. In short, many of the underworld journeys of these mortal heroes parallel the divine journeys of the gods. Archaic stories about the heavenly and underworld journeys of the gods and mortal heroes upheld the three-fold model of the cosmos.

Pagan and Judeo-Christian stories of journeys to the underworld and heaven share the common desire to authenticate religious ideas and beliefs about the nature of the gods, the afterlife and the immortality of the soul. Theological ideas related to the existence of the afterlife and the immortality of the soul permeate ancient literature. Terms such as "the afterlife,"

Introduction

"the underworld" and "heaven" tend to be abstract and difficult to envision. As a result, stories were used to elucidate the meaning of these concepts. Mythical tales and vignettes related to marvelous journeys into the unknown realms of the cosmos provided a symbolic vehicle that gave shape to these religious ideas.

Throughout history, many individuals and religious institutions have insisted upon the existence of a supernatural realm lying beyond the world of the senses and have told stories to give substance to their beliefs. The sacred realm has been described in a variety of ways; frequently, it has been conceived as the home of the gods and other spiritual beings; likewise, it has been described as the place where souls go when a person dies. In both ancient and modern times, the subject of the afterlife and what happens to a person upon death has always been a popular subject. In modern parlance, the term "underworld" connotes something negative and uninviting and indeed many ancient underworld narratives speak of an inhospitable place under the earth where souls of deceased human beings would go upon death. However, in many ancient narratives, another lower region below the earth is described and it is filled with light and is the home of the gods. Many narratives suggest that souls judged to be worthy in the next life will go there. In these accounts, the dark and light sections of the underworld are adjacent to one another. For example, in the *Aeneid*, the lower realm is divided into different sections ranging from evil regions filled with doom and gloom to other more hospitable regions filled with light and joy.

An Overview of the Book

Given the pervasiveness of otherworldly narratives throughout the history of Western literature, this book in no way intends to present a comprehensive discussion of all the extant material. Only a representative sampling of ancient and medieval mythological, poetic and philosophical narratives that throw into sharp relief the modalities of spiritual awareness have been selected. The fact that the texts selected for discussion originate from various locations and historical epochs including ancient Greece, Rome and medieval Europe, illustrates an important point, namely, that

Introduction

the fundamental constituents of religious experience extend far beyond the boundaries of a single historical or cultural milieu.

In respect to the ancient period, the focus of the discussion is upon both pagan and Judeo-Christian literary material originating from the Near East and Greco-Roman world. In respect to the medieval period, the focal point is Norse and Anglo-Saxon mythological literature dating from the early period up until the 9th century CE, especially a few narratives originating in the context of pagan Europe. It should be noted that several ancient and medieval otherworldly journey narratives have been left out of the discussion. The ancient Greek story of Theseus' sojourn to Tartarus has been omitted. Likewise, the Babylonian goddess Bell's underworld journey is not considered. Several medieval stories are excluded from the discussion, including the Irish Cuchulain's underworld journey as well as the British narratives regarding the underworld journeys of Arthur, Gwydion and Amathaon. Material arising after the time of early Middle Ages, including those medieval Islamic narratives pertaining to Mohammad's night journey, are not included in this work.[20] Furthermore, although Dante's *Inferno* presents the classic narrative description of an underworld journey, it has been excluded from consideration because it was written in the late Middle Ages.

Following this introduction, the remaining chapters examine various primary sources that provide detailed descriptions of otherworldly journeys. Since many cosmological ideas appear in these narratives, Chapter One focuses upon the main features of the ancient cosmological outlook. To accomplish this objective, a few ancient Near Eastern and Greco-Roman creation myths are discussed. Some of the stories to be reviewed include the Babylonian story of creation entitled *Enuma Elish*, the Biblical creation story in the Book of Genesis, the creation myth appearing in the *Theogony* as well as Norse creation narratives found in the *Prose* and *Poetic Eddas*. Chapter Two focuses upon "numinous experience" as it appears in several ancient Near Eastern and Greco-Roman otherworldly narratives. In numinous experience the divine is something that is "Wholly Other" from the profane world. Traces of numinous experience can be identified in several ancient narratives such as in Book XI of *The Odyssey* which presents an account of Odysseus' journey to Erebus. Several ancient Near Eastern narratives are examined as well, including certain portions of the *Egyptian Pyramid Texts* and the Hebrew Bible. The focus of Chapter Three is upon

Introduction

mystical experience and those otherworldly narratives which provide descriptions of this kind of religious experience. Whereas numinous experience involves a confrontation with supernatural beings existing outside of oneself, mystical experience occurs within the locus of the inner self. A plethora of paranormal phenomena including out of body experiences and dream visions of the gods are reviewed in this chapter. Chapter Four discusses a third form of religious awareness referred to as "spiritual transformation." In ancient times, the phenomenon of spiritual transformation represents the central theme of several otherworldly journey narratives including the Sumerian myth entitled *Inanna's Journey to the Underworld*, the Babylonian myth entitled *Ishtar's Descent to the Underworld*, the Greek *Homeric Hymn to Demeter*, and the Egyptian *The Myth of Isis and Osiris*. Some of the rituals associated with these stories are also examined. Chapter Four also includes a discussion of Apuleius' *Metamorphoses* as well as the Norse tale of Baldr's descent to the underworld. Chapter Five is entitled "Courageous Journeys in the Face of Death." Accepting of the reality of suffering and death represents the fourth modality of religious experience. Two epic poems originating from two different historical settings exemplify this category of religious experience. Even though these narratives originate in highly divergent cultural settings, they share many thematic commonalities. In both *The Epic of Gilgamesh* and *Beowulf*, each protagonist undertakes a journey to the underworld where the overwhelming powers of death are confronted. Chapter Six explores the intellectual apprehension of the sacred as it is described in two ancient documents, namely, Plato's *The Myth of Er* and Cicero's *Dream of Scipio*. Each narrative tells the story of an individual's otherworldly journey to the heights of heaven where spiritual wisdom is attained. Chapter Seven focuses upon the journey to moral awareness. Frequently, otherworldly journey narratives encourage moral behavior in this life by showing the fate of the soul in the next life. In the ancient Near East, many tales of underworld journeys and heavenly ascents explore the theme of ethical obligation. Some of the sources examined include *The Egyptian Book of the Dead*, the Zoroastrian document *The Menok*, as well as various Hellenistic Jewish and early Christian texts including the Book of Enoch and the Gospel of Peter. The book then moves to its conclusion, followed by chapter notes, a bibliography and index.

ONE

Ancient Cosmologies

Cosmologies of the Ancient Near East

One of the primary goals of this book is to show how the archaic cosmological perspective is reflected in the stories of otherworldly journeys originating from the ancient Near East, ancient Greece, Rome and the Germanic world. A preliminary step in achieving this goal is to discuss how the three-fold view of the universe is embedded in various ancient and medieval creation myths. In archaic creation myths, the universe is divided into three separate and distinct zones or spheres.[1] Each realm is populated by its own gods and goddesses and each has its own distinct religious rites associated with the worship of these divinities. There are gods associated with the sky, the underworld and earth. In addition, each of the three cosmic realms is in close communication with the others. How the intricate network of communication takes place between the three cosmic realms is outlined in detail in many mythic narratives.

Ancient Mesopotamian Cosmology

Since no single ancient document provides a complete picture of the three-fold cosmological model, several documents need to be examined. In ancient Mesopotamia, the closest thing to an all-inclusive description of the birth of the cosmos and its inhabitants is provided by the Babylonian *Epic of Creation, Enuma Elish* ("When on high"). Earth and the heavens are born out of a primeval watery chaos. As one of the three parts of the cosmos, the watery chaos becomes transformed later in the Homeric epics into a shadowy place beneath the earth where the souls of the dead reside. After that, in Judeo-Christian times, the underworld is

Journeys to the Underworld and Heavenly Realm

once again transformed into a place of punishment of souls and the home of Satan.

It is believed that the Babylonian creation story was recited annually during the New Year's celebration each year. Since a certain degree of cultural continuity exists between the various civilizations of ancient Mesopotamia, including Sumerian, Akkadian, Assyrian and Babylonian society, a document such as the Babylonian creation myth highlights some of the general features of the cosmological outlook of the ancient Mesopotamian people. Originating during the second millennium BCE, this text describes the creation of the sky and earth out of the primordial waters. Most of the myth focuses upon telling the story of a great struggle taking place at the beginning of time between the gods of watery chaos and the gods of the sky and earth.[2]

The myth begins by stating that in the beginning the heavens and the earth did not exist. Only Apsu, the god of the subterranean waters and Tiamat, the mother goddess existed. Apsu represented a sea of fresh water and Tiamat was the salty ocean. When these the two bodies of water mingled together, the world and all the things in it were created:

> When the skies above were not yet named
> Nor earth below pronounced by name,
> Apsu, the first one, their begetter
> And maker Tiamat, who bore them all,
> Had mixed their waters together,
> But had not formed pastures, nor discovered reed-beds.[3]

When the waters of Apsu and Tiamat commingled, two gods named Lahmu and Lahamu came into being. Then, two other gods named Anshar and Kishar were formed who "prolonged the days and added on the years."[4]

Their son was the sky-god Anu who subsequently begot the earth-god Nudimmud, the "master" who possessed wisdom, understanding and strength. All these gods lived in the Abode of Heaven, but Tiamat, the goddess of the watery depths was deeply troubled by the never-ending comings and goings of these gods from the world above down into the watery depths of her world. Because of this, Tiamat and her husband, Apsu decided to murder the other gods. When Ea, the earth god learned about Apsu' plot, Ea killed Apsu. Afterward, in the watery depths another god named Marduk was begotten. Marduk was chosen by the other gods of the sky to lead the final assault against Tiamat, the earth mother. In her

One. Ancient Cosmology

defense, Tiamat created eleven horrible monsters and equipped them with venomous fangs to assist her in battle against her foes. Then Marduk killed Tiamat with an arrow. From the deposed carcass of Tiamat, Marduk created the heavens and the earth.[5] Following the creation of the sky and earth, Marduk created the race of human beings.[6]

Sky gods such as Marduk and Anu figure prominently in many ancient cosmogonies. Symbolic images of the sky and the heavens are universally reflected in the mythological traditions of the world. Connected to this celestial symbolism is the belief that divine beings exist in the heavens who are responsible for the creation of the world and function as its guardians. Often these gods are regarded as high gods who are seen to possess divine wisdom. Frequently, they are responsible for establishing the moral order of earthly communities. Sky gods were always considered to be known as supreme deities perhaps because the sky itself symbolizes power and force.

Ancient Egyptian Cosmology

Numerous creation myths abound throughout the religious traditions of ancient Egypt.[7] One of the most important creation myths of the Middle Kingdom (2050–1710 BCE) came to be known as the Heliopolis creation myth. It features a mythic description of the birth of the nine gods of the Ennead of Heliopolis. The creator-god Atum who is said to have climbed out of the dark waters of chaos at the beginning of time. After ascending to the top of a great hill, Atum brought the gods Shu (air) and Telnut (moisture)into existence. Then Shu separated the earth from the sky and the earth god Geb and the sky god Nut were born. These two gods had four children who were called Isis, Osiris, Seth and Nephthys.

Like Babylonian cosmology, Egyptian creation myths express the idea that the cosmos is divided into three realms. The first cosmic realm is heaven which is the domain of the gods. The second cosmic zone is the watery abyss. The third realm of the universe is the earth which is the home of human beings. In many Egyptian creation myths, the earth emerges out of the watery abyss at the beginning of time. Sun-worship is one distinctive aspect of ancient Egyptian religion that was an outgrowth of the three-fold cosmology. As early as the fifth dynasty, the religious landscape of Egypt began to change because certain popular gods such as Atum, Horus and Re began to take on the attributes of one another. The result of this merging of divine identities was the birth of several new sun-gods such as Amon-Re who ultimately served to strengthen the power and authority of the pharaoh over his people. Shu, the god of the atmosphere was originally a god of the sky who later became identified with the sun. It is likely that other Egyptian gods such as Amun originally were sky gods. Although sun-worship was a major religious force in ancient Egyptian society because of its political associations with the pharaoh and priesthood of Heliopolis, it never attained such a high status elsewhere in the ancient Mediterranean world. In ancient Mesopotamia and the Greco-Roman world, sun-worship existed only in a secondary role to other forms of religious worship.

The Cosmology of the Hebrew Bible

The fundamental elements of a three-fold view of the cosmos are clearly manifested in the cosmological outlook of the ancient Israelites. A primary emphasis on the sky is reflected in the worship of Yahweh, with various manifestations of Yahweh's power having celestial and atmospheric associations. For example, storms are a primary way that Yahweh reveals his power. His voice is described as thunder and lightning and is referred to as Yahweh's fire or his "arrows."[8] Probably the best example of Yahweh's sky associations appears in the Book of Exodus where God reveals His covenant to Moses on Mt. Sinai. According to tradition, Moses is the author of Torah which includes the first five books of the Hebrew Bible (Genesis, Exodus Leviticus, Numbers and Deuteronomy), but modern scholars generally believe these Biblical books came into existence shortly after the time of the Babylonian exile sometime in the 5th century BCE. When God appears to Moses, "there was thunder and lightning to flash, with a thick cloud over the mountain. "[9] The account continues by saying that "Mount Sinai was covered in smoke, because the Lord descended on it in fire."[10] Elsewhere in the Book of Genesis, Yahweh's covenant with the descendants of Noah is symbolized by a rainbow. "I have set my rainbow in the clouds, and it will be the sign of the covenant between me and the earth ."[11]

According to the Genesis narrative, it is through the actions of God that the heavens and earth emerge out of a chaotic formless mass. In fact, Biblical scholars have identified two separate and distinct creation stories

One. Ancient Cosmology

which are interwoven into the opening chapters of the Book of Genesis. Water plays a significant role in the first one. In the first creation narrative (Gen1.1–2.3) at the beginning of time the world is described as a formless mass. The Genesis creation myth has elements that are like the Babylonian creation myth: through the actions of Yahweh, the creator-god, this formless, watery mass is shaped into the cosmos. The Biblical author describes the creation of the world in somewhat ambiguous terms. In the first creation story in Genesis 1.1 God is portrayed as a designer of the universe who gives shape and structure to the earth and the heavens. Like many Sumerian creation deities, Yahweh simply orders the world to come into existence and it comes to pass.

> In the beginning God created the heavens and the earth. Now the earth was formless and empty, darkness was over the surface of the deep, and the Spirit of God was hovering over the waters. And God said, "Let there be light" and there was light. God saw that the light was good and he separated the light from the darkness. God called the light "day," and the darkness he called "night." And there was evening, and there was morning—the first day.[12]

After separating light from darkness and creating the day and night, God created the sky by forming an expanse between the waters.

> So God made the expanse and separated the water under the expanse from the water above it. And it was so. God called the expanse "sky".... And God said, "Let the water under the sky be gathered to one place, and let dry ground appear." And it was so. God called the dry ground "land," and the gathered waters he called "seas".[13]

In addition to the similarities existing between the Genesis and Near Eastern creation myths, there are also some important differences. In the Babylonian creation myth, the universe comes into existence because of a violent clash between the gods. Genesis describes a more peaceful creation. Even though the Israelites believed that numerous secondary gods existed in the background, they also believed that only one primary god, namely, Yahweh was responsible for bringing the universe into existence. In the Biblical narrative, no other god except for Yahweh is involved in the creation of the world. As a result, Yahweh's creative function lifted him up above all the other gods in the minds of the people. In the Babylonian creation story, a series of gods including Tiamat and Marduk are involved in a bloody battle that brings about the creation of the cosmos. In the Biblical creation story, it is through the supernatural power of one supreme god, namely,

Yahweh that the world comes into existence. Another significant difference between the two accounts is that in the Genesis story all the creative actions of Yahweh are proclaimed to be "good" whereas none of the creative activity of the Babylonian gods is described in such terms. In this respect, the Genesis account is unlike its Near Eastern counterparts.

The Greco-Roman Cosmology

The pervasiveness of the three-fold cosmic model extended from the ancient Near East into the Greco-Roman world as evidenced by various Greco-Roman creation myths.[14] Most notable among these is Hesiod's 8th century BCE myth of creation appearing in the *Theogony*. The *Theogony* provides a mythological explanation for the birth of the gods. Hesiod's creation account shares some similarities with other creation myths of the ancient Near East. Like several Near Eastern creation narratives, Hesiod proclaims that only a formless mass described as "Chaos" existed at the beginning of time and that the gods and their offspring came into existence as part of a mysterious emanation of Earth (*Gaia*) out of the Void. In many Near Eastern creation narratives, an original male god is responsible for creating all the other gods as well as the earth and the sky. Hesiod's account differs from the Near Eastern myths because he assigns a female divine principle, namely, Mother Earth (*Gaia*) as the divine agent responsible for creating the other gods through a series of emanations.[15] Fertility cults emerged in ancient times as an outgrowth of the mythological idea that the earth played a key role in the creation of the cosmos. Just as numerous sky gods were associated with various astronomical objects such as the sun and celestial phenomena including such things as thunder and lightning and solar and lunar eclipses, likewise, the religion of the earth had its own divinities some of whom personified various natural processes of the earth including the fertility of crops. Within agricultural communities of the ancient world, a close connection existed with nature that led to a belief that the entire natural world was filled with life and vitality.

In Greece, one of the main divine representatives of the archaic sky religion was the god Ouranos who was eventually forgotten in the minds of the Greek people and replaced by Zeus and the Olympian religion of classical times. In Hesiod's creation narrative, the sky god Ouranos is described as drawing near to earth and spreading out in every direction, bringing night with him and enveloping the entire earth in darkness.[16] Sky (*Ouranos*) and Earth (*Gaia*) exist as a divine pair. First, Earth (*Gaia*) gives birth to Sky (*Ouranos*) and from the sacred union of the earth and sky all the other gods including Oceanus, Hyperion, Theia, Themis, Phoebe and Kronos as well as the Cyclops were born.

Like the Babylonian creation myth (*Enuma Elish*), the *Theogony* describes the creation of heavens, the earth and the underworld in the context of a bloody battle between the gods. When the three sons of Gaia, Obriareos, Kottos and Gyges angered their father Ouranos, they were imprisoned below the earth where they sat for a long time in suffering and pain until Gaia advised Zeus to free them to participate in the war against the Titans.[17] In the history of Greek religion eventually *Ouranos* is replaced by Zeus, whose name is etymologically related to the shining light of the sky. Zeus' primary weapon was the thunderbolt. He is called Hyetios (rainy), Urios (he who sends favorable winds), Astapios (he who sends lightning) and Bronton (he who thunders). Among his many attributes, Zeus is the heavenly father who presides over earthly communities and is the guardian of law and order in the world. It is from Zeus that earthly rulers obtain their power and authority. His Roman counterpart is the sky god Jupiter who uses magic to accomplish his ends. When Gaia's sons were released from below the earth, a great cosmic battle ensued between Zeus and the sons of Cronus against the treacherous Titans. The battle reaches cosmic proportions when Zeus descends from the sky upon his foes with his lightning and thunderbolts. At the end of the great conflagration, Zeus and the sons of Cronus are victorious and the Titans are locked away down in the misty gloom, "in a place of decay, at the end of the vast earth." The chasm where they are imprisoned is described by Hesiod as so vast that a man would not reach its bottom even if he were to travel downward for a whole year.

> And there are the sources and extremities of dark earth and misty Tartarus, of the undraining sea and the starry heaven, all in order, dismal and dank, that even the gods shudder at; a vast chasm, whose floor a man would not reach for a whole year if once he got inside the gates, but storm wind upon terrible storm wind would carry him hither and thither. It is a cause of fear even for the immortal gods, this marvel. And there stands the fearful house of gloomy Night, shrouded in clouds and blackness.[18]

Standing next to the vast underworld chasm is the son of Iapetos, Atlas, who is holding the broad heavens with his head and hands as Day and Night move across the sky. The lack of astronomical and scientific data about the sun and the solar system are reflected in Hesiod's mythological explanation of how the daytime passes into night on earth.

> One goes in, one comes out, and the house never holds them both inside, but always there is one of them outside the house ranging the earth, while the other waits inside the house until the time comes for her to go. One carries far-seeing light for those on earth, but the other, baleful Night, shrouded in clouds of mist cradles Sleep, the brother of Death.[19]

Norse Cosmology

The 2nd century CE astronomer and mathematician Claudius Ptolemy scientifically reformulated how the cosmos was perceived. In this Ptolemaic model, new astronomical information about the solar system was added to the cosmological picture.[20] Based upon Ptolemy's findings, the earth was seen to be at the center of solar system, surrounded by the moon, the seven planets, the sun and the stars. Despite Ptolemy's astronomical discoveries, archaic mythological thinking continued to remain in vogue in medieval Europe. One example of this is found in the Scandinavian poem entitled the *Eddas* composed in the 12th or 13th century CE in Iceland by Snorri Sturluson. The *Eddas* are divided into two parts, the *Prose Eddas* and the *Poetic Eddas*. In the *Poetic Eddas* a short narrative called the *Sibyl's Prophecy* describes the creation of the world out of primordial chaos and the birth and death of the gods in the final *Ragnarok*, i.e., the end of the world.[21] The story is told by the *volva* (a sibyl or prophetess) who is called forth from the dead by the god Odin. The Sibyl begins her story by saying that prior to the time when the earth or heaven came into being, only a giant named Ymir and a huge chasm existed.

> Early of ages when nothing was. There was neither sand nor sea nor cold waves. The earth was not found nor the sky above. Ginnungagap was there but grass nowhere.[22]

The term *Ginnungagap* refers to a great emptiness or void that holds the potential to bring everything into existence. After that, the Sibyl makes a special reference to an ash tree called Yggdrasill.

One. Ancient Cosmology

> I know an ash, It is called Yggdrasill, a high, holy tree, splashed and coated with white clay. From it come the dews that fall in the valleys. It will always stand green over Urd's Well.[23]

The historian of religion Mircea Eliade refers to this cosmic tree called the Yggdrasil as an excellent example of the symbol of the *axis mundi* that connects the three realms of the universe.[24] Yggdrasil took root in the depths of the underworld (Nifl-heim) next to a spring called Hvergelmir. Eventually it grew up into earth (Midgard) and continued growing upward into the heavenly realm (Asgard) of the gods in a place that was next to the Urdar fountain. The tree had three huge roots. An eagle was perched on top of one of the branches and could see everything happening in heaven, earth and the underworld so that he could tell the gods if anything important was happening. The tree was always green, and its leaves never withered away or fell off. Around the tree was the pasture-ground of Odin's goat, Heidrun, who supplied the heavenly mead of the gods. Nearby were the stags Dain, Dvalin, Duneyr and Durathor, from whose horns honey dew dropped down upon the earth and gave water for the rivers of the earth. At the bottom of the tree was a great dragon named Sidhu who was trying to destroy the tree by gnawing on its roots and thereby causing the downfall of the gods. The dragon was assisted by many worms living inside the tree that were trying to kill it. Scurrying up and down the branches of the tree was the squirrel Ratatosk. He was always stirring up trouble by telling the eagle and the dragon what the other one was doing. Since the cosmic tree connected the three cosmic zones, it was the job of the Norns or Fates to keep it in good condition by watering it every day with holy water taken from the Urdar fountain. Trickling down through the branches and leaves of the great tree, the water eventually came to earth to supply the bees with honey. At the foot of Yggdrasil in Nifl-heim stood the bridge called Bifrost better known as the Rainbow Bridge, which extended up to earth (Midgard) and into the heavens (Asgard). The bridge was made from fire, water and air; it provided a way for the gods to travel back and forth between earth or the Urdar well (ocean) and Asgard. Only Thor, the god of thunder refused to travel upon it because he was afraid that the weight of his hammer and the heat of his thunderbolt might destroy the bridge. Armed with his sword, the god Heimadall guarded the bridge day and night. The sound of his trumpet would announce when

Journeys to the Underworld and Heavenly Realm

the gods traveled across the bridge or if an attack of the Frost Giants was about to happen.

More details about the creation of the cosmos are provided in the *Prose Edda*. At the beginning of the story, King Gylfi of Sweden makes a journey to Asgard where he entered Valhalla. Inside Valhalla he encountered three gods sitting on three thrones. The king proceeded to ask the three kings some questions. First the king asked the three gods which of the gods in Asgard was the oldest. One god named High replied that it was "All-Father."[25]

> High replied "He lives through all ages and governs all things in his realm. He decides all matters, great or small." Then Just-as-High said, "He made heaven, earth and the skies and everything in them." Then Third said, "Most important, he created man and gave him a living spirit that will never die, even if the body rots to dust or burns to ashes. All men who are righteous shall live and be with him in that place called Gimle or Vingolf. But evil men go to Hel and from there into Nifhel [Dark Hel], which is below in the ninth world."[26]

King Gylfi asked a few other questions about the creation of the world. The three gods explained that another world called Niflheim (Dark World) was created ages before the time when earth was created. At the center of Dark World there was a spring called Hvergelmir (Roaring Kettle). Many rivers flowed from this spring including the Gjoll river which flowed to the gates of Hell. Before the Dark World was created, another world called Muspell existed in the southern region. It had incredibly hot flames that made passage through it impossible. A poisonous river of hot embers flowed out of Muspell that hardened into ice. A great thaw happened on the border between warm Muspell and the northern colder portion of Ginnungagap and this was the place where life first occurred.

The three-fold view of the cosmos serves as a backdrop to many archaic myths including the Babylonian creation myth (*Enuma Elish*), the story of creation in the Hebrew Bible, the creation myth of Hesiod's *Theogony* and the Norse story of creation in the *Prose* and *Poetic Eddas*. The archaic model of the universe provided the formal setting for much of action described in many ancient and medieval otherworldly narratives. As a form of literary expression, ancient and early medieval otherworldly narratives express the various modalities of religiosity. In the remaining chapters of this book, the ways in which these experiences of the sacred are conveyed in story form are examined.

Two

Numinous Otherworldly Journeys

Ways of Apprehending the Sacred

Several ancient and early medieval narratives that describe otherworldly journeys articulate a type of religious awareness that can be conveniently labeled as "numinous experience." In this chapter some of these narratives are examined. To accomplish this objective, first it is necessary to identify the characteristics of numinous experience and then explain the ways in which this type of religious experience is reflected in these narratives.

The characteristics of numinous experience can be distinguished from other types of spiritual awareness. The nature of religious experience and its variations have been the subject of great debate within the scholarly community for many years and has been defined and analyzed in various ways. Numerous typologies have been proposed. Regardless of how it is defined, there is no such thing as a "pure" religious experience, only those that have been interpreted by means of the religious beliefs that one has acquired. In the words of Steven Katz,

> There are no pure (i.e., unmediated) experiences. Neither mystical experience nor more ordinary forms of experience give any indication or any grounds for believing, that they are unmediated. That is to say, all experience is processed through, organized by, and makes itself available to us in extremely complex epistemological ways ... this feature of experience has somehow been overlooked or underplayed by every major investigator of mystical experience whose work is known to me. A proper evaluation of this fact leads to the recognition that in order to understand mysticism it is not just the question of studying the reports of the mystic, after the experiential event but of acknowledging that the experience itself as well as the form in which it is reported is shaped by concepts which the mystic brings to and which shape, his experience.[1]

Journeys to the Underworld and Heavenly Realm

Katz's statements are applicable to all the other modalities of religious experience, including numinous experience.

Classifying the various forms of spiritual awareness into different categories is a useful first step for making comparisons. However, the attempt to build a typology of religious experience poses certain problems. One of the most influential early 20th century studies in the psychology of religion is *The Varieties of Religious Experience*, written by the eminent American psychologist and philosopher William James. James identified several different types of individual religiosity including the religion of the healthy-minded, the religion of the sick soul, saintliness and mysticism. Unfortunately, the way in which James approached the subject lacked cross-cultural applicability because his examples were drawn primarily from western religion, especially Christianity. Expanding upon James' classification system, a six-part cross-cultural typology of religious experience has been implemented in this book, largely based upon the work of Ian Barbour and Frederick Streng.[2] One of the aims of this book is to demonstrate how each of the six categories of religious experience finds its corresponding literary expression in stories of otherworldly journeys. Otherworldly journeys consist of two kinds: underworld journeys and heavenly journeys. Each of the six categories of religious experience are reflected in one or more examples of otherworldly narratives originating in the ancient and early medieval world.

Supernatural encounters are often described as traveling to a world lying beyond this one. Awareness of the numinous is truly an earth-shattering event for those individuals experiencing it. Typically, a person responds with feelings of fear, awe and wonder. Many examples of the transformative power of the "wholly other" sacred reality appear throughout the history of religions. The Hebrew Bible's description of Moses' first meeting with God on Mt. Sinai in the Book of Exodus provides a classic example of this type of sacred encounter. At the sight of the burning bush, Moses drew closer to inspect this strange sight, but God called out to him to stand back.

> "Do not come any closer," God said. "Take off your sandals, for the place where you are standing is holy ground." Then he said, "I am the God of your father, the God of Abraham, the God of Isaac and the God of Jacob." At this, Moses hid his face, because he was afraid to look at God.[3]

Two. Numinous Otherworldly Journeys

Similar spiritual ideas concerning the overwhelming power of the divine appear in a variety of religious traditions. Even in the context of the indigenous religious traditions of the world such themes and motifs are commonplace. For example, among the Melanesian people of the Pacific islands, the term *mana* is used to refer to this holy power found in various objects in the world. Typically, mana can be manifested in almost anything in the world that manifests powerful attributes. For example, it can be displayed in a variety of inanimate objects such as rocks or mountains, but it can also be found in living things as well such as plants or animals. Originating in the east, the *Rig Veda* is one of the oldest religious texts of the world, dating from the time of the second millennium BCE. It describes manifestations of supernatural energy as they appear in certain natural phenomena such as the movements of the sun, wind and fire.[4]

Some of the ideas of the historian of religion Mircea Eliade are helpful for understanding the nature of numinous experience. According to Eliade, when one has an encounter with the sacred, one is transported out of the everyday world of ordinary experience and carried off to another transcendental realm inhabited by gods and other supernatural beings.[5] In a sense, the sacred exists in a realm that is entirely separate from the profane world. The exact meaning of the term "sacred" remains ambiguous because "as soon as you start to fix limits to the notion of the sacred you come upon difficulties."[6] The only definitive statement that can be made about the meaning of the term "sacred" is that it is the opposite of the profane. The sacred manifests itself through what Eliade calls hierophanies. These manifestations of the sacred, such as the burning bush in Exodus 3.5 of the Hebrew Bible, reveal the transcendent nature of the sacred. A *hierophany* is a "revelation of an absolute reality, opposed to the non-reality of the vast surrounding expanse."[7] Whenever the sacred appears in the world, a sacred space comes into being. In traditional societies, myths describe the absolute truth about the primordial events taking place at the beginning of time when the sacred first made its appearance in history. When the members of traditional society reenact these sacred events of the past by performing religious rituals, those mythic events are brought back to life and commemorated. The celebrants participate once again in those events in sacred time. Eliade refers to the ritual reenactment of the sacred events as the concept of the eternal return. By recalling the creation of

Journeys to the Underworld and Heavenly Realm

the world and the fantastic feats of mythical heroes, members of traditional society break away from the profane sphere and enter the sacred realm of the gods.

In archaic hunting societies, the figure of the shaman dominated the religious landscape. A shaman has the unique ability to experience trance-states in which he is carried off to the world of the gods of the upper and lower regions. There he receives prophetic religious knowledge and spiritual power. To become a shaman within the community, a prospective candidate had to undergo a kind of initiatory ordeal that involved an arduous descent into the underworld. Once the shaman arrived there, he would be confronted with horrifying monsters who inevitably would try to kill him. Usually the shaman suffered death and dismemberment by these evil creatures, but then he would be resuscitated and restored back to life by the gods. In many cases, the gods used various medicines and substances that were placed inside of the shaman's body to replace missing organs. Afterward, the shaman would travel back up to the celestial world of the gods and there he would acquire knowledge and wisdom from various mythic heroes and gods of the sky. Afterward, the shaman came out of his trance state with his newly acquired powers to heal and help his people to successfully hunt. Just as the shamans of pre-literate society participated in great initiatory ordeals as part of their underworld journey and even suffered a symbolic death and rebirth, likewise Orpheus and Aeneus underwent various kinds of ordeals and challenges while traveling into the "wholly other" netherworld.

In the ancient Mediterranean religious tradition, one way in which the mythic *katabasis* (underworld journey) was ritually reenacted was through the oracles.[8] The oracle of Delphi was one of the most well-known oracles in ancient Greek society that brought political and religious institutions together under one roof. Leaders of the polis would come to the oracle in search of advice to some perplexing civic issue. Once the Pythia (priestess of the oracle) was asked a question, she would then fall into a trance and then make some type of oracular utterance in response to the question. Sometimes the ambiguous nature of her oracular response would demand further clarification and interpretation. One of the most interesting aspects of the oracles from the point of view of the history of religions is that those participating in the oracles would engage in a kind of symbolic descent into the underworld.

Two. Numinous Otherworldly Journeys

In his *Description of Greece*, Pausanias discusses the rituals surrounding symbolic descent of those visiting the Oracle of Trophonius.[9] Drinking the water of forgetfulness and waters of memory represented two important rituals associated with this oracle. It was believed that drinking the waters of forgetfulness would help the candidate to forget all his memories of the past; drinking the waters of memory would help the candidate to remember everything happening during the descent. According to Pausanias, the candidate was required to climb down a long ladder leading into an underground oracular chamber. Once there he was told many things that would happen in the future. Afterward, the person would climb back up the ladder to the world above. Then the priestly officials would ask him to reveal everything he had seen and heard down below. Then, he was free to go.

Odysseus' Journey to Erebus

Allusions to numinous experience appear in various archaic myths describing journeys to the underworld. One representative example is found in Book Eleven of Homer's *The Odyssey*. Composed in Greece approximately at the end of the 8th century BCE, *The Odyssey* contains several scenes depicting Odysseus' encounter with the numinous spirits of the underworld.[10] No longer is there mention of a watery chaos, but instead there are references to a dark place below the earth where the souls of the dead live. A sense of mystery fills Odysseus' heart when he wanders into the depths of the Erebus to confront the ghosts of his deceased mother, Agamemnon and many other deceased heroes of the Trojan War. Later, at the end of the 1st century BCE, the Latin poet Virgil composes the *Aeneid* in which similar descriptions of Aeneus' numinous encounter with the supernatural are described as he travels down into the depths of the lower realm of the dead. Given the fact that *The Odyssey* is an extremely archaic document, and Virgil is trying to emulate much of its style and content, it is not surprising that each of these documents possesses archaic, shamanistic religious motifs.

The Odyssey tells the story of the Homeric hero Odysseus' long journey back home after the Trojan War. Heroes such as Odysseus, Achilles

Journeys to the Underworld and Heavenly Realm

or Hercules played an important role in ancient Greek religion. In certain cases, heroes attained their special status either because one of their parents was a god, as in the case of Hercules, or because of their amazing deeds, as in the case of Odysseus. Hero cults emerged in the ancient Greek religious tradition as a way of giving homage to certain mythological figures and evolved out of the cult of the dead.[11] According to the historian of religion Martin Nilsson, the family was an important institution in ancient Greece and one way this was expressed was through the cult of the ancestors.[12] The hero-cult was founded upon the belief that a dead person continued to exert a certain kind of spiritual energy or influence, but this numinous energy was only present at the location where the person was buried. It was believed that the "mana" or spiritual energy of the dead hero stays connected to the physical remains of the deceased person's body. It is likely that the spiritual basis of Greek hero cults is rooted in the primitive religious belief that a deceased person's soul exerts a significant influence upon the world of the living if certain rituals continue to be practiced.

Just as in the case of Near Eastern mythology, Greek mythology had a lot to say about heroes. Many Greek heroes were the byproduct of Zeus' numerous affairs with earthly women. Having one divine parent allowed heroes to perform a wide variety of amazing and supernatural feats. One illustration of the way in which the hero stands above the rest of humanity is provided by the tales describing the twelve labors of Hercules. Even after their death, heroes could continue to perform supernatural feats to those who gave homage to them. Throughout ancient Greece many hero cults sprung up at the burial sites of various deceased heroes. Worshippers would come to these holy places and pray to the spirit of the deceased hero, asking them to fulfill their various special requests.

There are numerous mythic narratives surrounding the legendary heroes of ancient Greece. In the case of Odysseus, one of his most legendary deeds involves his journey to the depths of the underworld. Because of all the dangers and difficulties involved, descending into the underworld and successfully making a return to the world above was something that an ordinary person would never try to undertake. Thus, Odysseus' success in performing such as journey illustrated his heroic nature. In Book ten and eleven of *The Odyssey*, Odysseus' underworld journey is described in detail.[13] Although Odysseus confronts the underworld as a living reality filled with strange beings and events, the narrative also contains information about various ancient Greek conceptions of the soul and afterlife. In the Homeric view, once the soul or psyche has made its descent down into Erebus or Hades, certain changes take place. Although the identity of a person is still recognizable, and their soul still goes by its earthly name, the soul of the person still appears as a lifeless, ghostly shadow. One passage in the *Iliad* states that "So even in death's strong house there is something left, a ghost a phantom—true, but no real breath of life."[14]

There are a few similarities between the Homeric conception of the underworld and the ancient Hebrew concept of *Sheol*. Just as the Homeric underworld is a place of shadows and darkness, likewise the Hebrew Bible describes *Sheol* as a huge, gloomy realm where the dead reside forever. According to the Bible, once the deceased descends into this shadowy realm, there is no going back; the Book of Job states "He who goes down to the grave does not return."[15] In the English translation, the word "grave" is used for the Hebrew word "Sheol." Like the Homeric conception of Hades, *Sheol* is a wholly uninviting place for as the prophet Job says,

> Turn away from me so I can have a moment's joy before I go to the place of no return to the land of gloom and deep shadow, to the land of deepest night, of deep shadow and disorder where even the light is like darkness.[16]

Since the realm of the underworld is "wholly other" and removed from the world on earth, special instructions are needed to enter such an unearthly region of the cosmos. Usually, these instructions are delivered by some type of supernatural messenger. In the case of Odysseus, it is the crafty witch Circe who provides the details about how to reach the lower realm. Circe tells Odysseus that to reach the underworld he must sail his ship across the vast ocean until he reached a mysterious island at the end of the earth where a grove of poplar trees is growing. Bodies of water such as stream of ocean or rivers such as the Gjoll river of Norse mythology or the River Styx of Greek mythology divide the sacred from profane reality and serve as a barrier to entry. Crossing the river sometimes requires the assistance of a boatman such as the grim Charon, the ferryman of the *Aeneid*, or Urshanabi, the boatman of *The Epic of Gilgamesh*. The fact that the underworld is separated off from profane reality is emphasized using

Journeys to the Underworld and Heavenly Realm

images such as the gatekeepers of the underworld and ferrymen who assist in crossing into the world below.

> When you have crossed with your ship the stream of Ocean, you will find there a thickly wooded shore, and the groves of Persephone, and tall black poplars growing, and fruit-perishing willows; then beach your ship on the shore of the deep-eddying Ocean and yourself go forward into the moldering home of Hades. There Pyriphlegethon and Kokyton, which is an off-break from the water of the Styx, flow into Acheron. There is a rock there, and the junction of two thunderous rivers. There, hero, you must go and do as I tell you.[17]

Carefully following Circe's instructions, Odysseus sets sail for the island. When Odysseus and his crew arrive, a few rituals are performed and immediately thereafter a series of ghostly apparitions begin to appear out of thin air to confront Odysseus. In archaic religion, manifestations of the numinous are frequently connected to the practice of divination and prophecy. Various types of divinatory beliefs and magical practices are reflected in *The Odyssey*. When Odysseus visits the underworld, the theme of divination appears when the prophet Teiresias suddenly stepped out of the mist carrying a golden staff. First the prophet asked Odysseus why he left the pleasant surroundings of the land of the living to come to the dreadful world of the dead. Then Teiresias manifested his prophetic powers by making a few predictions. He told Odysseus that he came to the netherworld to find a way back to his homeland in Ithaca. Then he issued a warning to Odysseus that he must not disturb Helios' cattle and sheep at the island of Thrinakia during his trip home because otherwise his ship and crew will be destroyed. Even if Helios' cattle and sheep alone are left alone, he will soon discover back home that countless suitors are courting his wife. If he decides to kill them all, he will be successful, but afterward he will need to travel to a faraway land to make sacrifices to the god Poseidon.

Wishing to speak to the ghostly image of his deceased mother hovering nearby, Odysseus asked the prophet if there was some way to allow her to speak to him. The prophet revealed a magical formula that involved the drinking of blood. He explained that any apparition would be able to answer any question truthfully if it was given blood to drink first. After informing Odysseus about the numinous power of blood, Teiresias retreated into the fog. Then the ghost of Odysseus' mother came forward and drank from the bucket of blood. Immediately she recognized her son.

Two. Numinous Otherworldly Journeys

She asked him why he would want to come to the world of fog and darkness since no one ever came there unless they had died. Traveling there would be a terrifying experience for any living person. Odysseus explained to his mother that duty forced him to come to the house of Hades. When Odysseus asked her about the circumstances of her death, she explained that her grief over her son's long absence had caused her to die. Being deeply moved by his mother's speech, Odysseus reached out to hold her in his arms, but each time he tried to do this the ghostly image of his mother fluttered out of his hands like a shadow. This perplexed him and so he asked her why he could not hold her in his arms. She explained that when a person dies all that remains is an immaterial soul that "flitters away like a dream and flies away."

After the spirit of Odysseus' mother departed, a succession of other spirits appeared to him, including the ghosts of the deceased wives and daughters of various kings and heroes. Gathering around Odysseus, each ghost took its turn in drinking from the bucket of blood and then spoke to him about their lives and the circumstances of their death. Eventually the soul of Agamemnon appeared out of the mist along with the souls of other warriors who died with him during the Trojan War. When Agamemnon tried to embrace Odysseus "there was no force there any longer, nor any juice left now in his flexible limbs, as there had been in time past."[18] Just as in his previous attempt to embrace the ghostly image of his mother, Odysseus quickly discovered that he could not hold onto Agamemnon's fleeting spirit either. Agamemnon described the circumstances surrounding his death. He told Odysseus that he did not die on the battlefield. He said that he had died "a most pitiful death" because he was murdered along with several of his companions by Aigisthos and his wife in their home. As a ghostly spirit, Agamemnon had the numinous power of prophecy. He told Odysseus that he would not suffer such a deplorable fate when he is re-united with his wife Penelope. He asked Odysseus if he knew whether his son was still alive, but Odysseus said he did not know.

Then several other souls appeared to Odysseus including the soul of Achilles. After speaking to Odysseus, Achilles retreated into the mist and then several other Trojan heroes appeared to Odysseus. Each of them told him about their sorrows. Then Odysseus turned his head and saw King Minos on his golden throne, passing judgment on the souls of those who confessed their sins. Then Odysseus noticed that various souls were being punished in different ways. For example, a giant named Orion was herding a group of wild animals in the asphodel meadow. Back on earth the giant had previously killed these animals in the mountains with his club. Next another giant named Tityos was sprawled out on nine acres of land. Two vultures were tearing apart his liver. Tantalos was standing in a lake up to his chin in water and unsuccessfully trying to drink some of the water. Every time he bent over to take a drink from the lake, the water vanished and then the earth would appear at his feet in its place. Above him were some fruit trees, but every time he would try to pick a piece of fruit the wind would blow the fruit out of his reach. Sisyphos was engaged in the horrendous job of using his strength to push a gigantic stone up a huge hill. Every time that he had almost gotten it up to the top of the crest of the hill, the force of gravity would cause the stone to roll back down the hill to the ground. Then the cycle repeated itself endlessly because Sisyphos would never give up in his effort to try to push the stone back up the hill only for it to fall back down the hill again.

In the distance Odysseus saw the image of the great hero Hercules who was holding a bow and arrow in his hands. When he spotted Odysseus, he asked him if he was on some type of heroic quest like his own twelve legendary labors. He reminded Odysseus that one of his twelve labors involved him coming down to the underworld to retrieve Cerberus, the hound of Hell and bring it back to earth. After Hercules retreated into Hades, Odysseus decided to return to his crew. After leaving the underworld, Odysseus and his men set sail across the stream of ocean to resume their trip back home to Ithaca.

Aeneus' Journey

The 1st century BCE Latin poet Virgil was heavily influenced by the writings of Homer. Whereas *The Odyssey* tells the story of the Greek warrior Odysseus' long circuitous, adventure-filled journey back to Greece, the *Aeneid* tells a similar tale of the long journey of a Trojan hero named Aeneas and his crew to Rome. Just as Odysseus demonstrated his heroic nature by performing various feats, including his journey to the underworld as part of his long trip home, likewise Aeneas also reveals his heroic nature in a similar fashion and traveled down into the depths of the netherworld as part of his long journey back to Italy. The two narratives have several parallels concerning the hero's descent into the underworld. Just as Odysseus encounters a variety of numinous beings and supernatural forces, likewise Aeneas has similar numinous meetings with friendly and unfriendly spirits of the dead.

Upon his arrival on the shores of Italy, Aeneas decided that he wanted to speak to his deceased father who resided in the underworld. Divine assistance is usually a necessity to make a successful journey to the shadowy world of the dead. In the case of Odysseus, this divine assistance was provided by the witch Circe who gave directions to Odysseus about how to find the underworld. The Sibyl of Cumae plays a similar role in the *Aeneid*. Not only does the Sibyl provides instructions for locating the underworld, but she also accompanies the mortal hero on his journey. In contrast to Circe's simple directions, the Sibyl's instructions are rather complex. When Aeneus discovered that the Sibyl of Cumae could help him in his quest to reach the world below, he searched for her inside an underground chamber of the temple of Apollo. Since the underworld is set apart from the profane world, entering it is not easy to accomplish. This point is underscored when the Sibyl told Aeneus that few mortals have ever succeeded in coming back across the river Styx and black Tartarus once they have entered the domain of the underworld. The Sibyl tells Aeneus that the entrance to the underworld is located near a tree with a golden branch.[19] To enter the underworld, one must first find the tree with golden bough and break the branch off from the tree. If the Fates have summoned Aeneas to the underworld, then the bough will break off easily, but otherwise he will fail since the branch is stronger than any metal.

Aeneus finds the golden bough when he looks up and sees two doves flying overhead heading toward some trees in the distance. Aeneas watched as he saw the birds land on top of the tree with the golden bough. Immediately, he went over to the tree and quickly broke off the branch, enabling him to traverse into the world below. Immediately following this, Aeneas set off to a nearby cave with mysterious vapors pouring out of it. This was the gateway to the underworld. Just as Odysseus performed a variety of rituals prior to entering the world below, Aeneus and the Sibyl

Journeys to the Underworld and Heavenly Realm

also perform a series of preparatory sacrifices at the cave's entrance. Odysseus entered the world below by himself alone, without any of his crew; likewise, Aeneus entered the underworld unaccompanied by his crew. Only the Sibyl came with him as his guide. At dawn, the Sibyl ordered everyone to leave the area except for Aeneas for only he was permitted to enter the numinous depths of the underworld.

> "Away, away, you uninitiated," the priestess shrieks, "now leave the grove: only Aeneas move ahead, unsheathe your sword; you need your courage now; you need your heart." This said, she plunges, wild, into the open cavern; but with unfaltering steps Aeneas keeps pace beside his guide as she advances.[20]

Then, the Sibyl and Aeneas plunged together downward into the dark cavernous recesses of the earth.

Just as Odysseus encounters a series of the ghostly images of the dead, similarly a variety of ethereal phantoms are seen by Aeneus during his sojourn underneath the earth. Arriving at the waters of Tartarean Acheron, Aeneus and the Sibyl meet a grim, white-haired ferryman named Charon who is the guardian of the rivers. Then Aeneus saw countless deceased souls, both young and old, nearby on the shore who were pleading with the ferryman to escort them across the waters to the land of the dead. Unfortunately, Charon refused to help them. The text echoes the Egyptian notion that those who fail to follow the proper burial procedures would not be eligible to taste the blessings of immortality. When Aeneas asked the Sibyl why the ferryman callously brushed many of them aside, the Sibyl responded that "the waves will only carry souls that have a tomb."[21] Those who are unburied or without a tomb "wander for a hundred years and hover about these banks until they gain entry, to visit once again the pools they long for."[22]

In many archaic underworld myths, the entrance to the underworld is usually guarded by various kinds of supernatural gatekeepers. In the case of Aeneus' journey, he is confronted with two guardians, namely, Charon, the ferryman of the river Styx and Cerberus, the three-headed dog. When Aeneus and the Sibyl approached the ferryman, he became angry and asked them if they had come to steal something out of the land of shadows. He warned them that "no living bodies can take their passage in the ship of Styx."[23] The Sibyl showed the boatman the golden bough, telling him that Aeneas had come to speak to his deceased father in the lowest part of Erebus. Immediately Charon no longer was angry and ushered Aeneas onto his boat. Upon their arrival at the entrance of the underworld, the pair got off the boat and immediately were confronted by Cerberus, the three-headed dog. Cerberus barked loudly and in a threatening manner at anyone who dared to come near the gate. This was the same supernatural "hound of Hell" that had been rescued by Hercules as part of his arduous twelve labors. The Sibyl outwitted the dog by throwing it a sweet cake dipped in a sleep-inducing drug. After the dog fell asleep, Aeneas nimbly passed through the entrance and descended into the world below.

The first region of the underworld was overseen by the deceased soul of King Minos, the first king of the Minoans who served as a judge of lost souls. Minos is also mentioned as a judge of souls in *The Odyssey*. In *The Odyssey*, Odysseus witnessed a few punishments being inflicted upon those who had sinned against the gods, such as Sisyphus, who endlessly pushed a boulder up a hill. Likewise, a few more details about the punishments occurring in the underworld are provided by Virgil. Unlike Homer, Virgil also offers a few more details about the pleasant aspects of the underworld, especially when he describes the Land of Gladness. As Aeneus and the Sibyl traveled on their downward journey, they heard the cries of the souls of babies in the distance and those who been falsely accused and condemned to die. Next, Aeneas encountered the souls of suicide victims. Although these souls longed to return to the land of the living, they were blocked from doing so by the waters of the Styx which hemmed them in. Finally, they reached a fork in the road. On the right side was the road to the land of the blessed called Elysium where the souls of the good and just reside, but on the left side was to the road to Tartarus, the place of punishment for the wicked. High up on a hill Aeneas saw a huge fortress that was encircled by a wall of raging flames. In the front of the fortress stood a large gateway and next to it were two gigantic pillars. The entrance of Tartarus was guarded by one of the three Furies who was called Tisiphone who remained sleepless during the day and night as she watched for anyone who tried to enter. Aeneus heard the blood-curdling cries of the wicked, the sound of dragging chains and the clanging iron echoing up from the depths of Tartarus. The road through Tartarus was quite dangerous; once Aeneus made it past the gates he had to sneak by

Journeys to the Underworld and Heavenly Realm

the hideous Hydra with its fifty venomous heads. Then, further down the road was the dwelling place of the Titans. At the time when the cosmos came into existence, they were the ones who were imprisoned by Zeus with his thunderbolts. Along the road Aeneus saw various lost souls who were being punished for their sins. Aeneas saw a black flint rock hanging from a precipice that was continually about to fall upon the heads of tortured souls of those who were permanently stationed below. He also saw many souls who were ravenously hungry and were seated at a great banquet table filled with food and drink. One of the Furies stood watch over the food and would not let any of them to eat any of the food. Various punishments were assigned to these sinners; some were forced to roll a giant boulder up a hill; others were made to sit motionless and could not move in any direction.

After seeing the many awful torments of Tartarus, the Sibyl told Aeneas that they needed to leave these troubled souls behind and make their way to the entrance of the Land of Gladness. Aeneas sprinkled some water on his body and took out the golden bough as he approached. The Groves of Blessedness was a place of light and beauty.[24] The ghostly phantoms of several glorious heroes of the ancient past appeared to Aeneas in the sunlight. Some souls were sitting quietly on the lawn having a picnic and others were gathered together in a grove of trees singing songs. There was a river in the middle of the field that flowed up into the world above. When the Sibyl asked one of the souls if they knew the whereabouts of Aeneas' father the ghost replied that it was impossible to find a soul in the land of the dead because no one had a fixed home there. He told them to climb on top of a hill so that they might be able to locate Aeneas' father somewhere in the Field of Gladness. After climbing a hill, they spotted Aeneas' father sitting in a valley deep in thought. As Aeneas approached, his father began to cry in joy at the sight of his son. Just as Odysseus was unable to grasp the ghostly image of his mother, Aeneus could not hold on to his father's ghostly image; "Three times he tried to throw his arms around Anchises' neck; and three times the Shad escaped from that vain clasp—like light winds, or most like swift dreams."[25]

Nearby crowds of people gathered by the river Lethe. Aeneus asked his father why they were there. His father explained that these were spirits who were preparing to return to earth in a second body after drinking from the river of forgetfulness. Anchises continued in a philosophic vein by saying that everything in the cosmos possesses a soul. The soul of a human being is encased in a harmful body and cannot perceive the light of heaven, but instead wallows in a world filled with fear and sorrow. Unfortunately, this suffering does not come to an end upon death because then the souls of the deceased are punished for all their sins in the afterlife. Some souls are hung up and suspended in mid-air to purify them by cosmic winds. For others, sins are washed away in a huge whirlpool or burnt in a gigantic fire. Afterward, a few souls may enter the Fields of Gladness where they will remain until the end of the world. However, most of the souls will stay in this heavenly place for a thousand years until they are sent to the world below to receive a new body. Prior to their departure, they drink from the river Lethe so that everything happening in the world above will be forgotten.

This part of the story sounds very much like passages in *The Myth of Er* where Orphic influences are reflected in Plato's discussion of the immortal soul and reincarnation.[26] Obviously, Virgil was familiar with the Platonic dialogues and Orphic spiritual ideas. When Anchises finished his theological monologue, Aeneas and the Sibyl decided to move closer to a throng of souls congregating near the river. Just as Teiresias the prophet revealed certain things to Odysseus about what would happen to him in the future, likewise Anchises used his prophetic powers to tell Aeneus about what would happen to certain souls in the future when they returned to earth in a new body. The soul of Silvius, Aeneas' last-born son, would be born to his wife Lavinia when Aeneas was old. His son would become a king when he grew up. One by one several other souls were identified by Anchises including Romulus, one of the founders of Rome, Augustus Caesar and Brutus and for each of them Anchises revealed the fate that awaited them after returning to earth in the next life. Aeneas noticed a mysterious unidentified soul and asked Anchises who that soul was. Anchises responded by saying "do not search out the giant sorrow your people are to know. The Fates will only show him to earth; but they will not allow a longer stay for him."[27]

As they wandered throughout the Fields of Gladness, Aeneas' father spoke about all the wars that Rome would fight in the future. Finally, Aeneas and the Sibyl came to two gates. The first gate was named the

Journeys to the Underworld and Heavenly Realm

Gate of Horn. It allowed a soul to exit the world of the dead and return to earth. The other gate was called the Gate of Ivory and through it false dreams were sent into the world by the spirits of the dead. Aeneas passed through this gate to return to his ship and crew who awaited him back on earth.

Hercules' Journey to the Underworld

Several numinous encounters are described as part of Hercules' mythic descent to the underworld while performing his twelfth labor.[28] In the iconic tale of Hercules' Twelve Labors, he is driven mad by the goddess Hera. As a result, he ends up killing his wife, Megara and his children. After regaining his sanity, he is filled with a deep sense of guilt over his actions. Turning for help from King Thespius, Hercules is purified of his sins and travels to the temple of Apollo at Delphi to find out how to atone for his sins. The Pythia tells him to go to Tiryns and serve King Eurystheus for twelve years. In return, he would be given the gift of immortality. Eurystheus orders him to perform ten labors. After Hercules performed these labors, the king claimed that Hercules would receive help from his nephew when he slew the Hydra and cleansed Augeas. Therefore, to fully pay for his debt, Hercules is commanded to perform two more labors, namely, to fetch the Golden Apples of Hesperides and to retrieve the hound of Hell, Cerberus. It is in the performance of the twelfth labor where Hercules descends to Hell. Cerberus was a three-headed dog that had the tail of a dragon and snake heads adorning his back. Prior to his departure to the underworld, Hercules went to Eleusis and asked Eumolpus the high priest to initiate him into the Eleusinian mysteries. After being cleansed from the killing of the centaurs, Hercules is admitted into the cult. Then he journeyed to Taenarum in Laconia where he found the gateway to the world below. When Hercules descends into the dark depths of the underworld, all the souls of the underworld who saw him became afraid of him and withdrew except for Meleager and the Gorgon Medusa. Instead of cowering in fear at the sight of the hideous Gorgon Medusa, Hercules drew his sword and prepared to fight her. Then the god Hermes intervened and immediately told him that there was no need to become worried because the Gorgon was only a ghost. Hercules encountered several other ghosts while in the underworld. At the gates of Hades, he encountered the ghost of Theseus and Pirithous who appeared with outstretched hands, hoping that Hercules might raise them up from the dead. Although Hercules could grab Theseus' hand, he had to let go of Pirithous' hand because an earthquake rattled it away. Continuing his underworld journey, he confronted a great boulder of Ascalaphus, the guardian of the orchard of Hades. After pushing it out of the way he continued his underworld trek until he stopped to see a great cow. Realizing that the souls of the dead might need blood to drink, Hercules decided that the cow needed to be slaughtered. Menoetes, the son of the mysterious spirit of Ceuthonymus, stood nearby and challenged Hercules to a wrestling match, but quickly Hercules defeated him by grabbing him around the waist and cracking his ribs. Finally, Hercules came to the place where the god Hades resided. Hercules asked permission to take Cerberus back to the world above. Hades granted him his wish under one condition: Hercules must learn how to control the dog without the use of his weapons. Then Hercules began his search for the dog and he found it at the gates of Acheron. Immediately he threw his muscular arms around the three-headed dog. A dreadful dragon living inside the dog's tail bit Hercules, but Hercules refused to let go until the dog finally gave up its fight. Then Hercules carried the dog off to the world above at the site of city of Troizen. Apparently, Demeter was not pleased with these events because she turned Ascalaphus, the caretaker of the orchard of the underworld into an owl. After showing Cerberus to King Eurystheus, Hercules' twelve labors were finished and so he returned the dog back to Hades.

Numinous Journeys to the Heavens and Underworld in Ancient Near Eastern Religious Traditions

Besides stories of underworld journeys, sometimes numinous experience finds expression in stories of spiritual ascension to the heavens. Several ancient Egyptian texts originating from the second millennium BCE speak about the journey of the deceased pharaoh's soul to the realm

Journeys to the Underworld and Heavenly Realm

of the gods. According to ancient Egyptian religious beliefs, such a journey to the world of the gods was made possible through the process of mummification of the body which allowed for the pharaoh's spiritual self to join the world of the gods. To some extent, the concept of the immortality of the soul became democratized and available to the average person during the Middle Kingdom of Egyptian history. However, immortality of the soul was possible upon death only if certain mummification procedures were followed, but the attainment of immortality was not typically connected to any visionary or mystical experiences. During the time of the Old Kingdom (2686–2181 BCE), the so-called *Pyramid Texts* reveal that immortality was reserved only for the pharaoh upon death. In the following passage taken from the *Pyramid Texts*, the spiritual self of the pharaoh is described to ascend to the heavens upon death.

> Thou ascendest to the sky as a falcon, thy feathers are (those of) geese (Pyr 913). King Unis goes to the sky. King Unis goes to the sky! On the wind! on the wind (Pyr 309). Stairs to the sky are laid for him that he may ascend thereon to the sky (Pyr 365).[29]

Heavenly journeys of this kind were not available for the average citizen in the archaic period, but eventually by the time of the Middle Kingdom a significant change was underway within Egyptian religion. *The Coffin Texts*, which were inscribed inside the coffins of the deceased during the Middle Kingdom, reveal that immortality of the soul had become a real possibility for any citizen, not just the soul of the pharaoh, if mummification procedures were undertaken. The ancient Egyptians believed that a human being was a mixture of both physical and metaphysical elements. A person's physical components consisted of their name and their shadow. The immaterial components were a person's *ka*, or life force, the *ba*, or personality and the *akh*, the spiritual aspect of the person. The Egyptians believed that once a person died, their *ba* and *ka* came together to form a spiritual union out of which emerged the *akh* or soul. It was the *akh* that continued to exist in the afterlife. In predynastic Egypt, the objectification of the soul is underscored by the fact that various objects such as vessels of food and weapons such as knives have been recovered from the graves of the deceased.[30]

In contrast to the ancient Egyptian belief that the deceased person's soul could join the gods in heavens, the ancient Mesopotamian story of the sage Adapa describes the ascension of a living person to the heavens.[31]

Two. Numinous Otherworldly Journeys

Heavenly ascents represent a common theme in ancient Mesopotamian literature. A few kings and sages are described as ascending to the heavenly realm. The earliest Mesopotamian sources mention the ascent of kings; the figure of King Etana is frequently mentioned who is described as the shepherd who established order throughout the land. There are also references to the heavenly ascent of kings Shulgi and Ishbi-Irra of Ur as well as the ascent of the god Dumuzi. The story of Etana is the oldest story of a heavenly ascent in the ancient Near East. He is described as riding on the back of an eagle in search of a magical herb that would enable him to find an heir to his throne. The tale contains part of a folktale that talks about an eagle and a snake who help one another hunt. The eagle is disloyal to the snake and has his wings clipped as punishment. In the story of Etana, the eagle makes up for his transgression by allowing Etana to climb on his back and fly up into heaven in his search for the magical herb.

Adapa is probably one of the most well-known ancient Mesopotamian figures connected to stories of heavenly ascents. There are approximately thirty-four texts referring to him that date from Babylonian times to the Hellenistic period. Many ambiguities surround the figure of Adapa which are partly due to the existence of numerous versions of the story. What is particularly interesting about the main features of story of Adapa is that it describes the ascension of Adapa's physical body to the realm of the gods as opposed to a spiritual ascent of his soul. When Adapa travels to the heavens he has a numinous encounter with the gods.

The text pre-dates various ideas about the immortal soul and is a good illustration of some of the more archaic conceptions of spirituality that existed in the ancient Mesopotamian world. The text consists of four main fragments. The oldest piece dates from around the 1400 BCE and comes from the El-Amarna archives. The other three were part of the Library of Ashurbanipal. The story of Adapa is set in the primordial past after a great Flood has destroyed much of the land. The text states that a man named Adapa visited the sanctuary of Eridu every day. Then one day he set sail at the holy pier of the New Moon to catch some fish for Ea's temple. Once he set off on his journey a great wind blew him off-course on the wide sea. Suddenly the wind capsized the boat and Adapa was submerged down into the depths of the sea. When Anu, the Sumerian god of the sky heard about Adapa's submersion in the sea, he ordered Ea, the god

Journeys to the Underworld and Heavenly Realm

of the ocean to search for him. When Ea found Adapa, he brought him back to Anu the king. The king ordered Adapa to go to heaven where he will meet two gods, namely Tammuz and Gizzida. Anu told Adapa that the two gods will offer him the bread and water of death, but he should refuse to eat or drink any of it.

After ascending to heaven Adapa met the two gods, Tammuz and Gizzida who immediately asked him why he appeared so sad and was dressed in mourning garb. Adapa explained that two gods had disappeared from the land. Then Anu asked Adapa if he was responsible for causing the south wind to stop blowing. Adapa explained that while he was out on the sea trying to catch some fish for his master, the south wind came up and blew him into the water. The two gods Tammuz and Gizzida listened to Adapa's story and decided to speak up in his defense. At the end of the story, Anu suggested that Adapa should eat some bread and drink some water, but he refused to do so.[32]

Heavenly ascensions of a living person are described in the Hebrew Bible. Numinous experience is highlighted in references to the first two prophets of the Hebrew Bible, namely, Elisha and Elijah. In 2Kings 2, Elijah ascends bodily into heaven in a great whirlwind. Elisha vows to never leave Elijah's side. When Elijah tells Elisha that the Lord has sent him to Bethel, the pair journey together to Bethel. When they arrive, the pair are greeted by a crowd. The crowd asks Elisha if he knew that Elijah was about to be taken up to heaven on that day. Elisha says that he knew, but asks the crowd not to speak about it. Again, when Elijah tells Elisha that the Lord has asked him to go to Jericho, once again Elisha refuses to leave his side and the pair set off for Jericho together. Upon arriving, once again a crowd asks Elisha if he knew that Elijah was going to be taken up to heaven on that day. Again, Elisha says he knows, but asks them not to speak about it. When Elijah tells Elisha that the Lord has sent him to the river Jordan, Elisha once again vows that he will not leave him and together they travel in the direction of the river Jordan. When they arrive, they see a group of fifty men "of the company of the prophets" standing in the distance. Elijah removed his cloak and struck the water with it and the water parted and the pair crossed over on dry land. Elijah asks Elisha if there is anything he can do for him before he is taken up to heaven and Elisha asks to receive a double portion of Elijah's spirit. Elijah says that Elisha's request is difficult to fulfill, but he will grant it to him if he stays to witness his heavenly ascension. As they continue walking along, suddenly a chariot and horses of fire appears in the sky and Elijah is instantly taken away up to the heavens in a great whirlwind. Afterward, Elisha tore off his clothes and grabbed Elijah's cloak that had fallen to the ground and struck the river Jordan with it. Suddenly the waters of the river part and Elisha safely crosses the river. Because the spirit of Elijah had descended upon Elisha, he continued to prophesize to the people throughout Israel.

Stories of numinous journeys to the underworld and heavenly realm have been the focus of this chapter. A variety of stories of otherworldly journeys from the Greco-Roman world and the ancient Near East have been reviewed. Numinous experience involves having contact with divine beings existing in a world beyond this one. A few parallels existing between various texts have been uncovered. The presence of these literary parallels and motifs suggests that some of the authors of later texts may have been familiar with material in the earlier texts. For example, Virgil's underworld narrative clearly reflects his acquaintance with Homer's account and may have helped to establish an informal literary tradition of stories of otherworldly journeys circulating the ancient and medieval world. The existence of a set of common literary motifs should not obscure the fact that a substratum of "lived religion" is expressed in these stories and narratives. That substratum was a multifaceted one that was made up of a variety of religious outlooks and perceptions.

THREE

Mystical Otherworldly Journeys

Mystical Experience Versus Numinous Experience

This chapter explores some of the ways in which stories of otherworldly journeys express a type of religious experience called mysticism. First, the nature of mystical experience needs to be identified, followed by a review of some of the ancient stories of otherworldly journeys which articulate this type of religious experience. Many of these texts offer vivid first-person accounts of paranormal experiences and out-of-body journeys of the soul to the heavenly realm.

Whereas numinous experience involves contact with supernatural beings existing outside of oneself, mystical experience, in contrast, typically involves finding the divine within oneself either deliberately through various means such as asceticism or spontaneously without any preparation. Whereas numinous experience involves experiencing God as "wholly other," mystical experience, on the other hand, is an inner psychological event occurring in the deep recesses of the mind. Sometimes the dividing line between these two types of religious experience can be hard to determine. Depending upon the religious tradition involved, mystics describe their inner experiences in various ways, but in many cases these experiences are reported to occur exclusively within the locus of the self.[1] It should be noted that in some instances mystical experiences have been described in theistic terms as encounters with supernatural beings existing outside the self. For example, in certain religious narratives an individual

Three. Mystical Otherworldly Journeys

may speak of traveling outside of themselves and ascending to the Godhead or traveling to a supernatural realm existing outside of oneself when in fact they may be experiencing an inner psychological event. In many of these cases, narrative accounts of these paranormal experiences reflect the underlying belief system of the individual as opposed to the fundamental constituents of the experience itself.

In the context of Hinduism and Buddhism, mystical experiences often result from the formal practice of yoga. Yogic meditation involves the effort to eliminate all forms of mental and physical distraction that hinder one's ability to contemplate the divine. As stated in the opening passages of the *Yoga Sutras* of Patanjali, it is through the practice of yoga that the mind achieves a state of tranquility and blissful consciousness. At this point all the distinctions between subject and object disappear and one attains a state of mystical awareness. In the final state of yogic meditation, one is said to reach a state of "non-duality" or oneness with the divine. In normal awareness, a person's consciousness identifies itself with the various sensory objects that it perceives, but in the highest states of yogic consciousness, the mind divorces itself from the world of sensory objects and stays within itself. The average person is caught up in a web of self-deception in which there is a failure to achieve the state of pure consciousness. Of course, for most people it is normal to believe that reality consists of the various physical objects existing in the world, including one's own thoughts and feelings. However, from the standpoint of the *Upanishads* and other spiritual texts of the eastern world, those who are in search of the ultimate truth seek to go beyond the boundaries of conventional wisdom. As the *Upanishads* states,

> The small-minded go after outward pleasures. They walk into the snare of widespread death. The wise, however, recognizing life eternal do not seek the stable among things which are unstable here.... That by which one perceives both dream states and waking states, having known (that as) the great, omnipresent Self, the wise man does not grieve.... He who knows this Self, the experiencer, as the living spirit close at hand as the lord of the past and the future—one does not shrink away from Him. This, verily, is that.[2]

Certain forms of mystical experience are differentiated from numinous experience because in the case of mystical experience the recipient does not encounter divine beings existing apart from oneself. As Ninian Smart points out, in certain forms of mysticism, such as those described

Journeys to the Underworld and Heavenly Realm

in Theravada Buddhism, the experience is not interpreted in terms of an encounter with a deity or supernatural being.[3] Certain aspects of the archaic religious worldview, including its anthropomorphic view of the gods and the three-fold view of the cosmos, stands in sharp contrast to the mystical perspective. For the mystic, God is not an anthropomorphic being who lives in some other mysterious realm beyond this world. Rather, the divine is found within oneself. Thus, mysticism, including various kinds of visionary experience, is characterized by the awareness of non-duality.

The British philosopher and historian of religion R.D. Zaehner once questioned the idea that an underlying unity exists among all the various examples of mysticism in the history of religions. He argued that some forms of Christian and Muslim mysticism do not qualify as examples of non-duality or oneness unlike what is found in Hindu and Buddhist mysticism. According to Zaehner, usually Christian and Muslim mystics do not typically describe their spiritual encounters with the divine in terms of a merging with the Godhead. Instead, they speak of developing a loving relationship with a supernatural being who exists strictly outside of themselves. For Zaehner, Christian and Muslim mysticism is a mysticism of "the love of God."[4] According to Zaehner, the only thing that the Buddhist, Christian and Muslim mystical traditions have in common is that each of them consider the mystical experience to be an "individual and personal affair."[5]

The problem with Zaehner's analysis of mystical experience is that it mistakes the doctrinal interpretation of a type of psychological experience for the experience itself. Describing mystical experience in terms of a "loving relationship" instead of the experience of oneness is likely to be due to differences in theological interpretations between Hinduism and Buddhism, on the one hand, and Christian and Muslim interpretations, on the other, rather than qualitative differences between various kinds of mystical experience. In all fairness to Zaehner, the relationship between mystical experience and its interpretation has puzzled many scholars of religion in the past. However, it is likely that many of the attributes which distinguish one style of mysticism from another can be explained in terms of doctrinal differences. These differences can be judged to be superficial in comparison to the underlying unity of the experiential contents of mystical experiences themselves that arise in various cultural contexts. In the ancient religious traditions of the Mediterranean world, many of those individuals who report having out-of-body experiences, visions of the divine and other types of mystical and paranormal experiences may talk about them in theistic terms, but this type of discussion primarily reflects doctrinal interpretations of the experience rather than actual factors related to the experience itself. Hence, there may exist a certain amount of overlapping between the ways in which numinous and mystical experiences are understood and described by the recipients of such experiences.

Although mystical experience can happen spontaneously, usually a set of rigorous procedures are consciously utilized to bring about these sorts of psychological events. These procedures include dietary restrictions such as fasting and vegetarianism, concentration and breathing exercises, the use of intoxicants as well as living a solitary life-style. In the final analysis, it is important to remember that there is no such thing as pure consciousness. All human experiences are processed perceptually and epistemologically by people in complex ways. Thus, mystical experience, like any other type of human experience, is conditioned by certain elements of an individual's culture and even the "doctrinal vocabulary" of a person's religious tradition.[6] Awareness of the sacred does not occur in a cultural vacuum and then given totally neutral, unbiased descriptions after their occurrence. On the contrary, one's religious values and beliefs surely have an impact on the way in which these occurrences are interpreted and ultimately described in literary accounts.

Orphism and the Intersection of Numinous and Mystical Experience in the Early West

Part of the problem with developing an adequate description of mystical states of consciousness is that the recipients of such experiences often admit that any description of their mystical encounters in words is inadequate. One of the noteworthy characteristics of mystical experience is that it is ineffable.[7] However, its ineffability is consistent with the idea that mysticism is essentially an experience of non-duality that is qualitatively different from ordinary experience. Non-duality can be interpreted in different ways in different religious and cultural circumstances. In the words of Ninian Smart, "some religious traditions or phases of traditions stress the powerful Other, the great Creator. Others stress more the inner quest, without reference to God. Others combine the two quests."[8] According to Smart, numinous and mystical experience represent the two primary strands of religious awareness which can be manifested in various ways. For example, in the case of shamanism, Smart distinguishes between the right wing and left wing of shamanism. The right wing of shamanism emphasizes the numinous experience of the Other whereas the left-wing represents a type of contemplative experience like the practice of yoga. The successors of left wing shamanism are the monks and nuns of various religious traditions; the representative successors of the right-wing of shamanism are the prophets and preachers of the Bible. In the ancient religious traditions of the west, mystical visions are often associated with various kinds of trance states, including nocturnal and waking dream visions of the gods, as well as out-of- body journeys of the soul to the underworld or heavenly realm.

Orpheus' Underworld Journey

One of the earliest references to visionary religious experience in the ancient west is found in the context of Orphism which emerges on the scene in Greece sometime in the seventh or 6th century BCE. In Orphism, numinous and mystical experience coalesce for the first time in the archaic west.[9] Much of Orphic mythology reflects elements of numinous experience whereas Orphic religious philosophy tends to focus its attention upon the pursuit of mystical experience. First, the numinous side of Orphism is examined as it appears in mythological narratives such as the story of Orpheus' underworld journey; afterward the visionary aspects of Orphism is examined in terms of its religious philosophy.

In Book Ten of the *Metamorphoses*, the 1st century Latin poet Ovid narrates *The Story of Orpheus and Eurydice*. It is one of the most popular underworld narratives of Greco-Roman literature.[10] In the story, Orpheus journeys to the land of the dead where he has several encounters with various supernatural beings such as Hades, the god of the underworld and Charon, the boatman of the River Styx. As a legendary figure of the Orphic religious tradition, Orpheus was regarded as the founder of the mystery-religions. He was a healer, a musician and possessed the miraculous ability to journey into the underworld to bring back the dead to life. In many ways, he possessed many of the strange and mysterious characteristics of a shaman. According to Ovid's account, Orpheus' wife Eurydice was walking alone one day across the grassy lawn when she was suddenly bitten on the ankle by a snake. Immediately she disappeared and when Orpheus learned of her disappearance, he fell into a deep state of grief. Finally, he decided to retrieve her by traveling on the River Styx down into the depths of the underworld. Passing through the portal called Taenarian, he saw many ghostly spirits. When he met the king of the underworld, he sang a song while strumming on his lyre. The lyrics explained that his wife had been bitten by a venomous snake and died. He decided to descend to the underworld to find her and take her back to the world above. The song concludes with Orpheus pleading for Eurydice's temporary return to earth. If this is not possible, then he will stay with her forever in the world below rather than leaving her again.

When Orpheus' emotional plea ended, an eerie silence engulfed the underworld. The Furies wept and even Sisyphus stopped pushing his rock up the hill. The King of the underworld could not refuse Orpheus' request to see his wife and so Eurydice was permitted to come forward to greet Orpheus. The king stipulated that there was only one condition for her to leave: on their return to the world above, Orpheus must not look back in the direction from which he came until he passed Avernus. If he did, then all would be lost. Then, the pair departed and began their long, steep climb back up to the world above in silence. At one point, Orpheus became afraid that Eurydice might slip and lose her footing and so he looked back at her to make sure that she was there. Instantaneously she disappeared. Orpheus reacted in shock. He went to Charon the boatman and asked him to take him back down to the underworld again to retrieve her, but the boatman refused his wish. Then he sat down on the banks of the River Styx and for seven days he cried about the cruelty of the gods of Hell. Finally, he went to Rhodope and Haemus where he lived alone for three years. While sitting in a quiet, shaded grove of trees and flowers, he strummed gently upon his lyre and sang his sad songs about his lost love.

Orphic Cosmology

Orphism had its own unique brand of cosmology which became incorporated into its mystical philosophical outlook. According to Orphic mythology, the Titans were afraid of Dionysus Zagreus because he was the offspring of Zeus and Persephone. The Titans decided to murder him by eating his flesh. When Zeus learned of this great travesty, he attacked and killed the Titans. Human beings were borne out of the ashes of the Titans. Thus, human beings are made of two halves. One half is good and the other is evil. The good half is the result of the Titans consuming the divine god Dionysus Zagreus. The evil half is the result of humanity's birth from the burnt cinders of the wicked Titans. Initiates into the Orphic mysteries sought to find their divine nature by disassociating themselves with the wicked side of human nature. To achieve immortality and salvation, first one had to become initiated into the mysteries of Orpheus and then practice asceticism and vegetarianism to free oneself from the prison of one's corporeal shell. According to the Orphic mystical outlook, to find one's true spiritual identity, each person had to liberate their Dionysian soul that was being held hostage in its bodily prison. As part of the epilogue of the Orphic cosmology, it is told that the Titans had failed to eat the heart of Dionysus Zagreus. When Athena found Dionysus Zagreus' heart, she gave it to Zeus who swallowed it, leading to Dionysus' rebirth through his mother Semele. In Orphism the reborn Dionysus plays a key role in helping human beings purify themselves of their Titanic nature and enabling them to discover their true Dionysian self. This ascetic portrayal of Dionysus in Orphism is quite different from the way in which the god is conceived in the cult of Dionysus of classical Greece. Like Orpheus, Dionysius made a descent into the underworld in search of his mother Semele. In his description of the temple of Artemis in Troizen, Pausanius states that

> In this temple, there are altars of the legendary gods who rule the underworld: they say this is where Semele was brought back by Dionysos from Hades and Herakles brought up Hades' dog. I am convinced Semele never died in the first place, since she was Zeus' wife....[11]

In its point of origin in the 6th century BCE, the Orphic movement emerged as a reaction against the nascent skepticism displayed in various pre–Socratic schools of Greek philosophy. Various Pre-Socratic philosophers such as Heraclitus and Empedocles advanced rationally based theories regarding the origin and nature of the cosmos. Instead of solely relying upon popular mythic conceptions of the universe, these philosophers put their trust in reason for solving many of the unexplained mysteries of the cosmos. In addition to proposing a few cosmological theories, the Pre-Socratics moved on to the subject of religion. Once again, several rational arguments were developed regarding various theological and philosophical issues such as the existence of the gods. In the last half of the 5th century BCE, a few skeptics emerged on the scene such as the sophist Protagoras, Gorgias and Prodicus, who claimed that there is no good reason for believing in the gods since it is impossible to rationally prove their existence.

Despite the force and popularity of these skeptical arguments, the Orphics still believed in the divine, even though they categorically rejected the baseless anthropomorphic conceptions of the gods of earlier times. They took things a step further in that they not only wanted to prove the existence of the gods, but they wanted to discover a way to experience the divine directly. In Book Two of the *Republic,* the classical Greek philosopher Plato mentions Orpheus along with a famous singer named Mousaios and some of their Orphic followers. In the *Republic*, Adeimantos claims that some of these "mendicant prophets" of Orpheus cater to the superstitious whims of the rich by carrying out magic rites and sorcery. Following the written advice of Orpheus, these vain holy men make sacrifices to the gods and champion the mysteries for the reparation of sin and the securing of the blessings of immortality. In the next life, those who have lived a life of goodness will participate in a great drinking party, but those who have lived a life of iniquity will suffer grave punishments.

> Still grander are the gifts of heaven which Mousaios and his son vouchsafe to the just; they take them down into the world below, where they have the saints lying on couches at a feast (symposium), everlastingly drunk, crowned with garlands; their idea seems to be that an immortality of drunkenness is the highest mead of virtue. Some extend their rewards yet further; the posterity, as they say, of the faithful and just shall survive to the third and fourth generation. This is the style in which they praise justice. But about the wicked there is another strain; they bury them in a slough in Hades, and make them carry water in a sieve, also while they are yet living they bring them to infamy, and inflict upon them the punishments which Glaucon described as the portion of the just who are reputed to be unjust; nothing else does their invention supply. Such is their manner of praising the one and censuring the other.[12]

It is likely that Plato's doctrine of the immortal soul was derived from Orphic ideas concerning the imprisonment of the soul in the body (*soma-sema* doctrine).

Journeys to the Underworld and Heavenly Realm

The Orphic Gold Plates, the Cult of Dionysus and the Orphic Hymns

A good deal of documentary evidence about Orphism is found in the later part of the Hellenistic period as opposed to earlier classical times. The mystical dimension of the Orphic religion become clearly expressed at this point. In later Hellenistic-Roman times, mystical journeys to the beyond are mentioned in the *Orphic Gold Plates*. The *Gold Plates* paint an optimistic picture of the afterlife in comparison to earlier depictions from Homeric times. One tablet from Thurii, South Italy dating from the third or 4th century BCE reads,

> But so soon as the spirit hath left the light of the sun, Go to the right as far as one should go, being right wary in all things. Hail, thou who hast suffered the suffering. This thou hadst never suffered before. Thou art become god from man. A kid thou art fallen into milk. Hail, hail to thee journeying the right road By holy meadows and groves of Persephone.

Another tablet from the same period and location states,

> I come from the pure Queen of those below, And Eukles and Eubuleus, and other Gods and Daemons: For I also avow that I am of your blessed race. And I have paid the penalty for deeds unrighteous. Whether it be that Fate laid men low or the gods immortal Or ... with star-flung thunderbolt. I have flown out of the sorrowful, weary circle. I have passed with swift feet to the diadem desired. I have sunk beneath the bosom of the Mistress, the Queen of the underworld. And now I come a suppliant to holy Persephoneia, That her grace she sends men to the seats of the Hallowed. Happy and blessed one, thou shalt be god instead of mortal. A kid I have fallen into milk.[13]

In classical times, examples of mystical ecstasy can be found in the cult of Dionysus; in Hellenistic times, additional examples appear in the mysteries of Dionysus. Dionysius, the god of wine was unlike any other Olympian god. In contrast to Orphism's emphasis on asceticism and vegetarianism, worshippers in the cult of Dionysus became intoxicated by drinking wine to achieve a state of *entheos*, that is, divine possession. Dionysius' association with wine included his ability to perform various wonders and miracles. On certain holy days Dionysius was said to produce miracles with wine. In one instance, a fountain of wine flowed by itself from the ground because of the god's power.[14] Pausanias records that a miracle took place at the festival of Dionysius at Elis. When priests brought

Three. Mystical Otherworldly Journeys

empty jars into the temple and left them there overnight, the next day they all were miraculously filled with wine.[15]

Later in Hellenistic times, the mysteries of Dionysius continued to be connected to certain forms of ecstatic religious expression. In addition, Orphic ideas regarding the nature of the soul and spiritual rebirth became imported into the mysteries of Dionysius in the Hellenistic-Roman period. New religious rituals were introduced in the mysteries of Dionysius for inducing ecstasy. For example, there was the *Bacchanalia*, an orgiastic festival of feasting, drinking and dancing. By participating in the great celebration, initiates became filled with the god (*entheos*). The *omophagia* was another popular ritual of the Dionysian mysteries which involved the aberrant practice of tearing apart an animal such as a goat and then eating its raw flesh and drinking its blood. An important religious doctrine associated with the *omophagia* was the belief that Dionysius was present in animal flesh that was eaten and the blood that was drunk.

Many Orphic ideas are reflected in a collection of Hellenistic religious poems called the *Orphic Hymns* which were written sometime during second and 3rd century BCE. In these poems, ancient Orphic beliefs related to the journey of the soul to the divine become intertwined with Hellenistic astrological ideas. One hymn states,

> Ouranos, father of all, eternal cosmic element, primeval, beginning of all and end of all. Lord of the universe, moving about the earth like a sphere, home of the blessed gods. Your motion is a roaring whirl, and you envelop all as their celestial and terrestrial guard. In your breast lies nature's invincible drive.[16]

Hymn Six discusses the role of the stars in determining the fate of humans;

> Heavenly stars, dear children of the dark Night on circles you march and whirl about, O brilliant and fiery begetters of all. Fate, everyone's fate you reveal, and you determine the divine path for mortals as, wandering in midair, you gaze upon the seven luminous orbits.[17]

In the mysteries of Dionysus as well as other mystery religions of Hellenistic times, a variety of archaic cosmological ideas are combined with various astrological and soteriological themes. By the time of late antiquity, a major objective of many western religious philosophies was to liberate the soul from the body to enable the soul's return to a divine world existing beyond the planets and stars. This idea of the heavens as a place of spiritual refuge was clearly present in the late antique religious thought of the Gnostics, and the Neo Platonists.

In late antiquity and medieval times, Christians of western Europe continued to believe in the idea of the underworld, but in the Christian context it was seen exclusively as a place of eternal punishment. In many respects, the contours of the universe remained the same as it had been articulated in the myths of ancient times; the cosmos was still divided nto three zones, but now a mixture of scientific and religious ideas was added to the model. As a result, a new way of seeing the world began to emerge. Earth stood in the middle of the cosmos, with the stars and planets above. Mythical ideas about the underworld continued to persist, but more and more interest was developing about the celestial world above. In these times there were many who searched for a direct experience of the gods by means of their dreams and visions. More emphasis was placed on one's personal relationship to the divine instead of the state. This movement away from collectivism toward individualism represents one of the most important religious developments occurring in the ancient Mediterranean world. In Hellenistic times, the focus upon individual salvation is prominent in the popular mystery-religions. With its characteristic emphasis upon individual salvation and the blessings of immortality, the mystery-religions represent a form of religious expression that is qualitatively different from the traditional forms of religiosity of earlier times and represents a cataclysmic shift in the religious thinking of the era.

Visionary Journeys in the Hebrew Bible

One of the earliest examples of visionary experience in the Hebrew Bible appears in the Book of Genesis. Genesis 28 describes the patriarch Jacob's vision of heaven which comes to him in the form of a dream. The patriarch Jacob was traveling from Beersheba to Haran. After a while he stopped for the night to rest and he placed a stone under his head to serve as a pillow. Then he lied down and went to sleep. While he was asleep a mysterious stairway appeared in one of his dreams that extended all the way from the earth up into the heavens. Angels were ascending and descending the stairway. At the top of the stairs God looked down at Jacob and proclaimed:

> I am the Lord, the God of your father Abraham and the God of Isaac. I will give you and your descendants the land on which you are lying. Your descendants will be like the dust of the earth and you will spread out to the west and east, to the north and to the south. All peoples on earth will be blessed through you and your offspring. I am with you and will watch over you wherever you go, and I will bring you back to this land. I will not leave you until I have done what I have promised you.[18]

Upon waking from the prophetic dream, Jacob he realized that he had spent the night in a place that was a sacred gateway of heaven. Therefore, he decided he needed to consecrate the ground where he had slept.

> Early the next morning Jacob took the stone he had placed under his head and set it up as a pillar and poured oil on top of it. He called that place Bethel, though the city used to be called Luz. Then Jacob made a vow, saying "If God will be with me and will watch over me on this journey I am taking and will give me food to eat and clothes to wear so that I may return safely to my father's house, then the Lord will be my God and this stone that I have set up as a pillar will be God's house and of all that you give me I will give you a tenth."[19]

Other visionary narratives in the Hebrew Bible had an impact on early Christian literature. For example, many themes and motifs mentioned in the *Book of Daniel*, re-appear in the *Revelation of John* in the New Testament. Other examples of this type of ancient visionary literature include the *Book of Enoch*, *Syraic Baruch*, the *Shepherd of Hermas* and the *Gospel of Peter*.

Heavenly Journeys in the Greco-Roman World

In the Greco-Roman world of late antiquity, mystical visions and other types of paranormal experiences are described in a multitude of narratives, but the psychological genuineness of many of these accounts has been questioned by scholars. The psychological authenticity of the visionary experiences described in such documents as the *Book of Daniel* in the Old Testament and the Egyptian *Corpus Hermeticum* can be questioned on the grounds that these texts contain a large amount of theological embellishment. Nevertheless, at the time when these texts were written, there were many individuals who were reaching out in various novel ways

Journeys to the Underworld and Heavenly Realm

for a direct encounter of the divine; undoubtedly, this thirst for contact with the divine is reflected in these texts. Likewise, in the Greco-Roman world there was an upsurge in mystical and visionary writings telling about journeys to the celestial realm. Although it is easy to dismiss these kinds of writings as fraudulent, it is more likely that many of those writing these texts had religious experiences and these experiences were described in an honest and truthful fashion. It would be wrong to jump to the conclusion that personal testimonies of this kind are entirely the product of literary invention.

One important late antique religious text in the Corpus Hermeticum was the *Poimandres*. The text describes a dialogue between the author and a mysterious revealer figure named Poimandres who possessed secret knowledge about the cosmos and the true spiritual destiny of humanity. Since the author had unyielding curiosity about spiritual matters regarding the nature of God and the cosmos, Poimandres agreed to inform him about all the things that he wanted to know. Poimandres' message can be summed up in the following way: this material world that we live in and everything in it including the body is evil and corrupt. The first step in finding one's true salvation is to attain knowledge of one's true spiritual origins, (*Gnosis*). Once a person has attained knowledge of their true spiritual identity, then they will immediately understand the need to undertake the second step in the road to salvation which consists of completely detaching one's spiritual self from the material world and everything in it, including one's own physical body. Once a soul detaches itself from the material universe, then it is free to return to its heavenly origins. This last stage in attaining salvation involves a spiritual ascent or journey to the heavenly realm of the divine.

Numerous other Gnostic texts from the period of late antiquity describe the cosmic landscape witnessed by the soul as it makes its way back to the Godhead. In *Allogenes the Stranger*, a Gnostic text from the Nag Hammadi library, there is a description of one such ascent to the heavenly realm.

> While I was listening to these things as those there spoke them, there was within me a stillness of silence, and I heard the blessedness whereby I knew [my] proper self. Then I ascended to the Vitality as I sought it. And I mutually entered it and stood, not firmly but quietly. And I saw an eternal, intellectual, undivided motion, all-powerful, formless, unlimited by limitation. And when I wanted to stand firmly, I

Three. Mystical Otherworldly Journeys

ascended to the Existence, which I found standing and at rest, resembling and similar to that which was covering me. By means of a revelation of the indivisible and the stable I was filled with revelation.[20]

Like the 4th century CE Neo-Platonic philosopher Plotinus, Allogenes believes that the divine cannot be described in words. Therefore, he employs a "negative theology" for discussing the nature of the divine:

> He is neither Divinity nor Blessedness nor Perfection. Rather he is an unknowable entity, not an attribute. Rather he is something else superior to Blessedness and Divinity and Perfection, for he is not perfect, but he is another thing that is superior. He is neither boundless nor is he bounded by another. Rather he is something superior. He is neither corporeal nor incorporeal, neither great [nor] small, neither a quantity nor a [quality]. Nor is he something that exists that one can know; rather he is something else that is superior that one cannot know.[21]

Although it is likely that Gnosticism may have originated prior to the time of early Christianity, many of its central theological teachings gradually infiltrated into the early Christian Church.[22] As a result, some early Christian Gnostic documents describe heavenly ascents such as the second or 3rd century CE narrative entitled the *Ascension of Isaiah*.

> And while he was speaking by the Holy Spirit in the hearing of all, he suddenly became silent and his consciousness was taken from him and he saw no more the men who were standing before him, his eyes were open, but his mouth was silent and the consciousness in his body was taken from him; but his breath was still in him, for he saw a vision. And the angel who was sent to make him behold it belonged neither to his firmament nor to the angels of glory of the world, but had come from the seventh heaven.... And the vision which he saw was not of this world, but from the world which is hidden from all flesh....[23]

In early Christian literature, visionary ascents to heaven were not unknown. Even a superficial reading of the New Testament letters of the Apostle Paul indicates that he was a deeply religious person. Given the fact that Paul was a Christian, many of his religious experiences were described in theistic terms. Prior to his conversion, Paul was a persecutor of Christians. The story of his dramatic conversion to Christianity is described in Acts 9.1–9. As Paul was traveling down the road to Damascus, he had a numinous encounter with the risen Jesus. Paul was hoping to bring any Christians he found in Damascus back to Jerusalem to stand trial for blasphemy. Suddenly there was a brilliant flash of light from the heavens and a mysterious voice spoke the words

Journeys to the Underworld and Heavenly Realm

> "Saul, Saul why do you persecute me?" "Who are you, Lord?" Saul asked. "I am Jesus, whom you are persecuting," he replied. "Now get up and go into the city, and you will be told what you must do."

The effects of such ethereal confrontations with the sacred can be extreme. In the case of Paul, he was struck blind for three days. During this time, he was unable to eat or drink anything. More importantly, Paul had a conversion experience. In 2 Corinthians Paul describes a mystical journey to the upper reaches of heaven. Paul states that on one occasion he was the recipient of the visionary experience in which he traveled to the "third heaven."

> I must go on boasting. Although there is nothing to be gained. I will go on to visions and revelations from the Lord. I know a man in Christ who fourteen years ago was caught up to the third heaven. Whether it was in the body or out of the body I do not know—God Knows. And I know that this man—whether in the body or apart from the body I do not know but God knows was caught up to paradise. He heard inexpressible things, things that man is not permitted to tell. I will boast about a man like that, but I will not boast about myself, except about my weaknesses.... To keep me from becoming conceited because of these surprisingly great revelations, there was given to me a thorn in my flesh, a messenger of Satan, to torment me.[24]

There is little doubt that the phrase "a man in Christ "refers to Paul himself. Some Biblical scholars have suggested that when Paul uses the phrase "a thorn in my flesh" he is alluding to some unknown illness such as epilepsy, malaria or a disease of the eyes. In the Acts account, Paul encounters the risen Jesus and in 2 Corinthians he is taken up to the "third heaven." Although Paul states that he came upon supernatural beings and places that existed outside of himself, most likely these experiences happened entirely within the realm of his own psyche. As a result, they should be classified as examples of mysticism instead of "numinous experience."

Pagan and Christian Visionaries of the Ancient World

Even though visionary experiences such as the one mentioned in 2 Corinthians should be interpreted as internal psychological events, frequently the recipient of these experiences believes that some form of esoteric spiritual knowledge has been conferred upon them by an external

Three. Mystical Otherworldly Journeys

supernatural source. Even the Neoplatonist philosopher Plotinus claimed to have had an experience of non-duality in which his soul merged with the divine on more than one occasion. Although Plotinus was very indebted to Plato for many of his ideas, he tended to reinterpret Platonism in a highly spiritual way. For Plotinus, philosophy and asceticism provided the gateway to higher levels of intuitive knowledge of the divine. Plotinus stated that humans would only attain incomplete knowledge of the divine through intellectual and philosophical activity. However, only by means of merging with the One was it possible for the individual to see the divine in its entirety. On several occasions Plotinus claims that his soul left his body and became one with the higher realm of the spirit. Then, after reaching the upper heights of the cosmos, his soul was sent on a return journey back to his body. After regaining his normal state of mind, he was left in a state of bewilderment because he did not exactly understand what happened to him and how he was able to return to his normal state of consciousness.[25]

> Many times it has happened: lifted out of the body into myself, becoming external to all other things and self-centered ; beholding a marvelous beauty; then, more than ever, assured of community with the loftiest order; enacting the noblest life; acquiring identity with the divine; stationing within It by having attained that activity; poised above whatsoever in the intellectual is less than the Supreme; yet, there comes the moment of descent from intellection to reasoning, and after that sojourn in the divine, I ask myself how it happens that I can now be descending, and how did the Soul ever enter into my body, the Soul which even within the body is the high thing it has shown itself to be.[26]

Likewise, Porphyry, Plotinus' biographer, also admits to having a similar type of experience of non-duality in which he "drew near to this God and was made one with him."[27]

An examination of Plotinus' writings reveals that his mystical experiences had a direct impact upon his philosophical outlook. As previously mentioned, one of the chief features of mystical experience is that the exact nature of the experience itself cannot be adequately described in words. Similarly, ineffability is one of the fundamental ideas associated with Plotinus' philosophy. Plotinus claimed that knowledge of God provided human beings with their salvation, but surprisingly nothing could ever be definitively said about the divine. Since God exists in another world that transcends the world of sense-experience, Plotinus argued that

Journeys to the Underworld and Heavenly Realm

ordinary language cannot be used to express the true nature of the divine. Therefore, Plotinus employs a "negative theology" to talk about the divine. Rather than saying what the divine is, Plotinus prefers to speak about what it is not. Given the fact that a deep gulf existed between this world and the next, it was up to human beings to find a way back to the Godhead. Fortunately, Plotinus found a way back by pointing to a series of divine emanations that connected the world of the divine with the world of sense-experience. At the top of the divine hierarchy was "the One" or God and emanating from the Godhead was the *Nous* or Mind followed by the World Soul. Since the One exists in another realm beyond the world of ordinary sense experience, ascending back to the One is a rather strenuous process requiring the purification of the soul. Plotinus believed that the key ingredients for finding one's way back to the Godhead were living a virtuous life and practicing asceticism. These activities eventually enable the soul to shed its corporeal shell and begin its long road of ascendance to the divine. Given his emphasis on "the One," it is not surprising that Plotinus is considered one of the most spiritual philosophers of western civilization.

In classical and Hellenistic times, some spiritual wanderers experienced mystical visions while participating in various forms of earthly pilgrimage. In some ways, earthly pilgrimages in the pagan world involved ritual reenactments of mythological underworld journeys. Although earthly pilgrimage is an external form of behavior, internal changes within the self can result when one participates in this type of religious ritual. In some cases, intense religious experience can become one outcome of earthly pilgrimage. Pilgrimage usually involves various kinds of ordeals for its participants. An important primary source for understanding pilgrimage in ancient times is found in Book II of Herodotus' *Histories*.[28] In Book II.58, Herodotus states that the Egyptians were among the first people to make "solemn assemblies and processions and approaches with offerings to the temples." One of the most jubilant of these processions occurred at the city of Bubastis in honor of the goddess Artemis. Another great procession to the temple of the goddess Isis regularly took place at the city of Busiris, located in the middle of the Nile Delta. A third "solemn assembly" occurred at the city of Sais for the Greek goddess Athena.

In the Hellenistic-Roman period, individual pilgrimages as opposed to collective pilgrimages became a popular form of religious expression

Three. Mystical Otherworldly Journeys

and was often linked to the pursuit of visionary and mystical experience. The cult of Asclepius was a popular healing cult in the Greco-Roman world, with its main sanctuaries located at Epidaurus, Pergamum and on the island of Cos in the Aegean Sea. People from all walks of life would make pilgrimages to the temple of Asclepius in search of healing from their various physical ailments. One of the most important religious rituals occurring at the temple of Asclepius was the rite of incubation. Incubation involved the practice of sleeping in the temple sanctuary at night to obtain some form of miraculous cure for one's illness.[29] One of the most ardent devotees of the cult of Asclepius was the 2nd century CE Greco-Roman pagan sophist Aelius Aristides. Originally Aristides' interest in the cult was based upon his expedient desire to be miraculously healed from his various physical problems, but soon a deeply religious bond began to blossom between himself and the god. The spiritual dimension of his dream visions becomes explicit in several passages in the *Sacred Tales* where Aristides experiences divine epiphanies of Asclepius and other gods and goddesses. The close continuity between Aristides' dream experiences and his daily waking life provides one reason why many scholars are convinced that the dreams recorded in the *Sacred Tales* are authentic. Aristides considered the world of his dreams to be an open doorway into the world of the divine. Aristides' most powerful spiritual encounters with Asclepius take place while Aristides is hovering in a pre-conscious state between waking and sleeping consciousness. Although Aristides' religious experiences clearly originated within his own psyche, a close reading of his diary reveals that he believed that his dreams enabled him to contact a supernatural realm filled with divinities such as the healer god Asclepius. Thus, in the case of Aristides, numinous and mystical experience become difficult to separate and distinguish from one another.

Aristides' earthly search for physical healing at the temple in Pergamum soon evolved into a search for a religious vision. His religious quest is somewhat representative of the times. In Greco-Roman times, there were many who were searching for some form of direct contact with the gods, either through their dreams, divination, gnostic revelation or other form of mystical and visionary experience. Another earthly pilgrim was the 1st century CE medical doctor Thessalos of Tralles whose visionary experiences are recorded in a letter addressed to Caesar Augustus. Although the letter mentions several medical issues that plagued Thessalos, the main topic is his earthly travels and his search for spiritual enlightenment. Embedded within this strange document is a detailed description of Thessalos' personal religious quest for a vision of the god Asclepius. In distinction to Aristides' dream diary, which contains abundant descriptions of several dream epiphanies of the god Asclepius, Thessalos's account concentrates upon a description of a single waking epiphany of a god. Thessalos received his vision of Asclepius in the context of this world as opposed to traveling to the heavenly realm of the gods. In his vision, the god asked him what it was that he desired and Thessalos told him that he needed to know why certain medicinal plants and herbs that he gathered were not effective. Asclepius explained that he had failed to collect the plants and herbs at the appropriate times and locations; this was why the plants and herbs were useless. The letter concludes with Thessalos making the decision to resume his search for the necessary medicinal plants and herbs.[30]

Alchemical visions were popular in late antiquity. The 3rd century CE alchemist Zosimus of Panopolis was the recipient of a series of visions in which he journeyed to a strange world bearing little resemblance to the world of everyday experience. In this way, his visionary experiences were somewhat dissimilar to the dream visions of Aristides.[31] Another piece of literary evidence vividly portraying the experience of seeing the god is an inscription coming from the temple of Mandulis at a town called Talmis in Nubia.[32]

The 2nd century Christian martyr St. Perpetua of Carthage, North Africa, was another recipient of strange, symbolic dream-visions. A few days before her martyrdom at the hands of the Romans, she experienced a series of four dream visions which are described in a text entitled *The Martyrdom of Saints Perpetua and Felicitas*.[33] Unlike Aristides, Perpetua was not an earthly pilgrim, nor did she experience any divine epiphanies. However, she did have "religious dreams" in the sense that the characters and events of her dreams have spiritual significance. Further, there is no reason to deny that her diary is an accurate rendering of her dream experiences.

The focus of this chapter has been visionary and mystical experience and some examples of how this type of religious experience became expressed in various narratives describing otherworldly journeys. It has been noted that identifying mystical experience and distinguishing it from

Three. Mystical Otherworldly Journeys

numinous experience is sometimes problematic. In numinous experience, the divine exists outside of oneself; in mysticism, the divine is found within the parameters of the psyche. Strains of mystical experience appear in a variety of settings in the ancient western world including the cult of Dionysus and Orphism. In terms of stories of otherworldly journeys, Orphic texts refer to mystical flights of the soul to the heavens. Likewise, Orphic influences were detected in Plato's doctrine of the immortal soul. Later, in the period of late antiquity, the Neo-Platonist philosopher Plotinus admitted that on several occasions he experienced dramatic mystical flights of the soul. Visionary experiences were recorded in Gnostic writings as well and in certain books of the Hebrew Bible such as in the Book of Daniel. In Hellenistic and Roman times, many religiously inclined individuals such as Aelius Aristides and Thessalos of Tralles used their dreams as a means for developing a close bond with the gods. Encountering the sacred can bring about a complete transformation of an individual's self-perception. In the next chapter, the nature of spiritual transformation is explored in further detail.

Four

Journeys of Spiritual Transformation

Spiritual transformation is a central theme of many religious narratives originating in ancient and medieval times. The process of spiritual transformation brings about a kind of internal metamorphosis for the individual, either temporary or permanent, involving a shift in values and perceptions; therefore, it has often been understood as a kind of spiritual journey that, in some instances, can lead either to the heights of heaven or the depths of hell. Stories of spiritual transformation were popular in antiquity and medieval times. Sometimes stories of spiritual transformation provided accounts of arduous journeys to heaven and hell undertaken by gods or mortals; sometimes, otherworldly journeys were not involved.

These stories emerged out of certain conditions related to the experience of encountering the sacred. Those who report making contact with the supernatural world often claim that they see their lives in new and different ways. This psychological consequence can impact how people act and function in the world.[1] The spiritually transformative nature of apprehending the holy is not restricted to any one religious tradition; on the contrary, it is widespread throughout the history of religions. The characteristics of this spiritual transformation can vary from person to person. As a third form of religious experience, spiritual transformation often springs from the first two modes of religious awareness, namely numinous and mystical experience. In the great monotheistic religious faiths of the western world, the concept of "spiritual transformation" is often connected to the phenomenon of religious conversion. William James describes conversion as:

Four. Journeys of Spiritual Transformation

> the process, gradual or sudden by which a self hitherto divided and consciously wrong, inferior, and unhappy becomes unified and consciously right, superior and happy in consequence of its firmer hold upon religious realities. This at least is what conversion signifies in general terms whether or not we believe that a direct divine operation is needed to bring such a moral change about.[2]

In the context of Christianity, the conversion experience is usually preceded by a period of spiritual crisis for the individual that finally becomes resolved when the person fully commits to their new religious path. This acceptance of the new spiritual path brings about feelings of inner peace due to the resolution of the person's spiritual predicament. The conversion process involves the total commitment of the individual involving the complete transformation of their life; this means that all of one's past religious associations are given up. This was not the case in the pagan religious traditions of the ancient Mediterranean world.

One example of the popularity of stories of spiritual transformation in antiquity is provided by the 2nd century CE Roman satirist Lucian in his narrative entitled "The Death of Peregrinus"[3] Although Peregrinius never journeys to heaven or hell but remains on earth until he dies, his story provides an excellent example of the protean nature of pagan religiosity. Unlike the religious exclusivism of the Judeo-Christian tradition, which required individuals to give up any past religious associations, in ancient times the pagan faiths had no such requirement; one could adhere to a multiplicity of religious faiths simultaneously. For example, one could be initiated and belong into any number of religious cults at the same time. The tale begins with an account of some background about this peculiar character. As an adult, Peregrinus wandered from place to place throughout the ancient world having one adventure after the other. At one point in the story, his wanderings led him to Palestine where he decided to become a Christian for a short period of time. Very soon afterward, he convinced the Christians there that he was a priest and prophet. To convince them of his spiritual authority he expounded on several esoteric doctrines and wrote several books so that eventually he was held in high regard, almost as a god. Soon Proteus was arrested and put in jail. His Christian congregation tried to free him, but was unsuccessful. The Christians clamored to be near to him since he was seen to be a "modern Socrates." Christians throughout the world came to visit him in jail, bringing him dinners to enjoy while he remained in prison. While Peregrinus

Journeys to the Underworld and Heavenly Realm

remained in jail, money poured in from the Christian community and eventually he was released. Under the protection of the Christians, Proteus lacked nothing and once again he set out on his wanderings around the ancient world. Eventually the Christians caught him eating some forbidden meats and they decided to have nothing more to do with him. Then he went to Egypt. Giving up his Christian faith, he shaved his head, and rubbed mud on his face so that the people there would perceive him as a pagan holy man. Then he shocked the public with a series of extravagant follies. Then he departed Egypt and took a ship to Italy. His behavior became so obnoxious in Rome that that the city prefect banished him from the city precincts. Finally, Peregrinus traveled to Greece where he tried to instigate a revolt against Rome by condemning one of the officials of Olympia for causing famine and drought. Because of this he was almost stoned to death, but was able to escape by remaining by the altar of Zeus. For the next four years he worked on a great speech in honor of Zeus which he delivered at the Olympic games. During this time Peregrinus had lost a lot of his popularity and fame. Therefore, he devised a plan to get back into the limelight. He announced that at the next games he intended to cremate himself in a funeral pyre. Finally, the day arrived and Peregrinus arrived at Olympia. The audience listened as Proteus gave a speech about all the adventures of his philosophical life. His grand conclusion was that since he had lived a life like Hercules, he needed to die like Hercules as well. He said that he desired to teach humanity how despicable a thing that death is. Although he thought that the audience would not allow him to get near the funeral pyre, many people approved of his resolve. After many delays, finally around midnight Peregrinus announced that his suicide was about to occur. The crowd followed him two miles down the road to a large hole in the ground filled with wood. Crying out to the gods he leapt into the blazing pyre.

Religious exclusivism, which was a conspicuous element in Christianity, Judaism and Islam, was clearly absent in ancient paganism. The story of Peregrinus provides a good example of non-exclusive nature of pagan religiosity. Other prominent theological differences between paganism and the three, great monotheistic religious traditions of the West can be noted. Unlike the three great monotheistic religions of the west, the pagan religions of antiquity did not possess an authoritative set of orthodox teachings nor did it possess an official canon of authoritative religious documents. Ancient Greek religion did not even have an official priesthood, even though Egyptian and Roman religion did. Portions of some ancient, pagan religious narratives such as Plutarch's *Myth of Isis and Osiris* and the Babylonian myth of creation may have been recited during various religious celebrations, but an official-canon did not exist in ancient paganism.

Even though pagan religiosity did not include the requirement of giving up one's previous religious associations when joining a new religious group, this should not lead one to the erroneous conclusion that various forms of spiritual transformation were entirely absent from paganism. In the pagan religious traditions of the ancient Mediterranean world, various forms of spiritual renewal appear in connection to the reenactment of sacred myths and rituals. Instead of using the term "conversion," a better term for describing spiritual reorientation in the context of Greco-Roman paganism is "religious adhesion."[4] In describing the phenomenon of spiritual transformation, Ian Barbour admits that we are used to thinking about it in Christian terms, but it is found in other religious traditions as well.

> In the lives of some individuals, acknowledgement of guilt has been followed by the experience of forgiveness. Others have described a transition from brokenness and estrangement to wholeness and reconciliation. Some experience a healing of internal divisions or a restoration of relationships with other persons. Such reorientation and renewal, whether sudden or gradual, may lead to self-acceptance, liberation from self-centeredness, openness to new possibilities in one's life, a greater sensitivity to other persons, or perhaps dedication to a style of life based on radical trust and love. Such transformative experiences are prominent in the Christian tradition, but parallels are found in many traditions.[5]

The significance of spiritual transformation in the pagan religious landscape is underscored by its heavy presence as a thematic element in many Greco-Roman regenerative myths. Here various gods and goddesses frequently are mythically portrayed as journeying to heaven or hell. In the ancient mystery-religions, participants identified with the dying and rising gods and experienced a kind of spiritual death and rebirth which resulted in the attainment of immortality. In their original classical Greek form, the mysteries were celebrated at a small town called Eleusis, situated about ten-miles outside of Athens.[6] The mysteries derived their name from the fact that only those who freely chose to become initiates or *mystes* were permitted to witness the secret ceremonies surrounding the cult. Initiates of the mysteries were required to swear under the threat of death never to reveal to anyone what took place in the inner-most sanctuary during the final stages of the initiation ritual. The initiation ritual began with a long ten-mile procession filled with pomp and circumstance from Athens to Eleusis. Prospective members had to participate in a fast from all types of food and drink. The next day and for several days afterward, various other rituals were performed at Eleusis. For example, a sacred drama was enacted and religious objects related to the cult were revealed to the initiates. Given that the initiates were sworn to secrecy, one can only speculate regarding the actual nature of the sacred drama and objects revealed. Some have speculated that these things may have had something to do with the events described in the Homeric Hymn to Demeter.

In Hellenistic times, the mystery-religions enjoyed a kind of spiritual renaissance due to a combination of several sociohistorical factors. Very soon after the time Alexander's conquests, the civilized world underwent a tumultuous process of social change. In the realm of religion, several important developments took place, most notably the onslaught of the eastern religions into the west. In many ways, the Hellenistic mysteries were like the old Eleusinian mysteries of classical times, except that the Hellenistic mysteries introduced the worship of a whole new set of eastern gods and goddesses such as the Egyptian goddess Isis, the Persian god Mithra along with a variety of new strange myths and outlandish religious practices. In certain cases, there is evidence of "spiritual transformation." The 2nd century CE Roman writer Apuleius provides some interesting details about the mysteries of Isis in his novel entitled the *Metamorphoses*. Prior to discussing Apuleius' narrative, a few other mythic accounts related to the spiritual concept of "death and rebirth" is examined.

The Journey of the Sumerian Goddess Inanna to the Underworld

In ancient paganism, spiritual transformation involved identifying oneself with the dying and rising gods. A review of the mythic tales of

Four. Journeys of Spiritual Transformation

various dying and rising gods will help to clarify the nature of those spiritual experiences connected to these narratives. Regeneration of vegetation is a central theme in many of the archaic religious cults of the ancient world. Cosmologically speaking, the death and rebirth of agriculture is analogous to the theme of the death and resurrection of a god. This theme is mentioned in several Near Eastern and Greco-Roman narratives. Usually the gods and goddesses of these stories have underworld associations and attributes. In the world of ancient Mediterranean paganism, a god or goddess from one religious tradition frequently became equated with a deity of another religious tradition. For example, in the mysteries of Isis, the Egyptian goddess Isis became identified with Demeter, the goddess of the Eleusinian mystery-religions.

As previously noted, the tri-partite cosmology of the ancient world appears regularly against the background of a variety of mythic narratives. Throughout the ancient world many archaic agricultural rituals focused upon the changing of the seasons and the fertility of crops. Fertility rites were among the most popular and widely practiced religious ceremonies of the ancient western world. Various myths associated with these agricultural rituals appear in the ancient Near East, Greece and Rome. Some of these myths portrayed the changing of the seasons in symbolic terms as a descent or disappearance of a god or goddess into the underworld followed by their subsequent return to the land of the living.

In some of these agricultural myths, a male god such as Osiris underwent a death and subsequent resuscitation and return to life. Through the saving actions of Isis, Osiris was reborn to become the chief Egyptian god of the underworld and a perennial symbol of the immortality of the soul. However, in the Isis-Osiris myth as well as many other of these stories of dying and rising gods, an underworld journey is not always the most significant part of the story. The most significant part of the tale is the rebirth of the god and return to earth. Back on earth, a variety of negative consequences ensue when the god or goddess descends into the lower realm. For example, when all the crops on earth begin to decay, this sets into motion an attempt to rescue the deity from the clutches of the underworld. The character who attempts to rescue the goddess can either be a divine assistant of the goddess or some other deity. Usually the character who seeks to rescue the goddess asks for assistance from several sources, but

Journeys to the Underworld and Heavenly Realm

is turned down, but eventually assistance is found. Usually a male god is the one who ends up offering help and the help comes in several forms. Perhaps some agent of the god is sent on a mission.

Originating from the second millennium BCE, the Sumerian text entitled *Inanna's Descent to the Underworld* is one of the earliest mythological stories describing an underworld journey of a goddess.[7] Power is the central theme of the story of Inanna's descent. By means of conducting a successful descent and return to the land above, Inanna extends her divine power. However, her success comes at a price. Before the goddess can return to the world above, a substitute must be provided. Like the basic economic model found in society, some kind of compromise must be reached. For the goddess to be released, something must be given up. Before the goddess can return to the upper realm, the exchange must be agreed upon.

At the beginning of the story, Inanna realizes that once she enters the underworld, she may have some trouble returning to the world above because her sister Erishkigal, the queen of the underworld might try to kill her. She tells her assistant that if she does not return in three days, she should go to the temple of Enlil and ask for help. When the goddess arrives at the gate to the underworld, she is stopped and interrogated by Neti, the gatekeeper. Neti asks her to identify herself and explain the reason why she wants to travel upon "the road from which no traveler returns." Inanna explains that her sister's husband had recently passed away and she desires to attend his funeral. After getting permission from the goddess Erishkigal, Neti allows Inanna to pass through each of the seven gates of the underworld. Before going through each gate, Inanna is ordered to remove an article of clothing. Just like any other aristocratic member of Sumerian society, the goddess adorns herself with fine clothing and jewelry. In the case of the goddess, each article of clothing represents one of her divine powers which she willingly gives up one by one to meet the demands of the underworld gods. Finally, at the seventh gate she removes her royal robe and she is completely naked.

The Sumerians believed that to gain entrance into the underworld, one had to meet certain mandatory requirements such as dressing in clean clothes and remaining quiet.[8] Prior to entering a religious temple, one was required to wear the proper clothing and present oneself in a purified state. Similarly, *Inanna's Descent to the Underworld* mentions that certain

Four. Journeys of Spiritual Transformation

stipulations were imposed upon the person who wished to leave the underworld. The main requirement was that a substitute had to be found to take the person's place in the underworld. Upon Inanna's arrival, she was subjected to a harsh judgment by the Anunnaki, the judges of the underworld. Then her sister, Erishkigal, the Queen of the underworld, decided to transform her into a corpse and hang her from a hook on the wall. The idea that a divinity could be easily transformed into a corpse illustrates the anthropomorphic way in which the Sumerians portrayed their gods in many texts. In ancient Sumerian religion, the gods appear to be vulnerable to death just like mortals. However, unlike humans, only gods could be brought back to life.

Meanwhile, back in the land of the living, Ninshubur, Inanna's assistant was beginning to become worried about the goddess' absence. After a period of three days, she decided to go to the holy shrine of Enlil to ask for help from the god. Refusing to listen to Ninshubur's request, Enlil responded by saying, since Inanna desired to journey to the underworld, therefore she was destined to remain there. After Enlil denied her request, then Ninshubur went to the god Enki to plead for help. Enki decided to send two tiny, fly-like creatures down into the underworld to rescue Inanna. After slipping through some cracks in the gates of the underworld, these two minuscule creatures found their way to the throne room of the Queen of the underworld. There they saw the Queen sitting on her throne moaning in pain. When she saw the two tiny creatures she asked them what they wanted. They said they came for the corpse of Inanna. She agreed to give them the corpse and then the two tiny creatures sprinkled some food and water on it. Suddenly, Inanna awoke and was alive again.

Returning to earth was not as easy for Inanna as coming back to life after having been transformed into a corpse. When she decided to get up and leave, she quickly discovered that she could not move because some hostile demons and judges of the underworld were holding her down. They told her that no one was permitted to leave unless a substitute was provided to take their place. Although they would gladly take Inanna's assistant in exchange for Inanna, she refused. Finally, it was agreed upon that Inanna's husband, Dumuzi, would serve as her substitute, but he objected to the idea. The text concludes with a description of a compromise: Dumuzi must remain in the underworld during the first half of the year and for the second half of the year another unidentified female would take Dumuzi's place. This arrangement is like the compromise reached in *The Homeric Hymn to Demeter* where Persephone was required to spend a one-third of the year in the underworld and the other two-thirds in the world above.

The Babylonian Goddess Ishtar's Descent to the Underworld

The theme of spiritual transformation re-appears in another ancient Mesopotamian story entitled *The Descent of Ishtar to the Netherworld*. This mythic narrative is the later Babylonian version of the earlier Sumerian story of *Inanna's Descent to the Underworld*.[9] Later in the history of ancient Mesopotamian civilization, the Akkadians and Assyrians identify Inanna with the goddess Ishtar. As the high goddess of Babylonian religion, Ishtar becomes a much more powerful deity than Inanna and possesses a higher place in the divine pantheon in comparison to Inanna.

The Babylonian story of Ishtar is much more than simply a Semitic translation of the older Sumerian myth because it frequently embellishes many elements of the earlier Sumerian version of the myth. Whereas Inanna goes to the land of the dead to attend her brother-in law's funeral, Ishtar travels there to reunite with her consort Tammuz. Unlike her Sumerian counterpart, Ishtar does not die and come back to life even though her underworld descent and subsequent return to the land of the living is a symbolic representation of the agricultural cycle and the changing of the seasons.

Ishtar displays her strength in various ways throughout the story. In Babylonian times, both the god Marduk and goddess Ishtar gain ascendancy within the hierarchy of the gods. Ishtar is a much more imposing figure than her Sumerian equivalent, Inanna. The motif of the gateway to the underworld is used in a manner that underscores Ishtar's lofty position in the Babylonian pantheon. Unlike the Sumerian account, there is no need to bother with laying out instructions about what should be done if the goddess does not return to the land of the living. The assumption is that she can handle any situation that may arise and so nothing is said

Four. Journeys of Spiritual Transformation

about what to do if she does not make it back to the land of the living. She simply departs and upon reaching the gateway to the underworld Ishtar displays her power by threatening to knock down the gates if they are not immediately opened.

> "Open your gate for me to come in! If you do not open the gate for me to come in, I shall smash the door and shatter the bolt, I shall smash the doorpost and overturn the doors, I shall raise up the dead, and they shall eat the living: The dead shall outnumber the living!" The gatekeeper made his voice heard and spoke, He said to great Ishtar, "Stop, lady, do not break it down! Let me go and report your words to queen Ereshkigal."[10]

Without hesitation, Queen Ereshkigal ordered the gates of the underworld to be opened. Like the earlier Sumerian version of the myth, Ishtar is required to remove various articles of clothing as she passes through each of the seven gates. After passing through the seventh gate, Ishtar is confronted by the Queen of the Underworld. Rather than immediately turning into a corpse, Ishtar is attacked by "the sixty diseases" that attack her eyes, her sides, her heart, her head and feet. Back on earth things have changed for the worse due to Ishtar's descent. None of the crops will grow and famine has descended upon the land.

At this point in the Sumerian account, Ninshubur, Inanna's assistant asks for divine assistance and the god Enki sends two tiny creatures to help free Inanna. In the Babylonian version, a priest named Papsukkal asks King Ea for help in releasing Ishtar so that she would be able to restore the land to its former state. Ea creates a eunuch named Asushunamir to go down to the land of the dead to find Ishtar and bring her back. The story concludes with Ereshkigal allowing Ishtar to be released. Since Ishtar is a much more powerful deity than Inanna, neither demons nor the judges of the underworld can hold her down. Unlike the Sumerian version of the myth, the various articles of clothing and jewelry that were previously taken from the goddess are given back to her as she exits each of the seven gates. Whereas in the Sumerian myth, a substitute is required for Inanna to be released, in the Babylonian version a ransom must be paid in exchange for Ishtar's release. Perhaps a ransom is suggested instead of a substitute because there would be no substitute for the great goddess Ishtar. In the final lines of the myth, Ishtar's male consort Tammuz is briefly mentioned.

Journeys to the Underworld and Heavenly Realm

The Homeric Hymn to Demeter

Ancient Greek mythology also told similar stories about a god disappearing into the underworld and subsequently re-appearing in the land of the living. One such story is the 8th century BCE Greek myth entitled *The Homeric Hymn to Demeter*.[11] Despite the parallels, the extent to which Homer drew upon ancient Mesopotamian sources is unknown. Unlike the myth of *Inanna's Journey to the Underworld*, most of the action in *The Homeric Hymn to Demeter* takes place on the earth's surface as opposed to the underworld and focuses upon a description of Demeter's frantic search for her kidnapped daughter, Persephone. However, the main theme of both stories is the disappearance of the goddess into the world below and her eventual release back to the world above. At the heart of each tale is the symbolic portrayal of spiritual transformation.

The Homeric Hymn to Demeter provided a mythological explanation for the foundation of the Eleusinian mysteries. At some point during the initiation ceremonies of the mysteries of Eleusis, *The Homeric Hymn to Demeter* probably was recited and provided the mythological context for the performance of the rites. Instead of focusing upon a single divine protagonist such as the moon goddess Inanna or her Babylonian counterpart Ishtar, the Homeric poem has two primary divine protagonists, namely, the Olympian goddess Demeter and her daughter Persephone. Once again just like in the myths of ancient Mesopotamia, the gods of ancient Greece are portrayed anthropomorphically. According to the story, Persephone was sitting in a meadow of flowers when something unexpected occurred. Suddenly, as she plucked a pretty flower, a crevasse of earth opened and out of the depths, "the many named son of Kronos, sprang out upon her with his immortal horses."[12] In an instant, Persephone was kidnapped and taken down to the depths of the underworld. Although her mother Demeter heard her daughter's cries, she could not see where Persephone had gone. For nine days Demeter conducted a fruitless search looking high and low throughout the earth for her missing daughter. Then, on the tenth day Demeter met Hecate who informed her that although she had also heard Persephone's cries, she did not see who had taken her away. Then the two deities flew off in search of the god Helios, hoping that he knew something about who had stolen Demeter's daughter. At Mt. Olympus,

Four. Journeys of Spiritual Transformation

Demeter found Helios who said that Zeus was to blame for Persephone's abduction because he had given Hades permission to take her to the underworld and make her his bride.

Grieving over the loss of her daughter, Demeter withdrew from Mt. Olympus and traveled down to earth to the city of Eleusis. Taking the form of an old woman, she decided to sit down and rest at the side of the road. When the four daughters of Keleos Eleusinides came by, they saw her sitting there. One of them asked her what she was doing there sitting on the side of the road. Demeter explained that she had been held captive aboard a ship of pirates. Fortunately, she had escaped the pirates and came to Eleusis. Then, the four women decided to bring Demeter to their house. Metaneira, the lady of the house immediately took a liking to her and asked her if she would be willing to help raise her son up until he reached the age of puberty. Demeter said she would be happy to bring up the child. Demeter took special care of the child in various ways such as by anointing him with ambrosia and holding him in her arms as she breathed sweetly on him. At night, she hid him from his parents in a blazing fire. When the child's mother learned of this she became alarmed and said "Demophoon, my child, this stranger hides you in a great fire, bringing me grief and painful care."[13] When Demeter heard this, she became angry. She said that she was planning to grant immortality to the child, but now that was impossible. Suddenly Demeter's physical appearance miraculously changed, revealing her divine identity to her astonished onlookers. Demeter commanded her onlookers to build a great temple. She told them that at that place her sacred rites would be performed in the future.

Meanwhile, Demeter remained sad about the loss of her daughter. In her grief, she brought a long harsh famine to earth that brought human beings to the verge of extinction.[14]

> Onto the much-nourishing earth she brought a year most dreadful and harsh for men; no seed in the earth sprouted, for fair-wreathed Demeter concealed it. In vain the oxen drew many curved plows over the fields, and in vain did much white barley fall into the ground. And she would have destroyed the whole race of mortal men with painful famine and would have deprived the Olympians of the glorious honor of gifts and sacrifices, if Zeus had not perceived this and pondered in his mind.[15]

When Zeus heard about Persephone's absence and the starvation occurring on earth, he sent golden-winged Iris to find Demeter and bring her

Journeys to the Underworld and Heavenly Realm

back to Mt. Olympus. When Iris found Demeter at Eleusis, she refused to go. Then Zeus sent other gods of Olympus to try to persuade her to come to Olympus, but she refused to budge. In her despair, Demeter said that she would never set foot upon Olympus again nor would she ever allow the grain of the earth to sprout forth again until she had her daughter back. Hearing this, Zeus sent Hermes to the underworld to talk Hades into releasing Persephone. In the underworld Hermes found Hades and Persephone together sitting on his bed. Hermes told Hades that he needed to let Persephone go because Demeter had caused all the crops of earth to stop growing and unless he released her, humanity would be destroyed. Having heard Hermes' pleas, Hades decided to let Persephone leave, but he was not ready to let her go completely. Hades devised a plan to make sure that Persephone had to go back to the underworld for a certain portion of the year. The plan was to give her a sweet pomegranate to eat. Then he took her in his chariot back to earth to the temple where Demeter was staying. As soon as Demeter saw her daughter she embraced her, but she immediately sensed that somehow Hades had played a trick on her. She asked Persephone a question.

> "Child, when you were below, did you perchance partake of food? Speak out, that we both may know. If your answer is no, coming up from loathsome Hades, you shall dwell both with me and with father Kronion, lord of dark clouds, honored by all the immortals. Otherwise, you shall fly and go to the depths of the earth to dwell there a third of the seasons in the year, spending two seasons with me and the other immortals. Whenever the earth blooms with every kind of sweet-smelling springflower, you shall come up again from the misty darkness, a great wonder for gods and mortal men. With what trick did the mighty All-receiver deceive you?"[16]

Then Persephone explained to Demeter how she was abducted from a meadow and taken to the underworld by Hades on his golden chariot. She said that before Hades allowed her to return home he tricked her into eating a pomegranate seed. When Zeus heard this, he decided that because she had eaten the fruit she had to spend one-third of the year in the underworld, but for the remaining two-thirds of the year, she would be able to be with her mother and the other the gods on Mt. Olympus. The terms instituted for Persephone's release are somewhat like the terms established for the release of Inanna and Ishtar. Persephone will have two homes, one on earth for two-thirds of the year and one in the underworld for a third

Four. Journeys of Spiritual Transformation

of the year. Demeter accepted the compromise of Zeus and once again, the whole earth "teemed with leaves and flowers."[17] Once again the crops began to grow again. Then Demeter went to the rulers of earth and taught them about her "awful mysteries."[18] The goddess,

> showed them the celebration of the holy rites, and explained to all.... the awful mysteries not to be transgressed, violated or divulged, because the tongue is restrained by reverence for the gods. Whoever on the earth has seen these is blessed, but he who has no part in the holy rites has another lot as he wastes away in dank darkness.[19]

The poem ends with Demeter and her daughter returning to Olympus to join the other gods.

The Egyptian The Myth of Isis and Osiris

From the standpoint of the mystery-religions, *The Myth of Isis and Osiris* is the Egyptian equivalent to *The Homeric Hymn to Demeter*.[20] Just as *The Homeric Hymn to Demeter* provides the mythological context for the Eleusinian mysteries, likewise *The Myth of Isis and Osiris* serves as the mythological backdrop to the mysteries of Isis. Like *The Homeric Hymn to Demeter*, most of the action of the myth occurs on the earthly plane as opposed to the underworld or heaven. In *The Myth of Isis and Osiris* once again the theme of spiritual transformation becomes articulated in mythic terms in the description of the death and subsequent rebirth of Osiris. *The Myth of Isis and Osiris* was recorded by the 2nd century CE Neo-Platonic philosopher Plutarch. According to the story, Osiris was the child of the earth-god Seb and the sky goddess Nut. In Greek mythology, his parents were identified as Cronus and Rhea. When Osiris was born, a voice cried out at the temple at Thebes that a great king was born. After Osiris' birth, then his mother gave birth to four other children including Horus, Typhon, Isis and Nephthys. After their birth, Horus married his sister Nephthys and Osiris married Isis.

As the legendary king of Egypt, Osiris established laws and taught the people how to worship the gods. When Isis discovered wheat and barley growing in the wild, Osiris showed the Egyptians how to cultivate these agricultural items which allowed them to overcome their cannibalistic

Journeys to the Underworld and Heavenly Realm

ways. At some point, Osiris decided to turn his control of Egypt over to his sister Isis so that he could travel throughout the entire world and teach the people everywhere he went how to grow crops and cultivate the land. Osiris accumulated great wealth as he traveled. When he decided to return to Egypt, he was hailed as a great god and worshipped by the people. This caused his brother Typhon to become jealous. Together with some of his associates, Typhon decided to murder Osiris. After secretly measuring Osiris' body, Typhon had a coffin custom made for him. Then he invited Osiris and some of his friends to a party. The coffin was brought into the gathering and Typhon told his guests that whoever could perfectly fit inside the coffin would receive it as a prize. Everyone tried to climb inside, but none of them could fit inside of it. The last one to try was Osiris. After he climbed inside, his conspirators quickly slammed the coffin lid down and nailed it shut. Then they took it and threw it in the Nile.

When Isis learned about Typhon's conspiracy and Osiris' disappearance, she became extremely upset and began to frantically search for her brother. On the advice of the god of wisdom she first went to the papyrus swamps of the Nile Delta. In the swamp, she came upon a mother and her child who had been stung by a scorpion and died. Taking pity on the mother, Isis brought the child back to life. Meanwhile, the coffin containing the body of Osiris had floated down the Nile and out to sea. It came to rest at a place called Byblos in Syria. At Byblos, a tall Erica tree grew up around the coffin and it became enclosed inside of the tree trunk. Not knowing that the tree trunk contained Osiris' coffin, the king of the country decided to cut the tree down and use it as a pillar for his home.

When Isis learned about the whereabouts of Osiris, she quickly traveled to Byblos. The portion of the myth describing Isis' time at Byblos resembles those sections of *The Homeric Hymn to Demeter* describing Demeter's encounter with the four daughters of the Lord of Eleusis. Just as Demeter sat by the side of the road near Eleusis disguising herself as a peasant, likewise Isis is portrayed as sitting at the side of a road disguised as a humble peasant woman. As she sat there, Isis began to cry and refused to speak to anyone passing by. In *The Homeric Hymn to Demeter*, Demeter was greeted by the daughters of the king and eventually becomes the nurse maid of the queen's child; likewise, in *The Myth of Isis and Osiris* Isis meets some handmaidens of the king of Byblos and is taken back to the palace

Four. Journeys of Spiritual Transformation

to serve as the caretaker of the queen's son. Fire plays a significant role in both stories. Just as Demeter hides the infant in a fire, similarly, Isis puts the infant into a fire to burn away all that was mortal in him. When the infant's mother discovered that Demeter was putting the child in the fire, Demeter cried out that immortality would no longer be given to the child. Then, she revealed her identity as an Olympian god. In *The Myth of Isis and Osiris,* similar events transpire. When the queen saw her child being burned by fire, she cried out and this prevented him from becoming immortal. Then Isis revealed her true nature and demanded to be given the pillar in which her brother was enclosed.

At this point, some differences between the two stories emerge. In *The Homeric Hymn to Demeter,* the goddess leaves Eleusis and continues her search for Persephone. Finally, after Zeus intervenes, Hermes travels to the underworld and convinces Hades to allow Persephone to return to earth for a portion of the year. In the *Myth of Isis and Osiris,* Isis is given the pillar containing Osiris' corpse. Then she removed her brother's coffin from the tree. Afterward, she wrapped the tree trunk in fine linen and gave it to the king and queen who placed it inside the temple of Isis in Byblos. Osiris' coffin was put inside a boat along with the king's oldest child and the boat sailed away. On her way back to Egypt, Isis stopped at the city of Buto. While she was gone, Typhon stumbled upon the coffin. Realizing that the coffin contained the body of Osiris, he grabbed the corpse, cut it up into fourteen pieces and scattered them everywhere. When Isis returned to the boat, she discovered that Osiris' corpse was gone. Once again, she began another search for the missing pieces of Osiris' corpse. Whenever she found one, she would bury it. This piece of the myth provided an explanation for why there are so many sanctuaries of Osiris scattered throughout Egypt. One legend claimed that Isis only buried a facsimile of a body part instead of a real body part so that people would be encouraged to worship Osiris in various places. In this way Osiris' real grave could not be found by Typhon. Since Osiris' genitals had been eaten by some fish, Isis made an image of it called an obelisk that was used in many Egyptian festivals.

In another legend transmitted by the 1st century BCE Greek historian Diodorus Siculus in his *Bibliotheca Historia,* Isis desired to make sure her that husband's grave was never found and so she devised a plan. After recovering all of Osiris' body parts except for his genitals, she made wax images of each of the god's body parts and gave them to the priests of many different countries of the world. As a result, people came to believe that Osiris was buried in their country and so they paid homage to the god in various ways. One way in which the god was worshipped was through the consecration of various beasts to the god. Whenever the consecrated animals died, the people staged a reenactment of their grief and mourning over the death of Osiris. One of the animals dedicated to Osiris was the sacred Apis bull. The Apis bull was sacred to the people of Egypt because it had helped in the sowing of seed in the ground and producing the wonderful benefits of agriculture.[21]

As a supplement to Plutarch's account, several additional local Egyptian legends surround the figure of Osiris. One account states that when Isis discovered the corpse of her brother Osiris, she sat down with her sister Nephthys and uttered a long sad lament which served as the prototype of all Egyptian lamentations for the dead in later times. The sun-god Ra heard their sad cries and sent the jackal-headed god Anubis down from heaven to help Isis, her sister Nephthys, Thoth and Horus find all of Osiris' body parts, piece them together and wrap all of them together in linen. After performing all the necessary rites, Osiris' body was brought back to life to reign over the land of the dead as the Lord of the Underworld.

The mythic account of Osiris' dismemberment, subsequent death and resurrection established in the minds of ancient Egyptians the idea that eternal life was a real possibility for anyone if certain mummification procedures were carried out in the same way as they had been carried out for Osiris. The funerary ceremonies performed upon the deceased in ancient Egypt duplicated those rituals enacted by Anubis, Horus and the other gods for the dead god. In a sense, every deceased person's mummy was Osiris and was subject to the same fate as Osiris. Just as Osiris came back to life, a similar kind of transformation was potentially available for any individual.

A few indigenous religious festivals and ceremonies were celebrated in ancient Egyptian society in connection to the death and resurrection of Osiris. One such festival was celebrated at the town of Sais in lower Egypt.[22] According to Egyptian tradition, Osiris' grave was in Sais where a lake was nearby. Once a year the suffering and death of Osiris was recalled there. Herodotus states that people mourned and beat their breasts to express their intense sadness over the god's death. Part of the festival involved the display of a statue of Isis. It portrayed her as a sacred cow with a golden sun fixed between its horns. Allowing the public to view the statue during the festival had symbolic value: it represented Isis' search for her deceased consort. Another important feature of the festival involved the nocturnal illumination of all the houses in the area. People fastened oil-lamps to the outside of their houses and the lamps burned throughout the night, suggesting a commemoration of the death of Osiris as well as all dead people in general. On the last day of the festival, people went down to the sea accompanied by priests who carried a shrine containing a golden casket. Fresh water was poured into the casket and the people would cry out that Osiris was found. The revived Osiris was symbolically embodied in the following way: the people took some vegetable mold and mixed it together with spices and water in order that it could be shaped into a moon-shaped image of the god which was dressed and robed. In this way, Osiris' death, Isis' search and discovery of her brother as well as his final resurrection were reenacted during the festival.

The Metamorphoses of Apuleius

The Myth of Isis and Osiris served as the interpretive framework for those participating in the Hellenistic mysteries of Isis. Just as Osiris suffered death and dismemberment and subsequently was re-vivified to become king of the underworld, those entering the cult of Isis experienced a similar kind of spiritual death and rebirth. In his satirical novel entitled the *Metamorphoses*, the 2nd century CE writer Apuleius provides information about the inner experiences of the initiates of the mysteries of Isis. Although the *Metamorphoses* is a fictional composition, nevertheless the descriptions in Book XI likely reflect some of the personal experiences of Apuleius and other initiates of the cult. Although elements of numinous and mystical experience are clearly present in Apuleius' novel, the main theme of the story relates to the spiritual transformation of Lucius, the main protagonist. In this sense, the *Metamorphoses* brings to life some of the spiritual ideas that are only hinted at in the story of Isis and Osiris. Once again, Apuleius' novel highlights

Journeys to the Underworld and Heavenly Realm

the popularity of themes related to spiritual renewal in the ancient Greco-Roman world. Most likely, Apuleius participated in the initiation rituals of the mysteries of Isis and drew upon his experiences in the cult to create the contents of Book XI of the *Metamorphoses*.[23]

The *Metamorphoses* presents a series of anecdotal tales and vignettes about Lucius who is magically changed from a human being into a donkey and wanders about the ancient world having one adventure after the other. In a sense, becoming a donkey is kind of a punishment analogous to a descent into Hell. His magical transformation back into human form at the end of the story represents Lucius' redemption. Throughout all his travels and misfortunes, the one thing that gives Lucius strength is his religious bond to the goddess Isis. Lucius' metamorphosis back into a human body symbolizes the religious transformation that takes place for those participating in the initiation into the mysteries of Isis.

At the beginning of Book XI, Lucius is awakened in the dead of night. Suddenly, he is overcome with feelings of joy and hope when he realizes that the goddess might finally appear to him in a divine epiphany and deliver him from all his travails and suffering. After falling asleep, the goddess appeared in a dream vision. When she spoke, she told Lucius that she was the queen of both heaven and hell;

> "Behold, Lucius," she said, "moved by your prayer I come to you—I, the natural mother of all life, the mistress of the elements, the first child of time, the supreme divinity, the queen of those in hell, the first among those in heaven, the uniform manifestation of all the gods and goddesses—I, who govern by my nod the crests of light in the sky, the purifying wafts of the ocean and the lamentable silences of hell—I, whose single godhead is venerated all over the earth under manifold forms, varying rites, and changing names.... Behold, I am come to you in your calamity. I come with solace and aid. Away then the tears. Cease to moan. Send sorrow packing. Soon through my providence shall the sun of your salvation rise."[24]

In addition, she told Lucius that if he were to become a devotee of her cult, he will receive many other blessings.[25]

> "You shall live blessed. You shall live glorious under my guidance; and when you have traveled your full length of time and you go down into death, there also (on that hidden side of earth) you shall dwell in the Elysian Fields and frequently adore me for my favours. For you will see me shining on amid the darkness of Acheron and reigning in the Stygian depths. More, if you are found to merit my love by your dedicated obedience, religious devotion, and constant chastity, you will discover that it is within my power to prolong your life beyond the limits set to it by Fate."[26]

Four. Journeys of Spiritual Transformation

In the morning, Lucius suddenly awoke from his dream and immediately was overcome by feelings of fear and joy when he recalled the contents of his nocturnal vision of the goddess. While he splashed his face with water, he thought about all the things the goddess had said to him the night before. He noticed a great religious procession passing by on the street. A long parade of colorfully dressed priests and worshippers were marching by carrying statues of many gods and goddesses. Finally, a priest came along who had been appointed by the goddess to bring about the restoration of Lucius' human shape. When the priest held out a garland of roses, Lucius ate them and was immediately transformed back into his human form. Some people standing nearby witnessed the miracle and marveled at the sight of Lucius' incredible metamorphosis. In unison, the entire crowd lifted their hands up to the sky and cried out in joy to the goddess. Lucius was so shocked that he could not speak. Then, he joined the long parade of believers as they continued their journey to the coast. Arriving there, Lucius and the others saw a boat docked at the shore. It was filled with various images and relics of the goddess. Many precious gifts and offerings for the goddess were placed inside the ship and then everyone watched as the ship sailed off into the distant sea. Next, Lucius and the others came to the nearby temple of Isis. Once Inside the temple Lucius was greeted by his parents who were overjoyed to be reunited with him since they had thought that he was dead. Then Lucius entered a private area of the temple where final preparations for his initiation into the cult were made. Doubt filled his heart about his ability to keep all the commandments of the goddess. That night he had a strange dream. In the morning, the temple priests interpreted the dream to be a positive sign from the heavens that all was well and that the gods had given their approval for his initiation into the mysteries. As a result, his courage was restored.

A few days later, the goddess once again appeared to him in a nocturnal dream vision and declared that the day had finally arrived for his initiation. She told him a priest named Mithras had been appointed to minister to him during his sacrifices. On the next day Lucius awoke and quickly sought out the old priest Mithras who took Lucius by the hand and led him to the gate of the temple. After performing a few morning sacrifices, the priest went inside the temple and retrieved some sacred books written in some unknown language. After reading certain passages from the books, the priest led Lucius back to the baths where he washed and purified himself. After that, Lucius was led back to the temple again where he presented himself to the goddess. Then he was told some things about the cult that were unlawful to repeat. Afterward, he was ordered to fast for a period of ten days. Ten days later a large group of priests arrived at the temple precincts bringing Lucius gifts. All those who were uninitiated were ordered to leave. Then Lucius was given a new linen robe to wear. A priest took him by the hand and led him inside to the inner most sanctuary of the temple. His initiation is described cryptically as a journey to heaven and hell.

> Perhaps, dear reader, you are keen to know what was said and done, I would tell you if it were permitted to tell. But both the ears that heard such things and the tongue that told them would reap a heavy penalty for such rashness. However, I shall not keep you any longer on the cross of your anxiety, distracted as you doubtless are with religious yearning. Hear therefore and believe what I say to be truth. I approached the confines of death. I trod the threshold of Prosperine; and borne through the elements. I returned. At midnight I saw the Sun shining in all his glory. I approached the gods below and the gods above, and I stood beside them, and I worshipped them. Behold, I have told my experience.[27]

The next day several priests dressed Lucius in fine linen and commanded him to stand upon a wooden pulpit in the center of the temple by a statue of Isis. In his right hand, he held a lighted torch and a garland of flowers was placed upon his head. Crowds of people gathered around to gaze upon him. For many days afterward, many feasts were held in the temple precincts in his honor. Several days later, after the religious celebrations had concluded, Lucius decided to return to Rome to visit his parents and friends.

    The nature of pagan religious adhesion is well-illustrated in the *Metamorphoses*. Like Peregrinus, Lucius is simultaneously connected to several religious cults. Back at Rome Isis appeared to him once again in a dream. This time the goddess told him to prepare for entry into a new religious order. Upon awaking, it dawned upon Lucius that although he had become a follower of Isis, he had not yet become a worshipper of her consort Osiris. That night a priest of Osiris entered his room, bringing with him some spears wrapped in ivy and some other things. The priest sat down in a chair and instructed Lucius about certain matters related to his entry into Osiris' cult. For several weeks, Lucius had to save some money to pay for his initiation. He had to sell his robe and practice law in the courts of Rome to be able to afford the entry fees. Finally, he had enough money to pay for his initiation into the cult. Shortly thereafter, he received another divine dream in which he was told to prepare for an initiation into a third cult. Initially, Lucius was overcome with doubt about the need to be initiated a third time, but in a vision the gods calmed him and made him understand that there was nothing unusual about being initiated so many times. Once again Lucius prepared for his initiation by abstaining from meat for several days. Then Osiris appeared to him in a dream-vision, telling him that he was divinely chosen to enter the college of the Pastophores and become one of Osiris' high priests.

A Dying God of Norse Mythology

Themes related to spiritual transformation and the dying and rising gods continue to re-appear in medieval times. As Christianity moved into the pagan communities of northern Europe during the Middle Ages, some interesting mythological permutations took place. For example, the intersection of Christian and pagan religious ideas is featured in one Norse myth entitled *Baldr's Descent to the Underworld*. Unlike other myths of the ancient Mediterranean world, this Norse myth proposes the novel idea that when a deity dies and descends into the underworld, that god may never return to the world above.[28] When the Norse god Baldr descended into the underworld, he was condemned to remain there forever.

In the early Middle Ages, the three-fold view of the cosmos, consisting of heaven, earth and the underworld, continued to prevail as the dominant worldview of the European cultural landscape and is reflected in Norse mythology. One important repository of Norse mythology is the *Prose Eddas*. Within this great mythological document, various portrayals of the gods and their activities are described. Like the gods of the Near East and the Greco-Roman world, the gods of Norse mythology are portrayed anthropomorphically. In the Middle Ages, Norse society was basically a warrior culture which placed a great premium on the masculine virtues of physical strength and bravery. The story of *Baldr's Descent to the Underworld* is filled with violence and supernatural imagery.

Journeys to the Underworld and Heavenly Realm

At the beginning of the story, Baldr seeks the advice of the gods because some ominous dreams were bothering him. After giving Baldr some help, they decided to have some fun. They told Baldr to stand in front of the entire assembly of the gods so that they could shoot arrows and throw stones at him. Every time Baldr was hit by an arrow or a stone, he was miraculously unharmed. This upset Loki so much that he devised a plan to seek revenge against Baldr. Disguising himself as a woman, he decided to visit the goddess Frigg. Frigg asked the woman what the divine assembly was doing. The woman said that they were shooting arrows and throwing stones at Baldr, but nothing appeared to harm him because the Aesir had made a pledge not to harm Baldr. Then the woman asked Frigg if all the Aesir had pledged an oath. She told him that some mistletoe was growing just west of Valhalla that was too young to require such an oath. When the woman heard this, she suddenly disappeared and went to fetch the mistletoe. Then Loki changed back into the image of a man and took the stick of wood back to the assembly of the gods. Loki noticed that one of the gods named Hod was not shooting arrows at Baldr and so he handed the twig of mistletoe to him and told him to throw it at Baldr. The wooden stick went right through Baldr and instantly killed him. When the gods witnessed this tragedy, they were speechless and began to cry.

The motif of a ransom re-appears in this Norse tale in a slightly different way. Frigg asked the gods if anyone was willing to ride on the Road to Hel to find Baldr and offer a ransom for his return to Asgard. Hermod the Bold volunteered. Taking Odin's horse, Hermod rode off for nine straight nights through a series of dark valleys before reaching the entrance to the world below. A golden bridge stretched across the River Gjoll that was guarded by Modgud, the gatekeeper. Modgud asked Hermod why he was traveling on the road to Hell since he was not dead. He explained that he was in search of Baldr who recently died. Then Hermod asked the gatekeeper if she had seen Baldr recently. She admitted that she had recently seen Baldr cross the bridge on his way to Hell. Then Modgud allowed Hermod to resume his journey to the depths of the underworld. Soon he arrived at a great hall. Inside the hall, Hermod immediately saw Baldr sitting on a throne of honor. The next morning Hermod awoke and introduced himself to the Lord of the Underworld. He asked him if he could take his brother back to Asgard because all the members of the Aesir were

Four. Journeys of Spiritual Transformation

in a state of mourning. The Lord of the Underworld said that if everyone back in Asgard was weeping for Baldr, then he would be allowed to return. Otherwise, he would have to stay in the underworld forever. Back in Asgard, the Aesir sent out messengers telling everyone to weep for Baldr so that he would be released. Then, all the animals, trees, stones and metals of the earth began to weep, and water flowed everywhere. While traveling back to Asgard, the messengers saw a giantess named Thokk sitting in a cave. When they asked her to weep for Baldr, she refused. Because of her refusal, Baldr's fate was sealed. He would never be able to leave the world below.

The Aesir blamed Loki for this unfortunate turn of events and so they decided to seek revenge. When Loki saw the Aesir coming to get him, he ran away and jumped into a river nearby. Loki changed into a salmon, but the Aesir used their fishnets to capture him. Next, they tied him up and positioned a poisonous snake above him so that the snake's venom would continually drip down upon Loki's face. Loki convulsed so violently that it caused earthquakes to happen everywhere on earth. Loki was left there, tied up in tortuous pain until the time of Ragnarok, i.e., the end of the world.

In this chapter, a third type of religious experience labeled as "spiritual transformation" was examined. In ancient times, it was a popular theme that circulated in many literary narratives, including stories of otherworldly journeys such as *Inanna's Descent to the Underworld, Ishtar's Descent to the Netherworld, The Homeric Hymn to Demeter,* Plutarch's *Myth of Isis and Osiris* as well as Book XI of Apuleius' novel, *Metamorphoses.* Many narratives associated with the mystery religions describe spiritual regeneration in terms of dramatic stories about the "dying and rising gods." In addition to numinous experience, mystical experience and spiritual transformation, the next chapter focuses upon a fourth type of religious experience related to the reality of death.

Five

Courageous Journeys in the Face of Death

Coping with Death and Suffering

Feelings of joy and happiness are not always experienced when an individual apprehends the sacred. Sometimes, becoming aware of the sacred has a darker side. A fourth way in which people experience the sacred is through the process of coping with the reality of suffering and death. Often, the death of loved ones can be a very painful event and can raise some important existential questions about life. The theme of coping with the reality of human suffering and death is repeatedly reflected in many mythic narratives of ancient and early medieval times, including stories of otherworldly journeys. If it is permissible to speak of "religion" as an independent force in culture and history, then, at the most fundamental level, one of its most important cultural functions, is to provide individual believers and communities with a meaningful perspective on death. It is left up to religious institutions to offer coping strategies for the incomprehensible problems of life including the experience of pain, suffering and death. Some of these coping strategies find expression in stories of otherworldly journeys.

Among the religions of the world, different strategies have been developed for handling the problem of death. In antiquity, the belief in the immortal soul was one important approach. Given the fact that people are frequently overcome with grief due to the death of loved ones, religious institutions, both in the past and present, provide a meaningful way for handling such tragic circumstances. The concept of the immortal soul, as

Five. Courageous Journeys in the Face of Death

it was articulated in ancient Greek philosophy and elsewhere, played a significant role in helping people to handle the negative feelings associated with death. By the time of the advent of the Common Era, several western religious traditions, including Christianity, Judaism and the Greco-Roman mystery-religions had adopted this belief as part of their doctrinal perspective. These traditions taught that despite all the injustice and suffering experienced in life, there was always the hope for a blessed life in the hereafter.

In eastern religion, the attitude of solemn detachment and withdrawal from the world was another popular strategy for dealing with life's insurmountable problems, including sickness, old age and death. In Buddhism, the main goal of human existence is to overcome suffering and attachment to the things of the world. The essence of Buddha's teachings is summed up in the Four Noble Truths. According to this doctrine, life is suffering (*dukkha*) which results from being attached to material objects. By learning to detach oneself from what one desires, one can finally overcome suffering. Eventually, one can achieve Nirvana and find release from the cycle of birth and rebirth. As Buddhism testifies, coping with suffering and death is a significant religious issue. Since the reality of suffering and death is a serious problem for human beings, many religious narratives focus attention on this theme.

In distinction to those religious philosophies which assert that a supernatural world exists beyond the grave, a second strategy admits that death cannot be overcome; after the physical body expires, there is absolutely no other form of spiritual existence for an individual. In this approach, human mortality must be accepted in its entirety. This second strategy for coping with death is the underlying theme of two great hero-myths, namely, *The Epic of Gilgamesh and Beowulf.*

In Chapter Three several literary motifs appearing in *The Odyssey* and *Aeneid* related to the underworld journey of the hero were noted. The current chapter demonstrates that the literary tradition of underworld narratives continues to develop well beyond the ancient world into medieval times. This chapter explores two great epics, namely, *The Epic of Gilgamesh* and *Beowulf.* Each of these two narratives originated in widely diverge contexts both historically and geographically. Whereas *The Epic of Gilgamesh* originated in ancient Mesopotamia, *Beowulf* originated

Journeys to the Underworld and Heavenly Realm

in medieval England. Despite these differences, comparative analysis yields a number of thematic commonalities. Both documents express the archaic stage of historical development in the west. Although differences exist between the two documents in terms of plot and composition, both the story of Gilgamesh and Beowulf share certain features related to their heroic quest. In their confrontation with evil, Gilgamesh and Beowulf represent "the good" for their respective communities. In their fight against evil creatures each of them is assisted by close friends. As the ruler of the ancient city of Uruk, Gilgamesh protects his community against "evil" by engaging in a successful battle against the snake-like creature inhabiting the forest called Humbaba. Beowulf is also called upon to display his heroic nature by defending not only his own people, but also neighboring tribes from the clutches of wicked, hellish creatures of the marshlands who have been attacking the people of the land. The goddess Aruru sends a friend named Enkidu to Gilgamesh and together the pair defeat Humbaba. In *Beowulf*, when Beowulf is near death, he is assisted by a fellow warrior named Wiglaf who joins him in the battle against Grendel's mother. One of the most important similarities between the two stories is the fact that in both tales each protagonist undertakes a heroic journey to the underworld to confront the grim reality of death. Gilgamesh travels there because he wishes to save his people by capturing the flower of immortality; Beowulf is somewhat more self-centered in his quest because he wishes to achieve fame, glory and to be remembered forever by his community and this is why he enters the subterranean landscape of the marshlands to defeat the evil creature menacing the community.

According to many archaic myths, the fate of human beings is fundamentally different from the fate of the gods; whereas death is the destiny of all humans, immortality is only allotted to the gods. Various hero myths portray the hero's extraordinary strength and bravery in confronting the overwhelming power of death in the depths of the underworld. In the archaic pagan religious traditions of the west, a different approach was taken to the issue of death in comparison to the great religious traditions of the world. Prior to the time when the doctrine of the immortal soul was popularly accepted throughout the ancient Mediterranean world, a fundamental distinction was made in many myths between the nature of the gods and humans. In these archaic narratives, the gods frequently were portrayed in anthropomorphic terms. Sometimes the gods behaved frivolously like weak human beings, but in comparison to mortals, the gods were always superior because they were immortal, but humans were not because they were subject to old age and eventual death. As a result, a variety of mythic tales arose that spoke about the reality of death and offered explanations regarding why it was that humans were mortal. The famous dictum of the Delphic oracle "Know thyself" came to mean: "Know thyself. Know that you are mortal."

Both Gilgamesh and Beowulf journey to the underworld to confront death, but each hero conducts their journey under different circumstances. In the case of the ancient Near Eastern hero Gilgamesh, he falls into a state of deep despair when his friend Enkidu dies. This tragic event leads Gilgamesh, the king of Uruk to search for the elusive flower of immortality. At the end of the story, it is through the loss of the flower of immortality that Gilgamesh eventually becomes reconciled to the fact that all human beings are fated to die. In the concluding portion of the medieval tale entitled *Beowulf*, the main protagonist Beowulf realizes that he will inevitably die in battle. Despite insurmountable odds, he chooses to single-handedly engage in a bloody battle to the death against a horrific dragon to protect his family and people. By means of his acts of heroism, Beowulf understands that he is fulfilling his destiny as a great warrior. Even though Beowulf dies in the end, it is through his heroic actions that he achieves a kind of symbolic immortality by being forever remembered in the mind of his community.

The Underworld Journey of Gilgamesh

In many mythic narratives, gods and goddesses travel to the underworld for a variety of reasons, but mortal heroes usually travel there in search of some specific thing or to achieve some lofty goal. In *The Epic of Gilgamesh* and the medieval tale *Beowulf*, each protagonist is searching for immortality, but each hero engages in this quest in a different kind of way. Gilgamesh descends into the underworld in search of the mysterious flower of everlasting life. By heroically defending his community against the onslaught of three horrific monsters, Beowulf hopes that he will never be forgotten by his community, even after his death.

Journeys to the Underworld and Heavenly Realm

In approaching *The Epic of Gilgamesh*, it is important to understand this mythic tale in the context of ancient Mesopotamian religion.[1] Life was brutal in ancient Mesopotamian times. As a result, human beings believed that they needed the protection of the gods for their very existence. The gods had made human beings out of clay. To show their gratitude, human beings were required to serve the gods by providing them with offerings of food and drink. Providing sustenance for the gods took priority over providing food and water for oneself and one's family. As a result, economic scarcity dominated ancient Mesopotamian civilization since there was little in the way of food and shelter to go around and most people were deprived of the necessities of life. Besides the ever-present threat of attack from roaming hordes of bandits, growing crops in the harsh desert environment was difficult. Since the divine world was conceived in mythic terms as a duplicate copy of the harsh life on earth, most ancient Mesopotamians expected very little in the next life. One thing that distinguished mortals from the gods was the fact that the gods were immortal, but humans were not. *The Epic of Gilgamesh* provided a mythological explanation for many of the dismal circumstances of human existence in the ancient Mesopotamian world.

The figure of Gilgamesh stands out as a good example in ancient Near Eastern religious literature of the mythological hero who travels to the underworld in search of immortality. Gilgamesh has many numinous encounters during his underworld journey that play a limited role in developing the plot. However, the main theme of the story is Gilgamesh's quest for immortality and his eventual acceptance of his own mortality. The circumstances of his mythic quest are described in the main body of the narrative. Gilgamesh's heroic status is defined by his heritage: he was two-thirds divine and one third human. He was extremely strong and gifted in the use of weaponry, but unfortunately, he was causing a multitude of problems within his own community. To pacify Gilgamesh, the goddess Aruru created a companion for him named Enkidu. After Gilgamesh and Enkidu became close friends, they decided to go on a long journey to kill a monstrous creature called Huwana who guarded the cedar forest. On their way home, the duo was confronted by Ishtar who asked Gilgamesh to marry her. When Gilgamesh rejected her offer, Ishtar flew into a violent rage. In her anger, she unleashed the sacred bull of heaven to attack and kill the

Five. Courageous Journeys in the Face of Death

pair. However, Ishtar's anger is thwarted when the two warriors successfully defend themselves against the bull and kill it. The outcome of the battle offended the gods and so they decided that Enkidu had to die.

Gilgamesh was crushed by Enkidu's death. It caused him to wonder if there was no escape from the inevitability of death. To find an answer to his question, Gilgamesh sets off on a long journey through the vast wilderness and into the underworld. When he arrives at a mountain range called the Mashu, he finds the entrance to the underworld and is greeted there by the Scorpion Men, the guardians of the underworld. The Mashu functions as the *axis mundi* of the world that connect the three cosmic realms.

> The name of the mountain is Mashu. When he reached the mountain Mashu, Which daily guards the coming out of [Shamash] Their upper part s [touch] the sky's foundation, Below, their breasts reach Arallu. They guard its gate, Scorpion-men Whose aura is frightful, whose glance is death.[2]

As gatekeepers to the underworld, the Scorpion Men represent a common type of character found in many underworld narratives. Gilgamesh was filled with fear when he confronts these guardians of the world below. When he explained to the Scorpion Men that he was on a quest for immortality one of them responded by saying, "It is impossible, Gilgamesh, Nobody has passed through the mountain's inaccessible tract. For even after twelve leagues The darkness is too dense, there is no light."[3] Ignoring these warnings, Gilgamesh revealed his heroic nature by continuing down the long dark path into the underworld below where no mortal had ever dared to go. After some time had passed, he began to feel the gentle north wind blowing on his face. Finally, he emerged from darkness and saw the sun rising in the east. Nearby he saw Shamash, the solar god who reiterated that it was impossible for any human being to find out about the secret of immortality and that he should give up his quest. Refusing to accept the futility of his search, Gilgamesh resumed his journey until he met a divine bar-maid named Siduri. Once again, he told her about the death of his friend Enkidu and how it had greatly saddened him. He explained that Enkidu's death had motivated him to set off on his long and arduous trip to defeat the powers of death. Siduri told him that his search for the secret of immortality would be extremely difficult for it involved a dangerous journey across the sea.

Journeys to the Underworld and Heavenly Realm

"There has never been a ferry of any kind Gilgamesh,
And nobody from time immemorial has crossed the sea.
Shamash the warrior is the only one who has crossed the sea: apart from Shamash, nobody has crossed the sea.
The crossing is difficult, the way of it very difficult,
And in between are lethal waters which bar the way ahead.
Wherever, then, could you cross the sea, Gilgamesh?
And once you reached the lethal waters, what would you do?
(Yet) there is, Gilgamesh, a boatman of Ut-napishtim, Ur-shanabi,
He—the "thing of stone" identify him—will be trimming a young pine in the forest.
Go, and let him see your face.
If it is possible, cross with him. If it is impossible, retreat back."[4]

In many religious narratives, the underworld is described as a sacred realm that is "wholly other" from the profane world. Many mythic accounts emphasize the transcendent nature of the underworld by using of certain foreboding images such as dark bodies of water that must be crossed such as the River Styx and mysterious ferrymen who assist in the crossing. After Gilgamesh found the boatman Ur-shanabi, he had him take him across the Waters of Death. After stepping on dry land, he met Utnapishtim who revealed something about himself. Unlike other mortals, Utnapishtim was given the gift of immortality by the gods after surviving a great flood. He was the only one who was given this precious gift and no other mortal would ever be given such a gift. After listening to Utnapishtim's story, Gilgamesh became tired and went to sleep for seven days and nights. While he slept, Utnapishtim told Ur-shanabi, the boatman to prepare for Gilgamesh's departure out of the underworld. After Gilgamesh woke up, the boatman took him to the washing place where he washed off all the grime and dirt from his body. Then Utnapishtim shared with Gilgamesh the secret of immortality.

"Gilgamesh, came, weary, striving,
What will you give him to take back to his country?
And Gilgamesh out there raised the pole,
He brought the boat near the shore.
Ut-napishtim spoke to him, to Gilgamesh,
"Gilgamesh, you came, weary, striving, What can I give you to take back to your country?
Let me reveal a closely guarded matter, Gilgamesh,
And let me tell you the secret of the gods.
There is a plant whose root is like camel-thorn,
Whose thorn, like a rose's, will spike [your hands]
If you yourself can win that plant, you will find rejuvenation."[5]

Five. Courageous Journeys in the Face of Death

Afterward, Gilgamesh began his long journey back to the world above. Along the way, Gilgamesh came to a river. Tying stones to his feet, he dived down into the deep water and spotted the plant of immortality. He plucked it from the bottom of the water. Cutting the stones from his feet, he quickly returned to the shore. Gilgamesh named the plant "Man Becomes Young in Old Age" and vowed to eat it so that he could return to the condition of his youth. After a long day's journey of thirty leagues, Gilgamesh and the boatman decided to stop and prepare to go to sleep for the night.

> At thirty leagues they stopped for the night. Gilgamesh saw a pool whose water was cool, And went down into the water and washed. A snake smelt the fragrance of the plant. It came up silently and carried off the plant. As it took it away, it shed its scaly skin. Thereupon Gilgamesh sat down and wept.[6]

With the theft of the plant of immortality, eternal life was lost forever. At this point, Gilgamesh realized that death is the fate of all human beings.

Beowulf

In contrast to *The Epic of Gilgamesh*, the medieval Anglo-Saxon poem entitled *Beowulf* presents a somewhat different picture of the hero's confrontation with death. The half historic and half legendary tale describes one Scandinavian warrior's heroic struggle against the overwhelming powers of evil. The story is set in early medieval Europe, a time when tribes and kingdoms are engaged in a violent battle for power and dominance. In this world the masculine virtues of bravery and brute, physical strength are valued above all other things. A variety of ominous and mysterious elements characterized the story of Beowulf. For example, the encounter between Beowulf and Grendel's mother in her underwater lair has pronounced numinous elements. Beowulf's magic sword used to defeat the evil creature and the descriptions of the misty, dank marshlands add an element of wonder and suspense to the atmosphere. However, the main message of the story is somewhat different from that of *The Epic of Gilgamesh*. In Gilgamesh's case, the loss of the flower of immortality leads to his acceptance of death. The main point of *Beowulf* is that although death is the lot of all human beings, the mortal hero has the power to establish a legacy for himself

Journeys to the Underworld and Heavenly Realm

through acts of bravery. In this way, the hero achieves a kind of symbolic immortality in the memory of the community.

The anonymous author of this epic medieval poem sets his narrative against the historical background of 6th century CE Denmark and southwestern Sweden. Prior to this time in the 4th century, Christianity had already become the official religion of the Roman Empire under the rule of Emperor Constantine. However, a variety of polytheistic beliefs and pagan, magical practices continued to thrive throughout medieval Europe well into the centuries following the fall of the Roman Empire. In addition to describing some interesting details about medieval European society, many Judeo-Christian and pagan mythological and religious symbols are interwoven into the story. As a result, a fascinating mix of history and fantasy is presented in *Beowulf*, with a heavy emphasis upon mythological symbolism. From a Judeo-Christian perspective, the marshland symbolizes Hell, a place existing below earth that is inhabited by horrific creatures such as Grendel, Grendel's mother and a horde of other evil Satanic demons. Grendel took the appearance of a giant male human being and his mother had the likeness of a woman. Nothing is mentioned about Grendel's father nor whether Grendel's parents ever produced any other offspring. Since the days of old Grendel and his mother lived in a marshy world of darkness. An underground mountain stream flowed nearby. Like a few other pagan and Judeo-Christian portrayals of hell, the marshy home of Grendel and his mother is referred to as a bottomless pit that was filled with many strange and terrifying things. When Hrothgar, the king of the land speaks about Grendel's home, he says the following:

> "It is not far from here, measured in miles, where the mere stands. Great trees hang above it, heavy with frost, woods held fast by roots overshadow the water. An omen of evil every night may be seen—flames on that flood. There is no one so wise that he can determine its bottomless depth. Though the heath-stepper, a stag with strong horns, seeking safety in woods was forced into flight, pressed hard by hounds, it would rather surrender its life on the bank before jumping in that water to protect itself. That is no pleasant place! Towering waves, surge upward on high, dark under clouds, when the wind whips up terrible storms, and the sky blackens with gloom as the heavens wail."[7](1361–1376)

The people of the territory have been under siege for many years by Grendel who is described in Biblical terms as a descendant of Cain. Every so

Five. Courageous Journeys in the Face of Death

often this evil monster crept out of the marshland and wreaked havoc and death upon the land. Many of King Hrothgar's warriors have been killed in their effort to defend the land from this awful creature. Finally, a young Scandinavian warrior named Beowulf enters the picture and offers his assistance to rid the land of this horrible beast originating from the dank marshes. Beowulf has a heroic past. Once when he was challenged to a swimming match with a boyhood friend, he killed nine sea monsters before swimming back to the shore.

In the story, Beowulf fights gallantly against the creatures of the underworld on three separate occasions. The first battle took place in Heorot, the great mead palace where all the warriors of the kingdom gather. One night while Beowulf and his fellow warriors were asleep in Heorot, the evil creature Grendel silently approached the warriors and launched its attack. A great battle ensued between Grendel and Beowulf and his warriors. Beowulf mortally wounds Grendel by tearing off one of the creature's claws. As a trophy of Beowulf's victory, the claw of the creature is hung up on the wall of the great mead hall. The next morning many warriors come from miles around to pay homage to the victorious warrior and see the great claw of the creature hanging on the wall. Then, a great celebration takes place and Beowulf is honored with many gifts for his brave deeds. Everyone is relieved to know that the evil creature has finally been killed.

Meanwhile, deep down in a dark marshland, Grendel's mother was seething with anger over the death of her son and plotting a second attack on Beowulf and the other warriors.

> The mother of Grendel, a female monster, was minded to cause misery. She was doomed to dwell in some fearsome waters, streams of cold as death, since Cain had committed the brutal murder of his only brother, both with the same father. He was fated to wander, marked for the murder, fleeing the joys of men, to dwell in the wasteland. From him descended doomed spirits of old—dread Grendel was one, that much-hated outlaw, who discovered Heorot a warrior on watch, all ready for battle. There the monster had seized ahold of the hero, but Beowulf bore in mind his marvelous strength, a wondrous gift which God had given him, so he counted on aid from the Almighty, for help and support. Thus, he defeated the demon, laid low hell's creature, and the wretched one departed deprived of joy, to seek out his deathplace, a fallen foe of mankind. And now came his mother, hungering for men's death, who desired to go on a sorrowful journey to avenge her son's death. (line 1258–1278)[8]

Journeys to the Underworld and Heavenly Realm

That night Beowulf left the mead hall and was sleeping nearby. Grendel's mother quietly crept into the hall while the other warriors were asleep. Suddenly everyone woke up and a great fight took place between Grendel's mother and the warriors. Unfortunately, Aeschere, one of Hrothgar's great warriors was killed during the fight. Before managing to escape from the hall and returning to her lair, the monster removed Grendel's claw off the wall and took it with her. The next day the warriors gathered together. Everyone agreed that Aeschere's death had to be avenged. King Hrothgar sent for Beowulf who gladly accepted the king's request for assistance in dealing with this menace to the community. Beowulf believed the best course of action for dealing with the loss of his friend Aeschere was to avenge his death.[9] A code of honor dictated the actions of the medieval warrior; like many other pagan heroes of the distant past such as Gilgamesh and Odysseus, Beowulf did not subscribe to the optimistic viewpoint that a blessed afterlife awaited the warrior upon his death. The medieval warrior Beowulf believed that a hero could only hope to achieve a form of symbolic immortality by performing noble acts of bravery. Then, the hero would be remembered in the minds of the community forever. In Beowulf's words, "Each of us must accept the end of life here in the world—so we must work while we can to earn fame before death. For a warrior, it is best to live on in memory after life has departed."[10] By means of boldly confronting death on the field of battle, the medieval hero would never be forgotten by his people.

Beowulf donned his armor, grabbed his great hilted sword called Hrunting and set off in the mere to confront the horrible beast. When Grendel's mother saw him, she quickly seized him, but his armor protected him from injury. Then she ordered a sea-wolf to grab Beowulf and carry him to the bottom of the mere to an underwater hall. In the numinous underwater hall, Beowulf confronted Grendel's mother. As she approached him, Beowulf immediately struck her with his sword, but he soon discovered that it was unable to cut through her skin. Throwing down the sword, he used his bare hands to fight the monster. When she tried to stab him with her dagger, once again his armor protected him. Then Beowulf spotted another large sword hanging on a nearby wall. Quickly he grabbed the weapon and was able to kill the monster by stabbing it in the neck. Afterward, Beowulf began a frantic search throughout the underwater hall for

Five. Courageous Journeys in the Face of Death

Grendel's corpse. When he found it, he cut its head off and then left with it in his hand. As he went, Beowulf's bloody mere sword began to slowly dissolve "into icicles of gore.... much like the ice when the Father loosens the bond of the frost, unfastens fetters on the waters, wielding power over seasons and times."[11]

Years later, Beowulf had become the king of the Geats. Once again, he was called upon to provide for the heroic defense of his people for a third time. In the wilderness nearby, a dragon stood guard in an underground fortress over a vast treasure trove that once belonged to a tribe of people that no longer existed. One day as the dragon was sleeping, a wanderer accidentally stumbled into the mysterious vault of fortunes. Noticing the dragon lying on the ground, the wanderer suddenly became frightened and ran out of the barrow, grabbing a precious golden cup on his way out. When the dragon realized that the man had stolen one of the dragon's precious treasures, he became angered and wanted revenge. Unable to immediately find the thief and punish him for stealing the golden cup, the dragon soon began a reign of terror that gripped the entire community living nearby. At night, the dragon would come out of its underground home and spew forth flames on many homes that burned to the ground. Many inhabitants were killed by the flames of the dragon. Then, every night, just before dawn, the dragon would return to its home. Initially when Beowulf heard about these attacks of the dragon, he thought that perhaps God was punishing him for breaking some ancient commandment. Then, realizing that the dragon had to be stopped at any cost, Beowulf decided to stand up against the dragon by himself. Having survived many brutal battles in the past, including his hard-fought victory against both the mighty Grendel and his mother, Beowulf realized that he had to face one final test at the end of his life. Before engaging the dragon in battle, Beowulf made one final speech to his fellow warriors.

> I have lived through many battles while in the strength of my youth, yet still I wish, as old protector of my people, to seek out this fight, to win great glory, if the man-slaying monster will come out of his cave to meet me in battle.... I would not wish to bear a sword, a weapon against the dragon, if I knew another way to fulfill my boast, to grapple with this beast, as I did against Grendel a long time ago. But here I will face a foe breathing fire, blazing and venomous —so I must do battle under shield and mail-shirt.... I bid each of you to wait near the barrow, protected by your mail-coats, proud warriors in arms, to see which of us two can better survive wounds

Journeys to the Underworld and Heavenly Realm

after the tumult of battle. This task is not yours, nor is it fitting for any other man, except me alone, to measure strength against the monster, in heroic war-deeds. With courage I will win a reward of gold treasures, or your king will be torn away from his people in a frightful slaughter.[12]

Once Beowulf found the dragon in its underground home, he approached it so that he could strike it with his trusty sword, but when the blade hit the creature's body, it was abruptly stopped by the creature's hard bone. Then, the dragon began to spew forth deadly flames toward Beowulf. All the warriors standing nearby fled in fear into the woods rather than stay there to help him. However, one warrior named Wiglaf felt remorse for leaving and decided to return to help Beowulf. When the dragon saw Wiglaf coming to help Beowulf, he attacked him with his fiery breath, melting Wiglaf's shield. Wiglaf's armor did not offer any protection against the flames. Nevertheless, the brave, young warrior did not give up, but continued to fight against the beast anyway. When Beowulf hit the dragon's head with his sword, the sword shattered into many pieces. Realizing his opportunity, the monster attacked Beowulf once again. This time the dragon "surrounded his neck with fierce sharp fangs, digging deep into his flesh to drain life from his body, as the blood streamed out"[13] Coming to Beowulf's defense in his time of need, Wiglaf showed great courage by inflicting a death blow to the creature in his lower extremities. Then the deadly fire of the dragon slowly began to die down. Together, Beowulf and Wiglaf had finally brought down the monster.

Beowulf's wounds were severe enough that they began to burn and swell. Realizing that the end was near, Beowulf told Wiglaf to go to the den of the dragon to make sure that the treasure was still there. When Wiglaf entered the dragon's den, he was amazed to find an incredible amount of valuable gold and jewels. He gathered some of the treasures in his arms and took it to show Beowulf what he had found. When he found Beowulf, Wiglaf washed the blood off from Beowulf's face and then Beowulf spoke his last words. First, he thanked the Almighty Lord for the riches of the barrow which he bequeathed to his people. Then, he told Wiglaf to build a funeral pyre near the coast so that those sailing by would see it. Beowulf gave Wiglaf the golden chain hanging from his neck, his war helmet and coat of mail, telling him that he would now be the king. After that, Beowulf passed away and "his soul traveled, forth from his

Five. Courageous Journeys in the Face of Death

breast, to the fame of the righteous."¹⁴ Wiglaf tried to revive Beowulf, to no avail. Then, he spoke strong words of condemnation to those cowardly men standing nearby who had deserted their leader in his time of need, saying that it was better to die than to live a life of shame. Afterward, the Geats realized that the treasure in the dragon's barrow was cursed. Therefore, it was decided that the best thing to do to avoid the curse was to remove it from the barrow and bury it with Beowulf. During Beowulf's funeral, his heroic actions were commemorated by singing of his great courage and bravery;

> They sang of his valor, and of his deeds of great strength, with all their power praising the hero—as it is fitting for a man with his words to praise his friendly lord, share the love from his heart, when the lord must go, passing beyond the bounds of his body.... They said that he was, among all the world's kings, the mildest of men, and the most kind in giving, the most gentle of men, and the `most eager for fame.¹⁵

Rather than experiencing the sacred through visions or other contemplative means, the closest that Gilgamesh and Beowulf ever come to apprehending of the sacred is through their face-to-face encounter with death. Both Gilgamesh and Beowulf descend into the depths of the watery abyss in their search for immortality. "Courage in the Face of Death" was the way in which these two mortal heroes experienced the sacred. Gilgamesh's courageous descent into the world below produced something totally unexpected. Although the flower of immortality was lost and death could not be defeated, such a fate could be ultimately accepted. It is through Gilgamesh's acceptance of human mortality that he achieves his true heroic status. Beowulf's quest is less altruistic in comparison to Gilgamesh. When Beowulf descends into the dank watery marshlands he held the selfish hope that he would always be remembered in the mind of his people for his heroism.

Attaining immortality through the performance of heroic actions is different from achieving immortality through asceticism or contemplation. This latter type of spiritual activity is frequently discussed by philosophers when they talk about the existence of an eternal soul and the afterlife. For Beowulf, when a person dies, there is no blessed afterlife. He consoles himself to this reality by realizing that he will always be remembered by his people. In the mind of Beowulf, there is no other kind of immortality that a human being can achieve. In contrast to Beowulf's

Journeys to the Underworld and Heavenly Realm

point of view, many philosophers have argued that a life of quiet contemplation is far preferable to a life of heroic action for a variety of reasons. For Plato, philosophy prepares one for death. Making sensible choices in the present life prepares a soul to make good choices in the next life. In the next chapter, the journey to philosophic wisdom is explored as it is articulated in the works of Plato and Cicero.

Six

The Journey to Philosophic Wisdom

Ultimate reality can be experienced non-rationally through dreams and visions, but it can also be experienced through a variety of other ways as well. Those who pursue the philosophical life approach the world of the sacred through their rational faculties. As a result, the intellectual apprehension of the sacred represents the fifth type of religious experience to be considered in this book. In the writings of some ancient and medieval philosophers, the quest for knowledge of the divine has often been articulated as a kind of philosophic journey. Hence, the heavenly journey to philosophic wisdom is the focus of this chapter.

The core beliefs and rituals of the major religious traditions of the west, including Judaism, Christianity and Islam are considered by their followers to be the direct revelation of God as recorded by their prophets and disciples in various sacred books and canonical writings. Under certain circumstances, this revelation can be ambiguous and in need of clarification. Under these conditions, human reason has been used as a tool for the interpretation of religious revelation. Due to the changing forces of history, the original message of a religious tradition can be lost or even forgotten. For it to be restored, additional support may be needed to withstand the challenge of dissenting voices from either within or outside of the religious tradition concerned. In the Christian tradition, the faith of the religious community has been fortified through the development of rational arguments for the existence of God. Looking at the world through the prism of the intellect, Christian philosophers and theologians have argued that a highly intelligent divine being exists as the source of the rational order and beauty present in the universe. One of the so-called

Journeys to the Underworld and Heavenly Realm

proofs for God's existence became known as the teleological argument or "the argument from design." According to this argument, the universe was fashioned by a supremely intelligent being who gave to his creation its rational order and structure.

In addition to the emotional side of religion, there is also a rational dimension of religion that is reflected in the development of complex religious doctrines and theological systems.[1] Further, the intellectual response to religious feelings and experiences is different from what William James calls "intellectualism" in religion which approaches the subject of religion purely from the standpoint of logic alone, without any reference to genuine religious feelings or experience.[2] On the emotional level of religious faith, many people are overcome with feelings of wonder and astonishment in the presence of the sacred, but this type of emotional response can also exert a significant influence in the development of one's intellectual thinking about God. If one has an unfailing faith in the existence of God, then one might also be inclined to seek some satisfactory intellectual grounds for justifying this kind of theological belief. Frequently, the intellect can become intertwined with various kinds of latent feelings and emotions.

The experience of the sacred often can be transmitted in intellectual terms. In numinous experience, feelings of awe and wonder can appear along with the realization that one is utterly dependent upon their God who is the source of all things including the order and beauty of the cosmos. In the mystical tradition, this awareness of overwhelming dependence is often expressed as an awareness of the presence of the divine power and energy within oneself. These types of religious awareness can alternately be described in rational terms as an intellectual apprehension of the sacred. In the words of William James,

> To redeem religion from unwholesome privacy, and to give public status and universal right of-way to its deliverances, has been reason's task.... even in soliloquizing with ourselves, we construe our feelings intellectually. Both our personal ideals and our religious and mystical experiences must be interpreted congruously with the kind of scenery which our thinking mind inhabits. The philosophic climate of our time inevitably forces its own clothing on us. Moreover, we must exchange our feelings with one another, and in doing so we have to speak, and to use general and abstract verbal formulas. Conception and constructions are thus a necessary part of our religion; and as moderator amid a clash of hypotheses, and mediator among the criticisms of one man's constructions by another, philosophy will always have much to do.[3]

Six. The Journey to Philosophic Wisdom

On the institutional level, theological controversies and disputes have frequently sprung up within religious communities regarding the implications of certain key doctrines. Within all the major religious traditions of the world, including Judaism, Christianity, and Islam in the West, and Hinduism, Buddhism, Taoism and Confucianism in the East, human reason has been used to illuminate certain key religious issues and ideas. For example, in the early days of the Christian Church, theological disputes arose within the Church regarding the true nature of Jesus Christ. In the 4th century CE, many members of the orthodox Church community were outraged with the heretical theological views of Arius, a priest within the Eastern Church. Arius stirred things up by claiming that Jesus of Nazareth was made of the flesh and was not divine at all. Therefore, Arius argued that Jesus should not be placed on the same spiritual level with God, the Father. Although many outliers including the Gnostics, supported Arius' views, others within the mainstream community disagreed. Then, in 325 CE Emperor Constantine organized the first ecumenical meeting of bishops at the city of Nicaea to resolve the disagreement. After hearing the arguments from both sides, the Council of Nicaea issued the Athanasian Creed which basically upheld the doctrines of Arius' chief opponent, Athanasius (296–373 CE).

On the personal level, when an earth-shattering encounter with the sacred happens to an individual, a period of quiet reflection may be needed for processing the event. Thinking and reflecting upon one's awareness of the divine involves the utilization of one's intellect. Some classical philosophers such as Plato have suggested that human reason plays a key role in apprehending divine truth. Greco-Roman philosophy addressed a variety of spiritual subjects, including the existence of the gods, the immortality of the soul and the afterlife. Rather than approaching these topics as a theologian would approach them, that is, purely from the standpoint of faith and belief, Greco-Roman philosophers tended to apply their intellect to these matters and were prepared to reject any metaphysical argument or theory that did not make rational sense to them. Although ancient philosophy dealt with many religious issues, such as the existence of God or the soul, it approached them differently than from a traditional theological point of view. In distinction to theological discourse, the traditional philosophical perspective does not assume the existence of any metaphysical entity including the soul or the gods. Rather, the goal of philosophy is to establish the rational grounds for holding such beliefs. At the outset theology is grounded in a faith in the existence of God and the immortal soul and then proceeds to elaborate various arguments to support those beliefs. In other words, theology is a faith-based inquiry whereas philosophy is not. However, in the later Hellenistic period, Greco-Roman philosophy had evolved in Roman society into something more than simply an intellectual activity. In short, philosophy was regarded as a highly desirable way of life.

The idealized image of the philosopher living a life of quiet contemplation was the quintessential life-style choice of many Hellenistic and Roman aristocrats. In this way, Greco-Roman philosophy functioned as a kind of quasi-religion in Hellenistic times by offering a life of quietude and withdrawal from the world as the exemplary means for solving many of the existential problems of the day. For many of those citizens enthralled with the philosophical life-style, the old traditional Olympian religion no longer held any value and had fallen by the wayside, leaving a spiritual void that needed to be filled. By Hellenistic times, several religious options were available for citizens of the Mediterranean world. Many found spiritual gratification in the various mystery-religions or Christianity; other superstitiously inclined individuals put their trust in the teachings of various holy men such as the 2nd century CE Neo-Pythagorean teacher and the wonder-worker Apollonius of Tyana whose exploits are described in Philostratus' 3rd century biography *The Life of Apollonius of Tyana*. Additionally, within aristocratic circles and the ruling class, there were those who demanded a more sophisticated approach to religious matters; for many of these individuals, Stoicism provided the answer. The appeal of Stoic philosophy is well represented in Marcus Aurelius' spiritual autobiography entitled the *Meditations*.[4]

The quasi-religious function of Greco-Roman philosophy is illustrated by the life of Dio of Prusa. During the period of the Flavian emperors of Rome (69–96 CE), Dio was a rhetorician and an enemy of various schools of philosophy such as Stoicism and Cynicism. However, during the reign of Domitian (81–96 CE), Dio was exiled from Rome and during this period of his life a dramatic religious change occurred. While staying in Greece, Dio paid a visit to the Delphic oracle and was ordered to travel

Six. The Journey to Philosophic Wisdom

the world. As a result, Dio became a worldly wanderer in pursuit of knowledge and wisdom. The philosophical treatise entitled "De Exilio" is the literary byproduct of his travels around the ancient world. Often comparing himself to noble figures such as Odysseus and Socrates, Dio saw himself "in the grand tradition and to some extent can be mentioned in the same breath as the great Greeks of the past."[5] In the words of Philostratus,

> He often visited the military camps in the rags he was wont to wear, and after the assassination of Domitian, when he saw that the troops were beginning to mutiny, he could not contain himself at the sight of the disorder that had broken out, but stripped off his rags, leaped on a high altar, and began his harangue with the verse: "Then Odysseus of many counsels stripped him of his rags."[6]

Among the upper classes of Greco-Roman society, philosophical activity was held in high regard because of its reliance upon logic and syllogisms. Various literary devices including aphorisms, dialogues and other forms of discursive writing were used by the Greek philosophers in presenting their arguments. The eminent classical Greek philosopher Plato (428–348 BCE) is notorious for his employment of the Socratic dialogue and his question and answer method which he used on a wide range of metaphysical, ethical and epistemological issues. At the core of Plato's teachings are the eternal, immutable forms of all things, existing in a transcendental world of pure ideas. Every object in the world such as a chair or a horse is modeled after its pre-existent image existing in a world of pure being. According to Plato's theory of forms, the eternal world of pure ideas was organized in a hierarchical fashion with the form of the Good standing at the highest point above all the others. It is up to human beings to try to apprehend the forms through the process of education. At the outset, one needs to try to apprehend the lower forms and then proceed to the higher ones such as the form of Truth, Justice and finally the Good. Coming to know the forms in this life prepares a person for an apprehension of the forms in the next life.

Plato's ideas concerning reincarnation and the transmigration of the soul reflects the influence of Pythagoreanism and Orphism.[7] In *Meno*, 81, c-d Plato claims that knowledge is really a process of recollection of something known in a previous life. The influence of Orphic dualism is manifested in the *Cratylus* and *Phaedo* where Plato says that the immortal soul is encased within the physical shell of a person's body. There it pays a price for the various sins it may have committed in a previous life. Upon death, when the soul detaches itself from the body, then it undergoes a judgment in the hereafter. Only on the condition that the soul is pure and free from sinful contamination will it find release and travel to the world of divine forms. Otherwise, it must return to earth and become reincarnated once again into another body.

The Myth of Er

A brief tale called *The Myth of Er* appears in Book Ten of Plato's *Republic*. Given the fact that similar stories of otherworldly journeys appeared in Homeric literature and other myths of classical Greece, perhaps Plato adopted this style of writing to suit his purpose of appealing to the literary and religious sensibilities of his Greek audience. Plato's employment of this narrative format clearly underscores his openness to other forms of written communication besides philosophic discourse.[8]

Even prior to the time of Plato, various Greek sophists of the 5th century BCE had adopted the literary style of inventing various myths. Even though Greek sophists considered themselves to be enlightened intellectuals who dismissed the validity of the traditional Olympian mythology, nevertheless many of them employed a type of writing called *mythopoeia* in which they created myths for the purpose of elucidating their thoughts on various subjects for their listeners. One such sophistical myth entitled "The Choice of Hercules" was composed by the 5th century BCE sophist Prodicus.

Although Plato accepted many of the criticisms of mythology made by previous generations of Pre-Socratic philosophers and sophists, he also borrowed the sophistic practice of combining his philosophic message with mythic tales and stories. However, Plato takes this practice to new heights, spinning various tales to express certain metaphysical ideas that would otherwise remain inexpressible if explained in discursive language. Generally, Plato's myths focus on some of his fundamental philosophical ideas including the destiny of the soul upon death or the creation of the world. Many of Plato's myths are non-falsifiable in the sense that they depict things that go beyond sense-experience such as the immortal soul,

Six. The Journey to Philosophic Wisdom

the gods, daemons and heroes. Some of the myths Plato invents include the Atlantis myth (*Timaeus* 21e-26d), the cosmological myth of the *Statesman* (268–274e), the myth of Theuth (*Phaedrus* 274c-275e), the *Phaedo* myth (107c-115a), the *Laws* myth (903b-905b), the myth of the androgyne (*Symposium* 189d-193d), the *Gorgias* myth (523a-527a), and lastly, *The Myth of Er* (*Republic* 614a-621d). In addition to inventing myths, sometimes Plato retells some traditional myths such as the story of Gyges (Republic 359d-360b) or the myth of Phaethon (Timaeus 22c7). In other cases, he combines a couple of traditional myths such as in the story of the Noble Lie (Republic 414b-415d) which combines the Cadmeian myth of autochthony and Hesiod's myth of creation.

One of Plato's invented myths is entitled *The Myth of Er*. In this story Plato describes the spiritual journey of a young Greek soldier named Er who suffers death on the battlefield. Upon Er's death, his soul detaches from his body and travels to the higher realms of the universe. After learning certain "secret" things about what happens to a person upon death, Er returns to earth and comes back to life. To appreciate why Plato inserts *The Myth of Er* at the end of his dialogue, it is important to understand the basic argument presented in the main body of the *Republic*.

In the *Republic*, Plato outlines the general characteristics of what he considers to be the ideal society. Using the character of Socrates as his mouthpiece, Plato argues that individual happiness is found in a life of quiet contemplation of the truth. Because Socrates advocated similar ideas to the Athenian youth, he was executed in Athens on the grounds of not giving recognition to the gods and "corrupting the youth."[9] Since individual happiness can only be achieved by embracing philosophy, Plato argues that society would do well to organize itself along similar lines. Unfortunately, this is usually not the case. Most societies are controlled by power-hungry rulers who seek to gratify their own materialistic desires and ignore the principles of justice and truth. This discussion raises some fundamental questions regarding the nature of justice which Plato does not fail to address. Plato notes that in actual practice the rulers of the state generally give priority to fulfilling their own needs and wants over against the needs and wants of the people. Instead of encouraging people to attain a true education grounded in a contemplation of the truth and justice, the greedy rulers establish corrupt educational systems to serve their own needs. Since most

Journeys to the Underworld and Heavenly Realm

people fail to come to a true understanding of concepts such as "the good "or "justice," they remain enslaved by their ignorance and love of money. Plato proposes a solution to this problem by advocating that a philosopher-king should be enlisted as the ruler of society. Since the philosopher-king possesses a higher understanding of the truth, he would be able to re-vamp social institutions, including educational institutions, in a fair and just way, so that they could serve the needs of the people instead of the ruling class. Thus, citizens of the ideal state could be encouraged to pursue a philosophic life instead of a life of materialistic gratification.

Plato's *Republic* concludes with the story of Er. Plato claims that even though the rewards of the philosophic life are not materialistic, there are substantial benefits, especially in the hereafter. Moreover, even though a just person receives many rewards in this life, such as a good reputation and the trust of many people, the rewards bestowed upon them in the hereafter are far greater than those received in this life. In telling *The Myth of Er*, Plato outlines some of the spiritual rewards of the next life. Er was a warrior who died in battle along with several other warriors. Ten days after their death the bodies of these warriors were picked up. Although the bodies of the other warriors had already begun to rot, Er's body remained intact and unchanged. After his body was placed on a funeral pyre a few days later, he suddenly came back to life and told the astonished bystanders standing nearby that he had returned from the dead. He explained that after he died, his soul had departed from his body and he traveled along with many other souls to a supernatural place filled with many wondrous things. In this new world, he came to a place where there were four openings; one door was for those souls coming out of the underworld; another door was for the souls that had recently died and were coming up from the earth; two other doors led to and from the heavens. Souls were continually entering and exiting out of each of the holes; the souls coming from the underworld were covered in dust and grime; the souls coming from the heavens were pure and unsoiled. Two judges stood nearby between the doors and judged all the souls coming before them. After a judgment was rendered, then the good souls would exit through the door on the right and the unjust souls would pass through the door on the left. Both the just and unjust were required to wear signs on their chests proclaiming whether they were good or evil souls.

Six. The Journey to Philosophic Wisdom

When it came time for Er to be judged, the judges told him that he had been selected to be a messenger for those still living back on earth. He was required to observe all the things going on in the heavenly realm so that he could tell the people back on earth about these things when he returned to earth. Er noticed that there was a constant stream of many souls entering and exiting the area; every time one soul exited through one of the doors leading to earth or heaven, another soul would appear through the second door. Appearing as if they had been on a long journey, these weary souls camped out in a nearby meadow where they awaited their judgment. Those who knew one another back on earth greeted one another; those coming up from earth would converse with the souls who had descended from the heavens. The souls from earth would ask the souls from heaven questions about what it was like in the upper realm. Some of those who had spent time in the underworld would tell tales about the horrors they had endured there. Most of these souls had spent one thousand years paying for their sins in the world below.

> For each in turn of the unjust things they had done and for each in turn of the people they had wronged, they paid the penalty ten times over, once in every century of their journey. Since a century is roughly the length of a human life, this means that they paid a tenfold penalty for each injustice. If, for example, some of them had caused many deaths by betraying cities or armies and reducing them to slavery or by participating in other wrongdoing, they had to suffer ten times the pain they had caused to each individual. But if they had done good deeds and had become just and pious, they were rewarded according to the same scale.[10]

In certain cases, some very sinful souls would never leave the underworld because of their horrible crimes. Whenever these souls tried to leave, an awful roar could be heard and then some awful, savage spirits would prevent them from departing. Frequently the savage spirits would beat them into submission, and then toss them into the depths of Tartarus. Whenever the roar sounded, everyone was fearful that it might be sounding for them. Relief would come when they realized the roar was for someone else.

After spending seven days in the meadow, on the eighth day the souls would arise and go on a journey to a place high up in the cosmos where a column of multi-colored lights shone down on the heavens and earth below. On the next day, the souls saw magnificent clusters of spiraled light revolving together in circles high up in the heavens. The Spindle of Necessity was hanging at the end of the concentric circles of light. On top of each circle of light a Siren stood and was singing a beautiful melody. The Three Fates, Lachesis, Clotho and Atropos were there also and were helping turn the spindles. Standing before the Three Fates, each soul was told the following:

> Ephemeral souls, this is the beginning of another cycle that will end in death. Your daimon or guardian spirit will not be assigned to you by lot; you will choose him. The one who has the first lot will be the first to choose a life to which he will then be bound by necessity. Virtue knows no master; each will possess it to a greater or lesser degree, depending on whether he values or distains it. The responsibility lies with the one who makes the choice; the god has none.[11]

Then some lots were given to the souls. Each soul, except for Er, picked up a lot that said when they would be able to select a new earthly life. Then models of various human and animal lives were placed before them. All kinds of options were available ranging from the life of a tyrant, a wealthy person or beggar, a strong person or someone who was chronically sick. There were the lives of famous men and women, beautiful people, athletes and noble aristocrats. Each type of life would invariably have a dramatic influence upon the soul choosing it, but this was unknown to the soul when he or she made their choice. Those souls possessing wisdom could distinguish between a good and a bad life and thus make a good choice. While the souls were pondering their decision, it was pointed out that a good life could be selected even for those who chose last. Unfortunately, the first soul to choose a new life was untrained in philosophy in his previous life on earth and lived virtuously out of habit instead of reflection. Failing to give much reflection about his choice, he picked the life of a tyrant destined to eat the flesh of his own offspring. Once he realized his mistake, he blamed chance and the *daemons* instead of his own deficiencies. Those souls who had spent time in the underworld and had seen much suffering and pain took their time in choosing their next life. It appeared to Er that those who had pursued philosophy while alive on earth would not have return at all to earth in another body. These souls would enjoy everlasting happiness in the heavenly realm.

Er realized that the way in which a soul chooses their new life depended entirely upon the quality of their previous life. For example, the soul that once belonged to the body of Orpheus chose the body of a swan.

Six. The Journey to Philosophic Wisdom

The Homeric heroes Ajax and Agamemnon picked the body of a lion and an eagle respectively. As chance would have it, the soul of Odysseus was the last to select a new life. Having forgotten the suffering of his previous life on earth, the soul of Odysseus sought out the life of a loner who worked in isolation from others. Some souls changed from animals into humans or vice versa. Unjust people wanted to become wild animals, but just people decided to become tame beasts. After everyone had made their choice, the souls marched in the order of their choices back to Lachesis. Each one was given a *daemon* to make sure that the soul's choice would be carried out back on earth. After passing under the Spindle of light to confirm its fate and after receiving the approval of the other Fates, Clotho and Atropos, then all the souls traveled together past the throne of Necessity and arrived at the Plain of Forgetfulness. There they camped beside the River of Unheeding for the night. Each soul was required to drink from its waters so that everything seen in the heavenly realm would be forgotten. On the other hand, Er was forbidden to drink from its waters since he had been instructed to tell the people back on earth about everything he had seen and heard in the hereafter. Then at midnight, suddenly there was thunder and a violent earthquake. Then all the souls were magically transported back to earth to be re-born into their new bodies. One of the souls was Er. Suddenly, he awoke as he was lying on his funeral pyre. Then he began to tell his amazing tale of the otherworld to his astonished onlookers.

The Dream of Scipio

It is a well-known fact that ancient Roman civilization was heavily influenced by classical Greece. In many respects, this influence was due to the deficiencies of Roman culture, especially in the arts and literature. As a result, much of Roman poetry and art is thematically and stylistically modeled after its classical Greek forebears. Greek mythology found a new home in Rome; there were many Latin versions of popular Greek myths. Homer's *Odyssey* had its Latin counterpart in the *Aeneid*. Just as *The Odyssey* narrates the story of Odysseus' arduous trip back home to Greece following the Trojan War, including a description of his

Journeys to the Underworld and Heavenly Realm

subterranean journey to Erebus, likewise, the *Aeneid* describes Aeneus' journey back to Rome and his sojourn in the world below the earth. The Latin poet Ovid's story of Orpheus and Eurydice recapitulates many of the thematic elements of *The Homeric Hymn to Demeter*. Many of the gods of the Greek pantheon found a divine counterpart in Roman religion. Zeus, the father of the Olympian religion became known as Jupiter in Rome. Poseidon, the Greek god of the sea became known in Rome as Neptune; many other Greek gods had their Latin equivalent in Roman religion.

Although major philosophical differences separate the thought of Plato and Cicero, Cicero's *The Dream of Scipio* serves as a fitting tribute to Plato's *Myth of Er*. Besides being a prominent Roman statesman and politician, Cicero (106–43 BCE) had an avid interest in philosophical and religious matters. At the end of the Roman Republic, Roman civilization was becoming more and more polarized both politically and religiously. There were those who favored the idea that political power should be held in the hands of the people and those who favored the opposite idea that political power should be held in the hands of the few or even a single person such as the emperor. In the realm of religion, a similar divide existed between those naïve individuals who put their faith in the efficacy of pseudo-scientific practices such as magic, divination, and astrology and other groups of educated citizens who ridiculed these religious practices.[12]

Although Cicero had a deep admiration for the Stoics and the Platonists, he was never able to completely accept the validity of many of their theological ideas. Cicero was practically minded and tended to favor a rigorous skeptical outlook; in short, he was deeply opposed to many popular religious beliefs and practices. Cicero's skeptical attitude is clearly articulated in his essay entitled *De Divinatione*, where he provides a critical commentary on various divinatory practices. Book Two largely focuses upon discrediting those who put their faith in the prophetic power of dreams. Rather than depending upon the unreliable prophetic power of dreams, Cicero claims that the scientific method is a preferable means for acquiring knowledge. In his lengthy essay entitled *On the Nature of the Gods* Cicero suspends his judgment and discusses various religious topics in an objective manner. Although he never endorses any one philosophical outlook, Cicero presents a somewhat dispassionate and neutral descrip-

Six. The Journey to Philosophic Wisdom

tion of the main schools of ancient Greco-Roman philosophy including Academic Skepticism, Stoicism and Epicureanism.

Although Cicero does not support many aspects of Plato's theological outlook, certain elements of Plato's doctrine of the immortality of the soul play a key role in the *Dream of Scipio*. Scipio was a warrior and a member the Fourth Legion of the Roman Army stationed in Africa during the Third Punic War. On one occasion Scipio happened to meet an old family friend, King Masinissa. That night, the two began a conversation about a variety of subjects that lasted well into the next morning. The king was well acquainted with Scipio's grandfather, Scipio Africanus, the Elder and he spoke about him incessantly, recalling all the things he had said and done. Finally, the young Scipio became exhausted and withdrew from the king. He immediately fell into a deep sleep. While Scipio slept, his grandfather, Scipio Africanus appeared to him in a dream. His grandfather told him not to be afraid and to remember everything that he was about to tell him. Pointing his finger toward Carthage, Africanus made a few predictions about what was going to happen to Scipio during the next two years. First, he said that although Scipio was just a soldier now, soon he would become a triumphant Roman general. After successfully campaigning in battle against many foreign enemies, he would return to Rome to discover that Africanus' grandson, Tiberius Gracchus was plotting against him to gain power. He admonished Scipio to remain steadfast in defending his country against these kinds of nefarious schemes. He continued his predictions by telling Scipio that when he turns fifty-six, he will find out that all the members of the Roman Senate, the citizens and even the allies of Rome will ask him to save the nation. At this point, Cicero injects the main point of the story:

> All those who have preserved, aided, or extended their fatherland have a special place assigned to them in heaven where they may enjoy an eternal life of happiness. For nothing done on earth more greatly pleases the supreme deity who rules the entire universe than assemblies or communities of men bound together by justice, which are called states. Their rulers and preservers go forth from here, and hither they return.[13]

When Scipio heard these words, he grew afraid because he thought that he might be seeing an apparition of his deceased grandfather. Then Scipio asked Africanus whether his deceased father, Paulus and other dead people were alive. Africanus responded in a philosophical way;

Journeys to the Underworld and Heavenly Realm

"Of course they are still alive," he replied. "They have taken their flight from the bonds of the body as from a prison. Your so-called life [on earth] is really death. Do you not see your father Paulus coming to meet you?"[14]

Just as Aeneus was saddened when he met his deceased father, Scipio's eyes were also filled with tears at the sight of the ghostly image of his father. As the two embraced, Paulus comforted his son by telling him not to cry. Then Scipio said that he would prefer to immediately join his deceased father on a permanent basis in the hereafter than to live a "dying life on earth." Cicero's philosophic dualism is clearly referenced in Paulus' response; unless the God who governs all things releases the soul from the body, a person cannot enter the heavenly realm. While a person is alive, their soul is joined to their body. During this time, it is the duty of every living person to cultivate the earth. The soul is the spark of life that originates from "those eternal fires which you call stars and planets, which are globular and rotund and are animated by divine intelligences, and which with marvelous velocity revolve in their established orbits."[15] Unless a soul is summoned by the divine intelligence of the cosmos, it must remain in its physical shell. A person must not "quit the life on Earth ... otherwise you will be seen to shirk the duty assigned by God to man." Africanus encouraged Scipio to devote himself to a life of service to his country, for such a path "is a highway to the skies, to the fellowship of those who have completed their earthly lives and have been released from the body and now dwell in that place which you see yonder."[16]

As Scipio stared out across the vast, starry sky, Africanus revealed to him some of the mysteries of the cosmos. Drawing upon his knowledge of Hellenistic astronomy, Africanus pointed to nine heavenly spheres, including the sun, the moon and the seven planets. Then he mentioned a popular astrological superstition that the region below the moon was an area where everything was destined to die and decay. Above the moon was the area of the eternal. He continued by explaining that earth occupied the ninth sphere. Although the earth does not rotate, it occupies the lowest point of the cosmos and therefore everything is drawn to it. As Africanus spoke, Scipio heard in the distance some strange music. Africanus explained to him that these sounds were the heavenly vibrations of the planetary spheres whirling along in their orbital path across the universe. While Scipio gazed down upon earth from his vantage point high up in

Six. The Journey to Philosophic Wisdom

the heavens, Africanus explained to him that it was better for him to fix his eyes upon the stars instead of earth because the earth was too small and insignificant in comparison to the other celestial objects. Africanus tried to put things in perspective for Scipio by pointing out that little or no contact or communication takes place on earth between different groups of people because each community is confined to small, habitable areas. Although many people laud the noble actions of heroes like Odysseus, Africanus claimed that the glorious deeds of a person would never be known to those living in the other parts of the world. Even if those acts of heroism were recorded for future generations, soon floods and other destructive forces of nature would eventually sweep these records away into oblivion and they would be forgotten. Rather than concentrating on achieving notoriety for oneself, a better course of action is to focus upon:

> your eternal home and dwelling place, and pay no attention to the foolish talk of the vulgar herd nor set your hopes on human reward for your great deeds. Virtue herself, by her own charms, ought to lead you on to true glory.[17]

In conclusion, Africanus reminded Scipio that only his spirit was eternal.

> Know yourself, therefore, to be a god—if indeed a god is a being that lives, feels, remembers, and foresees, that rules, governs, and moves the body over which it is set, just as the supreme God above us rules this world. And just as that eternal God moves the universe, which is partly mortal, so an eternal spirit moves the fragile body.[18]

In distinction to the souls of those who devote themselves to patriotic activities, those who pursue the pleasures of the senses go against the divine law. When these souls depart from their bodily shell, they fly about "close to the earth, and do not return to this place until after many centuries of torment."[19] At this point, Scipio awoke.

Scipio's journey to heaven taught him an important lesson: selfless devotion and service to the state is the best path for achieving everlasting life. In contrast, Plato believed that philosophy represented the gateway to the eternal life. In *The Myth of Er*, the importance of philosophy is vividly illustrated in Er's journey to the hereafter. Cicero takes Plato's ideas a step further by stating that unless philosophic wisdom is used to bring about positive political change for the sake of the state, it was a useless

Journeys to the Underworld and Heavenly Realm

activity devoid of any real practical value. Something more than pure reflection was needed for an individual soul to attain its highest potential and to achieve immortality. Action, as opposed to reflection, is needed, but not just any kind of action. The actions of heroic warriors such as Odysseus or Beowulf would be insufficient. According to Cicero, the type of action that was needed was political in nature. The heroic acts and feats of the individual would soon be forgotten unless they were taken for the greater glory of the state. For Cicero, only selfless political service devoted to the state would insure true immortality for the individual in the next life.

SEVEN

The Journey to Moral Awareness

Judgment in the Underworld

The sixth and last form of religious experience refers to the ethical dimension of religion. In the west, various ancient religious narratives depict the journey of the soul in ethical terms; in these narratives when a person dies, their soul is judged before God based upon whether the person lived a moral life while they were alive. In this chapter, the ethical dimension of religious experience is explored in terms of its expression in pagan and Judeo-Christian stories of otherworldly journeys. To accomplish this goal, it is first necessary to establish the connection between ethics and religious experience.

For *homo religiosus*, coming to an awareness of the sacred can have very strong moral implications. From the standpoint of the religious individual, behaving in a moral way is not entirely based upon the conventional standards of society nor is it founded upon one's own personal choice. It springs from an awareness of the holy. Ethical action is an outward expression of one's inner apprehension of sacred reality. Thus, religious people speak alternately in terms of fulfilling God's will or acting in conformity with cosmic law.[1] For those who have had an immediate experience of the sacred, the demands of their conscience cannot be ignored; certain moral and ethical obligations must be fulfilled.

As an outgrowth of coming to an awareness of the sacred, western religious traditions emphasize the importance of moral and ethical behavior as the fulfillment of God's will. God's teachings are inscribed in various sacred texts such as the Bible or the Koran. Many of the fundamental

Journeys to the Underworld and Heavenly Realm

religious beliefs and practices of Judaism underscore the importance of obeying God's law (Torah). Among the orthodox followers of Islam, submission to the will of Allah, as it is conveyed in the Koran, is all-important. In each of these religious traditions, morality is linked to one's faith and personal commitment to God. Thus, in Christianity life on earth is regarded as a moral test. One's actions on earth determines one's subsequent fate in the afterlife. Unless one has lived their life in accordance with the principles of truth and righteousness, their soul cannot expect to be judged worthy of a blessed afterlife. God offers spiritual rewards for those who have followed his moral edicts and issues punishments for those who have continually ignored his divine law. In many cases, the demands of the conscience take priority over the selfish desires of the flesh. In Judaism, the terms of God's covenant require individual believers to behave in certain moral ways. Prosperity and peace are given as the reward for those who follow the way of the Lord. In the Muslim faith, submission to God's will requires certain obligations to be fulfilled by believers. Muslims are obligated to profess their faith daily, engage in pilgrimage and alms-giving. It is the responsibility of the community to create a social environment that insures that God's will is followed. In the theistic religions of the west, a supreme creator god is responsible for establishing and maintaining a moral order that permeates the entire universe. Positive or negative consequences will occur for those who either follow or do not follow God's universal moral law. Many of these consequences take place in the next life when a soul is judged before God.

In contrast to the emphasis on personal responsibility and morality in the great religions of the west, the great eastern religious traditions, including Hinduism, Buddhism, Taoism and Confucianism, teach something different. Here, an impersonal divine force is at work in determining the ethical order of the cosmos. For example, in one of the Confucian Four Books, Confucius discusses how a righteous person exemplifies this impersonal principle of a universal moral order. In referencing the underlying principle of moral order in the cosmos, Confucius uses the term *chung yung*, usually translated as "the Mean." An unprincipled and vulgar person lives in a way that is a contradiction to the universal moral order. A good person is continually cultivating his goodness whereas a vulgar person has no fear of ethical edicts. Mencius, a spokesperson of Confucius reinforced Confucius' teachings by claiming that human beings do not require to be taught how to act morally; they have an innate ability to act in a correct manner. For example, every child naturally loves their parents and respects their brothers and sisters. In Confucianism, living a moral life and respecting others is equated with cultivating one's true self. In Hinduism, a similar idea is expressed in relation to following the *dharma*. The term *dharma* has come to mean various things throughout history. The word is derived from a Sanskrit verb that means "to secure" or "to uphold." Additional translations include "law," "truth" or "reality." In the early history of India, the term came to refer to what one ought to do, such as performing sacrifices properly. Gradually over a long period of time the ritual order was seen to reflect the social and cosmic order. At this point, the *dharma* came to mean the eternal law of the universe that is manifested whenever a person acts in a moral way. Given the infinite number of moral dilemmas that can arise, laws continually need to be reassessed and re-evaluated by sages and holy ones. In the Hindu tradition, the interpretation of law was done in accordance with key moral principles mentioned in holy books such as the *Rig Vedas*. The principles of morality and law were formalized and codified within Hindu society with the creation of law books such as the *Laws of Manu*.[2]

The Egyptian Book of the Dead

Becoming aware of one's ethical obligations comes to the forefront in some ancient Near Eastern stories and narratives describing otherworldly journeys. Examples of this appear in certain sections of *The Egyptian Book of the Dead* where the motif of the "gateway to the underworld" and the "guardian of the underworld" are mentioned.[3] *The Egyptian Book of the Dead* is a collection of funerary texts consisting of magical spells and formulae, incantations and hymns written over an extended period of time by Egyptian scribes for the benefit of the deceased. Many of its chapters were originally carved on the interior walls of pyramids or painted inside of coffins, sarcophagi and rolls of papyrus. According to the *Book of the Dead*, when a person died, their soul would journey

Journeys to the Underworld and Heavenly Realm

through the underworld (*Tuat*) and eventually arrive at a place called the Hall of Judgement. Three gods guarded the entrance: a doorkeeper, a lookout and a questioner whose job was to report a soul's arrival to Osiris. Besides these three divinities, a patron god watched over everything. To gain entrance into the Hall of Judgement, a soul had to repeat the patron god's name to the three guardians. After that, the soul would enter the Hall of Judgement and be judged by a group of deities whose job it was to determine whether an individual's life on earth was ethically sound and good enough for it to qualify for eternal salvation. If this was not the case, then it would suffer destruction at the hands of hideous monsters. To assist the deities in their decision, a deceased person's heart was placed on the Scale of *Maat*. On one side of the scales a feather was placed which represented *Maat* or justice and truth; a person's heart would be placed on the other side. If a balance was achieved on the scales, then the soul would be granted immortality. However, if an imbalance occurred, then a soul would be tossed into the eternal flames of *Tuat* and be destroyed. Undoubtedly, the potential of such a negative outcome would only serve to motivate people on earth to live in accordance to the moral dictates of their community.[4]

In comparison to other ancient Near eastern religions, ancient Egyptian religion had an unusually optimistic outlook about the destiny of the soul upon death since immortality was available for the individual. However, certain requirements had to be met, such as mummification and living an ethical life on earth, for the deceased to taste the blessings of eternal life. Ancient Egypt was the first civilization in the ancient Mediterranean world to substantially develop ethical ideas related to the judgment of the dead and the related concepts of heaven and hell. It was also the first religious tradition in the ancient Near East to consider the possibility that a pleasant afterlife was available to the average person. In contrast to the other negative portrayals of the underworld and afterlife in ancient Mesopotamian religion and the Homeric tradition, ancient Egyptian religion offered a far more cheerful viewpoint about the afterlife. Unlike the grim ancient Mesopotamian and Homeric characterizations of the hopeless fate awaiting the average human being, a far happier picture of the soul's destiny is presented in ancient Egyptian religion.

Seven. The Journey to Moral Awareness

The Journey to Moral Judgment in the Zoroastrian Afterlife

Zoroastrianism originated in the modern territory of Iran sometime during the seventh and 8th century BCE with the teachings of the prophet Zoroaster. Religious beliefs concerning the afterlife figure prominently in it.[5] One day when Zoroaster was a young man, an angel appeared to him in a vision and revealed to him some sacred truths. Among the many truths revealed to Zoroaster, a primary one was that the world was divided into two warring camps; on the one hand, there was "the Truth" and on the other hand there was "the Lie." Human salvation depended upon whether one affiliated themselves with the Truth as opposed to the Lie. Another important revelation given to Zoroaster was that God did not actually create the evil existing in the world. However, He did give human beings the power to make choices and this freedom of the will was the true source of evil. In his subsequent preaching Zoroaster stressed that the existence of evil cannot be blamed on God because God is the source of all the goodness. Instead, a wicked Spirit tempts human beings into committing various sinful actions and offenses against God. Therefore, it is up to human beings to turn away from evil and freely choose the path of righteousness. Zoroaster also taught that a blessed afterlife awaits those who give up their evil ways and follow the path of righteousness, but for those who do not turn away from their iniquity, the fires of Hell await them.

One Zoroastrian text entitled the *Menok* discusses what happens to a person's soul when their physical body dies.[6] In the text, the afterlife is divided into two regions: one realm is the place of punishment for those who have lived a life of wickedness and the other place was reserved for good souls. The text states that for three days after death, the soul will hover near the body; then it will travel across a great cosmic bridge into the realm of the sacred. While crossing the sacred bridge, the soul will be taunted by many kinds of evil spirits and demons. On the fourth day, a judgment of the soul will take place that is conducted by a mysterious figure called the "Requiter." Before a final judgment is rendered, the soul will encounter a beautiful young girl on the bridge. The girl will tell the soul

Journeys to the Underworld and Heavenly Realm

that she is not a beautiful girl at all, but a representation of the soul's good deeds.[7] The text states that after the girl leaves, then the soul will feel a fragrant heavenly breeze waft toward it. Then the soul will receive its judgment. If the soul receives a positive judgment, then it will step forward into the heavenly domains. The first step will take the soul to the first heaven of good thoughts; the second step will lead it to the second heaven of good words; the third step will lead it to the third heaven of good deeds, and with the fourth step the soul will arrive at the Place of the Endless Light that is filled with bliss. There the soul will be greeted by various gods who will ask the soul questions about its journey from those "fearful transient worlds where there is much evil ... which do not pass away and in which there is no adversary..."[8] The high god Ohrmazd usually interrupts the conversation by telling the gods not to ask the soul any questions because it has been separated from its body and has traveled on a long fearsome road. Then the great god describes the many ordeals that a soul has faced after a person has died. Upon death, a soul must endure three nights of terror "inflicted on him by Astvihat and other demons" as it hovers upon the Bridge leading into the afterlife. The good soul will join the gods but "the man who is damned dies, for three days and nights does his soul hover near his head.... And during those three days and nights he sees with his eyes all the sins and wickedness that he has committed on earth"[9] On the fourth day, a demon comes named Vizarah to bind the evil soul and drag it off to the Bridge of the Requiter. Urged on by the Wrath, the demon will attack the evil soul on the Bridge and then send it to "the nethermost Hell." Out of the mist an evil wench will appear and say

> I am no wench, but I am thy deeds,—hideous deeds—evil thoughts, evil words, evil deeds and an evil religion. For when on earth thou didst see one who offered sacrifice to the gods, then didst thou sit apart and offer sacrifice to the demons....[10]

The soul's first step will take him to the Hell of evil thought; its second step will lead to the Hell of evil words and the third step will take it to the Hell of evil deeds. Finally, the fourth step will take it to a confrontation with the Destructive Spirit and other demons who will mock the soul. Then the Destructive Spirit will order the demons to be silent and show no concern for this soul that has been separated from its body. Then the Destructive Spirit will tell the demons to serve the soul the filthiest food that can be found in Hell. After that, they will be ordered to bring it "poison, and venom, snakes and scorpions and other noxious reptiles (that flourish) in Hell" and they will serve him these things to eat.[11] The text concludes by saying that the soul will remain in Hell and suffer much torment and punishment until the "the Final Resurrection." Until that time, the soul must eat the awful food.

The text illustrates the fundamental Zoroastrian belief that when a person dies, their soul is separated from the body, but for a period of three days it stays close to the body. However, on the fourth day the soul receives a judgment on the Bridge of the Requiter. On the bridge, the "Requiter" examines all the words and deeds of a soul. If the good outweighs the bad, then the soul enters the heavenly realms. If the evil outweighs the good, then the soul is taken to Hell and remains there until the end of time when a general resurrection of the dead takes place.

Judeo-Christian Journeys to Heaven and Hell

In Greco-Roman times, underworld journey narratives found a new home in Hellenistic Judaism and early Christianity. Ethical concerns are reflected in various Judeo-Christian stories that portray the underworld as a place of punishment for one's sins. In comparison to the otherworldly narratives of the Greeks and Romans, the Judeo-Christian narratives heavily emphasize moral issues and ethical obligations. It is important to remember that in its early roots, traditional Judaism did not place much stock in a belief in an immaterial soul or the afterlife. According to traditional Jewish thinking, if one followed the terms of God's covenant, then one could expect to live a long and prosperous life on earth and this was God's reward for those living according to the terms of His covenant. Like many other ancient Mediterranean religious traditions, ancient Judaism focused primarily upon the community as opposed to the individual. There was little reference to the blessings of salvation for the individual in the hereafter. However, ideas pertaining to the immortal soul and individual salvation began to proliferate in later Hellenistic times. Then, the Mediterranean world saw an outpouring of new ideas about the soul and afterlife that originated in Greek philosophical circles. Many of these spiritual ideas

Journeys to the Underworld and Heavenly Realm

spread into the eastern Mediterranean world and had an influence upon Judaism during the Hellenistic period. Groups such as the Pharisees adopted the idea that the resurrection of the dead would occur sometime in the future when God's kingdom would descend upon earth. It is in this historical context that narratives describing journeys to heaven and hell begin to appear in the Hellenistic Jewish tradition. Many of these narratives were allegedly written by noteworthy patriarchs of the past such as Enoch.

Many important Jewish theological ideas related to the theme of death, evil and suffering emerge at the time of the Babylonian exile and are featured in the writings of the Hebrew prophets. Certain Hebrew prophets such as Jeremiah and Job served as the conscience of the people and spoke out against iniquity and injustice existing in the world. Realizing that the terms of the old Mosaic covenant were never going to be fulfilled through the performance of empty religious rituals, Jeremiah spoke about a time in the future when the kingdom of Israel would finally be restored. "'The days are coming,' declares the Lord, 'when I will bring my people Israel and Judah back from captivity and restore them to the land I gave their forefathers to possess,' says the Lord."[12] In the 5th century BCE, the Book of Job discusses the problem of evil and suffering that exists in the world. Situated in its historical context, the Book of Job came into existence against the background of the events of the 6th century BCE, a time when Judah was placed into captivity by the Babylonians. In commenting on the rise of individuality and the personal sense of guilt in the context of ancient Judaism John Hick states that

> So long as the stream of national life continued in full spate the individual was carried along in it, and the immortality of the nation did not require an individual immortality of its separate individual members. But, with the crushing Babylonian conquest of Judah in the 6th century and the exile of so many of Jerusalem's leading citizens, faith in continuing national existence was shaken and the individual became more conscious of his own personal status and destiny.... And with this dawning individual self-consciousness there came the agonizing question of God's justice to the individual, so powerfully and poignantly expressed in the book of Job.... In this situation belief in the resurrection of the dead (probably received from Zoroastrianism) spread among the Hebrews during the last two or three centuries before Christ.[13]

Although in the Biblical creation story God declares that his creation is good, it is difficult for Job to understand why it is that God would ever

Seven. The Journey to Moral Awareness

allow good people to suffer at the hands of the wicked. Job asks why is it that the wicked often thrive and rarely experience any negative consequences for their evil actions.[14] Job's struggle to understand Yahweh's mysterious action or inaction in the world appears in Biblical passages where he speaks about the fate of human beings upon death. From Job's perspective, there is no chance that things will ever be rectified in the next life since the afterlife is described in strictly negative terms. Job refers to a place called *Sheol,* a shadowy realm of the dead that is somewhat reminiscent of the Homeric underworld. This dark subterranean world is alluded to by Job in the following passage;

> Turn away from me so I can have a moment's joy before I go to the place of no return, to the land of gloom and deep shadow, to the land of deepest night, of deep shadow and disorder, where even the light is like darkness.[15]

Again, in the Book of Psalms there is a reference to *Sheol* in the following passage:

> For my soul is full of troubles, and my life draws near the grave (Sheol). I am counted among those who go down to the Pit; I am like a man without strength, I am set apart with the dead, like the slain who lie in the grave, whom you remember no more, who are cut off from your care....[16]

Instead of offering hope of a blessed life in the hereafter, Job says that the dead go to a dark and forbidding place that is filled with gloom, dust and desolation:

> If I say to corruption, "You are my father," and to the worm, "My mother" or "My sister," where then is my hope? Who can see any hope for me? Will it go down to the gates of death? Will we descend together into the dust?[17]

Traditional Judaism does not accept the doctrine of the resurrection of the dead.

> As water disappears from the sea, or a riverbed becomes parched and dry, so man lies down and does not rise, till the heavens are no more, men will not awake or be roused from their sleep.[18]

In Hellenistic times, a flood of new Greco-Roman religious and philosophical ideas poured into the eastern Mediterranean world, producing a flowering of new theological ideas regarding the nature of the soul and the afterlife. Although certain conservative Palestinian religious groups such as the Sadducees did not give credence to the idea of a resurrection of the dead, other groups such as the Pharisees were more accommodating and believed that sometime in the future a general resurrection of the dead would take place. Then God would usher in His kingdom on earth. The exact details varied; in some cases, the idea of a general resurrection of the dead was thought to come about in the distant future before the arrival of God's kingdom when the world would be "purified" of evil. In other cases, the new age was thought to come about in heaven as opposed to earth. Regardless of when and where the general resurrection of the dead would occur, Greek philosophical ideas such as Plato's ideas about the immortal soul played an important role in the development of these ideas within Judaism during the Hellenistic period. Concepts such as the resurrection of the dead and the imminent coming of the kingdom of God provided a springboard for the development of various Jewish and Christian stories describing heavenly flights and journeys to heaven and hell.

Otherworldly Journeys in Hellenistic Jewish Texts

The First and Second Book of Enoch

Because Enoch is a figure who was taken up to heaven in Genesis 5.18–24, he becomes one of the major focuses of attention within the Jewish apocalyptic tradition. After the time of the Babylonian exile, the idea of a blessed afterlife for the individual appears both in the first and second Book of Enoch which were written sometime between the second and 3rd century BCE. Both books are apocalypses that belong to *Jewish Pseudepigrapha*, that is, texts coming from the intertestamental period (2nd century BCE–1st century CE) attributed to some patriarchal figure of the Old Testament. Most *Jewish Pseudepigrapha* originated either in Palestine or Egypt. The apocryphal first Book of Enoch is the prototypical literary example of a heavenly ascent of an individual that speaks about a resurrection of a "spiritual" body. It serves as the literary model for other Judeo-Christian narratives coming after it that describe heavenly journeys such as the Book of Revelation in the New Testament. Enoch's account of heaven comes to him in the form of a magnificent symbolic vision. Engulfed in clouds and mist, Enoch was carried off in a vision to the heav-

Seven. The Journey to Moral Awareness

enly realm. Upon his arrival in heaven Enoch states that it was divided into two regions. One portion was filled with light and goodness. This was the dwelling place of angels and good souls. The other part was where sinners went for their punishment when they died.

In his vision Enoch met an angel who told him that when the end of the world arrives, God will send the Son of Man to set things right in the world, punish the wicked and reward the good. In those final days, the earth will bring back the dead and *Sheol* will give back those it has received. Then Enoch's spirit ascended to the upper reaches of the heavens where he saw "the holy sons of God" engulfed in flaming fire and a magnificent palace of God. Suddenly the entire palace disappeared, and a new house of God appeared that was even greater and loftier than the first one. Enoch went inside the house and found himself surrounded by sheep. Enoch saw a white bull with large horns and he watched as each of the lambs were transformed into white bulls. One of them became a great lamb with black horns on his head. Upon awaking from his vision Enoch wept tears of joy because he realized that all the lives of the faithful on earth will eventually be restored to join God and his Son for eternity.

Additional visions of heaven and hell are described in *The Book of the Secrets of Enoch* or *2nd Enoch*. A description of Enoch's journey through the heavens is included. Moral concerns dominate the narrative; during his journey Enoch observes the unfortunate fate of those who committed acts of evil during their life as well as the rewards that were given for those who lived a good life. Once again, hell is located above the earth in a celestial realm. The text begins by introducing a wise man who possessed the power to perceive heavenly things such as boundless light, God's divine throne and His many angels. Then, the narrative changes to a first-person account of Enoch's journey to heaven. One day when Enoch was three hundred and sixty-five years old he fell into a deep sleep while inside his house and suddenly two angelic figures appeared to him. The angels placed Enoch on their wings and flew him off to heaven. Upon his arrival in God's celestial kingdom, he realized that heaven was divided into different sections. Each heaven was either a pleasant place reserved for the righteous or a dark and evil place reserved for the punishment of sinners.

In the first heaven hundreds of angels appeared to Enoch and he was shown the course of the stars. The second heaven was filled with darkness.

Prisoners were hanging and were guarded by dark-looking angels who were weeping. When Enoch asked the angels about these tortured prisoners, the angels said that they were apostates who disobeyed God's laws. In the third heaven Enoch saw a beautiful multicolored Tree of Life whose roots descended to the earth. Flowing out of its roots were springs of milk and honey which poured into the Garden of Eden. Nearby was another realm created for those who committed sins such as worshipping false gods, fornication, murder and envy. This place was devoid of light except for the murky fire that was continually flaring up.

When Enoch arrived at the tenth heaven, he came upon God himself. God's face appeared "like iron glowing in the fire, emitting sparks, and burning."[19] Enoch admitted that he lacked the ability to describe in words the wondrous majesty of God;

> Who am I to tell of the Lord's unspeakable being, of his wondrous face? I cannot tell the quantity of his many instructions, his various voices. I cannot tell of the Lord's throne, great and not made by hands, nor of how many are standing around him, how many troops of cherubim and seraphim, nor of their incessant singing, nor of his immutable beauty. Who can tell of his ineffable greatness of his glory?[20]

Gabriel led Enoch to God's throne. Then Enoch's earthly clothing was removed, and he was anointed with a sweet ointment. Afterward he dressed himself in heavenly garments and he appeared like one of God's "glorious ones." The text concludes with the angel Pravil ordering Enoch to write down everything seen during his journey to heaven so that all the souls of humanity, even those born before the creation of the world, would know about it. The influence of Philo of Alexandria may be reflected in this passage since he also mentions the idea of the preexistent soul in his writings. Enoch dutifully obeyed the angel's orders and over a period of two months wrote three-hundred and sixty-six books about the things that had been revealed to him.

Baruch 2

Like the Book of Enoch, the *Apocalypse of Baruch* (*Baruch 2*) is filled with complex symbolism depicting otherworldly realms. In the Hebrew Bible, Baruch served as the scribe of the prophet Jeremiah. The *Apocalypse of Baruch* was written toward the latter part of the 1st century CE after the destruction of the temple of Jerusalem. The existence of evil in the world

Seven. The Journey to Moral Awareness

and God's punishment of sinners at the end of history is the primary concern of the narrative. The text describes a future age when God will wipe away all the evil in the world and establish his kingdom. The narrative begins with a sad lamentation over the circumstances of those living in the present age which are worse than the situation of those in *Sheol*. As Baruch loses consciousness and falls asleep, suddenly a strange vision unfolds in which he is swept away into the supernatural realm. In the vision, a great forest appears. A long vine is growing out of the top of some of the trees and at the bottom of the vine there is a fountain with water flowing out of it. Powerful waves pouring out of the fountain are destroying everything in their path except for one large cedar tree. A voice from the vine is telling the cedar tree to die since it has caused so much wickedness in the world. When he awoke, Baruch was confused by the vision and so he asked God for some help in interpreting it. God said that the forest represented the Word of God, but soon the earthly kingdom which destroyed Zion will be destroyed. After that, a third and fourth evil kingdom will arise and they will also be destroyed. The fountain and the vine are like the Messiah who will come into the world to establish God's kingdom.

4 Ezra

Another eschatological vision of a new age and the coming of the Messiah is presented in 4 Ezra, a 1st century CE Jewish Apocalypse. Like the Apocalypse of Baruch, the author of 4 Ezra is deeply upset about the destruction of the temple of Jerusalem by the Romans which occurred in 60 CE. In a vision, the angel Uriel tells Ezra that the destruction of the temple was the result of Adam's original sin and Israel's abandonment of God's covenant. The angel informs Ezra that sometime in the future God will balance the scales of justice. At that time the inhabitants of earth will experience a great panic. Then, a great cloud of moral confusion will descend upon the world. The truth will become hidden and faith will disappear. A few signs will appear that the end-times have arrived. The sun will shine at night. Blood will seep from wood and stones will speak. During the end-times, birds will act strangely, and the sea will spit out its fish. There will be earthquakes and fire everywhere. After a period of great distress and upheaval, heaven will open its gates upon the world.

Then, all sorrow and corruption will be wiped away. God will bring immortality to the world.

Seven days later Ezra had another strange nocturnal religious vision that was filled with drama. In the vision, a violent wind arose from the sea and out of the sea a man emerged engulfed in clouds. The man climbed to the top of a tall mountain and prepared to fight a great battle against some opponents. Rather than defending himself with a weapon such as a sword or spear, the man had a magical power that enabled him to send a great storm to descend upon his foes. Ezra saw a stream of wind and fire pour out from the man's mouth that burned his opponents to death. After that, the man came down from the mountain and called upon his supporters to come close to him. Some of these people were smiling and others who were in chains appeared sad. Then, an interpretation of this vision was given; the man of the vision represented the one sent to save God's creation. The wind and fire spilling from the man's mouth symbolized the days to come when God will deliver the earth from evil. One sign that the end is near is that many wars will be fought between various nations. At some point God's son will stand upon the summit of Mt. Zion and defeat his opponents. The wind and fire of the dream represents God's rebuke of the wicked. God's punishment is as powerful as a storm. God's law is like fire. It will burn evil doers. Those who gathered near the man from the sea represent the tribes of Israel who were held captive at one time by the Assyrian king and eventually were set free. When Ezra asks the angel why the man of his vision rose from the heart of the sea, he is told that just as one can neither seek out or know what lies in the deep part of the ocean, likewise no one on earth can know or see God's son or those who are with him until the time of his coming.

Otherworldly Journeys in Early Christian Texts

Like Jewish Apocalyptic writings, early Christian texts such as the *Shepard of Hermas*, the Gospel of Nicodemus, the Gospel of Peter and the Gospel of Paul also provide descriptions of heaven and hell. These narratives clearly serve a moralistic function of describing the fate of sinners and of the righteous. Whereas sinners are eternally punished in hell, the righteous are rewarded with everlasting life in heaven with God and his angels. Although Greco-Roman otherworldly narratives mention the idea that sinners are punished in the underworld, this ethical idea truly blossoms in early Christianity. Early Christian narratives develop the additional idea that in some cases the souls of the faithful can go to hell where they await the second coming of Christ. In these early Christian texts, heaven is always located above the earth and hell is always situated below the earth.

In many ways, early Christian writers depict heaven and hell in ethical terms as places of punishments and rewards. This type of portrayal is very similar to Jewish apocalyptic narratives and less like Greco-Roman otherworldly narratives, even though some Greco-Roman philosophical terminology has been imported into the narratives. Jewish apocalyptic writings such as Enoch I gave rise to later Christian apocalypses such as the Book of Revelation in the New testament and other apocryphal Christian documents such as the Gospel of Peter and Paul which also present accounts of journeys to heaven and hell. Some of these early Christian stories of otherworldly journeys reflect the eschatological belief that the kingdom of God was imminent. In the words of Willis Barnstone,

> the Christian apocalypse is an eschatological genre of writing in which knowledge of the End is the author's main aim. This knowledge, serving as a universal warning and hope, is conveyed through a journey to Hell and to Heaven, resulting in the disclosure of otherworldly secrets. Usually, the author recounts his vision as a rapture, that is an ecstatic ascent, outside of time, to other realms. To give authority to the vision, the apocalyptist (the author of the apocalypse) takes on the name of a great figure of the past, either an apostle or a patriarch of the Old Testament. To increase its prophetic value, the work is usually placed in the past; thus the prophecy of future history can be proved correct (because in fact these earlier events have already occurred).[21]

In its early period of development during the 1st century CE, the early Christian movement emerged onto the world stage as a small offshoot of Palestinian Judaism. Very soon the early Church experienced a remarkable transformation as it settled into the Roman world. In respect to the topic of the afterlife, many Palestinian Jewish ideas about the resurrection of the dead and the coming of the Kingdom of God filtered into the early Christian movement. Once Christianity was transplanted into the Roman world and became established there as a worldly institution, it underwent further change and development. Inevitably as the early Church moved out of Palestine into the Greco-Roman world, Greek and Roman religious and philosophical terms and ideas found their way into various teachings of the Church, especially regarding topics such as the immortality of the soul, the nature of God and the afterlife. Once these Greek philosophical terms and ideas became appropriated by leaders of the early Church, their meaning became transformed in the context of Christianity's emphasis on ethics and personal responsibility.

In the context of its Palestinian roots, early Christians believed that the coming of the kingdom was imminent. However, by the time of the 2nd century, many Church leaders realized that there was a delay in the *Parousia*. This realization led the Church to revise some of their ideas about the coming of the kingdom and the judgment of the dead, etc. Since the coming of God's kingdom was not going to happen in the immediate future, this left the leaders of the Church with the problem of explaining what happened to an individual immediately following their death. In addition, the Church needed to provide its followers with concrete reasons for receiving the sacraments and following the moral dictums of the Church. If the final judgment was not about to happen soon, but in the distant future, the Church needed to strengthen its position in the present age. Christians, especially new converts, needed to know what would happen to them immediately following their death. Would they go to heaven or hell?

To answer some of these pressing theological questions, the early Church developed its own brand of stories about the underworld and heaven. In many archaic underworld stories of ancient Greece and the Near East, the fate of human beings upon death was portrayed in strictly pessimistic terms. Humans were not eligible for immortality nor did they possess any supernatural powers. Humans were regarded as mortal and weak. Their time on earth was limited. In contrast, the gods had incredible supernatural powers and lived forever. The main thing that humans needed to realize was that they were mortal and not divine. In *The Odyssey* of Homer and Virgil's *Aeneid*, the souls of the dead dwelt in an unpleasant twilight world and nothing was blessed about it. In Hellenistic Judaism and early Christianity, this negative perception of the afterlife changes.

Seven. The Journey to Moral Awareness

Immortality and the resurrection of the dead is possible. In this way, Hellenistic Judaism and Christianity had something in common with the religious traditions of ancient Egypt. Likewise, rewards and punishments are seen to await the souls of the deceased in the afterlife. Many of these ideas are portrayed in vivid terms in various Judeo-Christian otherworldly narratives.

The central message of the early Christian Church was that Jesus was the Son of God who was sent to earth to redeem mankind. Seen in this context, the afterlife was the place where a soul went to receive either the blessings of eternal life or everlasting punishment for its sins based upon ones' behavior while alive on earth. These beliefs provided strong motivation for parishioners to receive the Church's sacraments and strengthen their resolve to follow the Church's strict moral code. Coming to know about the blessings of the righteous in heaven served a similar function. Perhaps reflecting the influence of the Zoroastrian religion, the early Church embraced the idea of two judgments. The first judgment took place immediately following a person's death. At that point, God would render his judgment and determine whether a person would be given eternal life in heaven or eternal damnation in hell. In addition to the first judgment, a second judgment would also take place at the end of history. With the coming of God's kingdom, a second, general resurrection of the dead would transpire. St. Paul made a distinction between heavenly bodies and physical bodies leading some to believe that the general resurrection of the dead involved the raising of spiritual bodies as opposed to physical bodies.

> But someone may ask, "How are the dead raised? With what kind of body will they come?" How foolish! What you sow does not come to life unless it dies. When you sow, you do not plant the body that will be, but just a seed, perhaps of wheat or of something else. But God gives it a body as he has determined, and to each kind of seed he gives its own body. All flesh is not the same. Men have one kind of flesh, animals have another, birds another and fish another. There are also heavenly bodies and there are earthly bodies, but the splendor of the heavenly bodies is one kind, and the splendor of the earthly bodies is another. The sun has one kind of splendor, the moon another and the stars another, and the stars differ from star in splendor. So will it be with the resurrection of the dead. The body that is sown is perishable, it is raised imperishable; it is sown in dishonor, it is raised in glory. It is sown in weakness, it is raised in power. It is sown a natural body, it is raised a spiritual body.[22]

Journeys to the Underworld and Heavenly Realm

Similar ideas appear in the Gospel of Mark 12.25 where Jesus discusses the resurrection of the dead with the Sadducees. Jesus seems to imply that there is only a spiritual as opposed to a physical resurrection of the body when he states the following; "When the dead rise, they will neither marry nor be given in marriage, they will be like angels in heaven."

There are further differences of opinion in the New Testament about the time when the final judgment of the dead will occur. On the one hand, in the "Parable of the Sheep and Goats," the judgment will happen when the Son of Man comes in his glory. (Matt:25–31–46) On the other hand, in the "Parable of Divas and Lazarus," it appears as if the judgment occurs at the moment of death when the soul travels either to Abraham's side (paradise) or to Hell (*Sheol*). (Luke16:22f) Early Christians resolved these two viewpoints by developing the idea of an interim period in which the souls of the dead would await the coming of God's Kingdom and the end of the world. Upon death, the individual would be judged and then sent to a place between heaven and Hades to await the Parousia. At the end of history, the souls of the dead would be resurrected from the dead to join the living in a final judgment. The details vary from one early Christian source to another. In Acts,20:35 only the righteous would be raised from the dead whereas in Acts24:15 the souls of both the just and unjust would be raised.

The Book of Revelation

The Book of Revelation in the New Testament speaks of a cataclysmic end of history in which God will destroy all the evil and bring about a new age involving two resurrections of the dead. As in earlier Jewish apocalypses, the central focus of the Book of Revelation is a description of a future age when God will wipe away all evil from the world and establish his kingdom. Written sometime at the end of the 1st century CE, the author explains in the introduction that while he was living on the island of Patmos an angel of the Lord appeared to him.

> I, John, your brother and companion in the suffering and kingdom and patient endurance that are ours in Jesus was on the island of Patmos because of the word of God and the testimony of Jesus. On the Lord's Day I was in the Spirit and I heard behind me a loud voice like a trumpet, which said: "Write on a scroll what you see and send it to the seven churches: to Ephesus, Smyrna, Pergamum, Thyatira, Sardis, Philadelphia and Laodicea."[23]

Seven. The Journey to Moral Awareness

John is the recipient of a series of heavenly visions in which he witnesses what will happen at the end of the present age. A fierce cosmic battle between God and Satan takes place.

> And there was a war in heaven. Michael and his angels fought against the dragon and the dragon and the angels fought back. But he was not strong enough and they lost their place in heaven. The great dragon was hurled down—that ancient serpent called the devil, or Satan, who leads the whole world astray. He was hurled to the earth and the angels with him.[24]

An angel of the Lord will come down from heaven and seize the dragon and lock him up for a thousand years in a vast pit. John states that the dragon will be imprisoned for one thousand years and during this period the first resurrection of the dead will take place; only Christian martyrs and others refusing to receive the mark of Satan will be raised from the dead in the first resurrection. The rest of the dead will not be raised until another one thousand years has passed. Then, Satan will be released from the abyss. At that point, Satan will gather all his forces of evil to launch a great battle against God and his army of angels. Satan and his army will attempt to destroy Christ's earthly kingdom. Ultimately, Satan and his legions will be defeated. A great fire from heaven will be unleashed upon the Satanic forces and Satan will be thrown into a lake of fire where the beast and the false prophets were tormented forever. Then, a second resurrection of the dead will take place. Those who have committed evil acts will be judged for what they had done while they were alive. Since their names were not in the Book of Life, therefore they will be thrown down into the pit where they will stay with Satan forever. The Book of Revelation discusses the aftermath of the second judgment in ambiguous terms.

> Then I saw a new heaven and a new earth for the first heaven and the first earth had passed away, and there was no longer any sea. I saw the Holy City, the new Jerusalem; coming down out of heaven from God, prepared as a bride beautifully dressed for her husband.[25]

The end of the old order is marked by the devil being thrown into a dark pit and locked away. Then, God will descend from heaven into the world to live among human beings in a spiritually transformed earth. At that time, a new heavenly city made from gold and jewels will descend upon earth to serve as God's home.

Journeys to the Underworld and Heavenly Realm

The Shepherd of Hermes

Christian apocalyptic writing continues to be popular in the 2nd century in the early Church. However, by this time, the Church community realized that the coming of God's kingdom might not be imminent. As a result, several new issues related to the establishment of the Church in the world needed to be considered. Some of these new issues and concerns are expressed in some of these 2nd century Christian apocalypses.

One important 2nd century CE Christian apocalypse is the *Shepherd of Hermes*. A series of visions are sent to Hermes that describe the need for all Christians to repent and prepare for the coming of God's kingdom before it is too late. Given the fact that there was a perceived "delay in the Parousia," the issue of repentance soon became an important issue in the early Church. While waiting for the coming of God's kingdom, people could still fall into the web of sin even if they were baptized. Therefore, repentance and ethical behavior were very important. Unlike other Jewish and Christian apocalypses, the *Shepherd of Hermas* does not focus primarily upon future events such as the end-times or the coming of the kingdom of God. Instead, the *Shepherd of Hermes* stresses the need for all Christians to repent in the present age. In the opening passage of the narrative, Hermas states that one day as he was passing by the Tiber river he saw a beautiful woman bathing in the river. At the time, he thought that she would make a wonderful wife. Then, several years later Hermes received a series of visions about the woman. The first vision begins as follows:

> After a certain time, as I was journeying to Cumae, and glorifying God's creatures for their greatness and splendor and power, as I walked I fell asleep. And a Spirit took me, and bore men away through a pathless tract, through which no man could pass: for the place was precipitous, and broken into clefts by reason of waters. When then I had crossed the river, I came into the level country, and knelt down, and began to pray to the Lord and to confess my sins.[26]

As he prayed, the heavens opened and suddenly he saw the same woman that he had seen before bathing in the Tiber. She told Hermas that she was taken up to heaven by God and could tell that he needed to repent for all his past sins. A year later Hermes returned to Cumae and had a second vision. The woman of the first vision appeared once again to him holding a little book in her hand. She asked Hermes if he would tell his fellow parishioners about everything that was written down in the book.

Seven. The Journey to Moral Awareness

Hermes admitted that he might not be able to remember everything in the book and so he asked her if he could make a copy of it. Giving the book to him, she pointed out that God will forgive those who ask for forgiveness. In the third vision, Hermes saw a beautiful stone tower surrounded by water. Many of the stones were on fire and some were falling into the nearby water. The lady of the first two visions re-appeared and explained the meaning of the vision. The tower represented the Church. Just as some stones were falling into water, some Christians will repent and be saved; just as some stones were on fire, some Christians will burn in the fires of Hell. The tower was built on water because God provides salvation to the elect. Then, she admonished Hermes to tell everyone what had been shown to him so that they would seek repentance and be saved. Twenty days later Hermas had a fourth vision. As Hermas was walking down a road, he saw a huge cloud of dust billowing up to heaven. Out of the cloud a huge beast emerged that resembled a sea monster. The creature's head had four colors consisting of black, gold, red and white. Putting his faith in God, Hermas passed by the monster unharmed. Then he saw a beautiful young bride dressed in white and he immediately realized that she represented the Church. She told him that God had protected him from harm because he sent his angel Sergi to hold the monster's mouth shut as he passed by. Hermas asked her what the four colors of the monster's head represented. She told him that the black represented the world; the red represented the fact that the world must perish; the gold represents those who will be able to escape from this world and the white is a symbol of the age to come where those who repent will be saved.

The Gospel of Bartholomew and the Gospel of Nicodemus

Besides the otherworldly visions described in the *Shepherd of Hermes* and the Book of Revelation, several other Christian apocalypses speak about otherworldly journeys to heaven and hell. The 3rd century CE document entitled The *Gospel of Bartholomew*, gives a much more elaborate description of Hell and the Devil than previous descriptions by providing a detailed account of Jesus Christ's descent into Hell. The author wishes to emphasize the need for all Christians to be on guard against the wily ways of Satan. Since the Kingdom of God is not imminent, Satan has additional opportunities to tempt Christians into a life of sin. By the 3rd century, the early Church had completely separated itself off from its Jewish roots in Palestine, but certain questions remained concerning its relationship to Judaism. Some of these issues appear in the Gospel of Bartholomew. One issue was Judaism's refusal to accept Jesus as the son of God. Another issue related to the status of the Jewish Patriarchs within the minds of the Church community. The description of their rescue from Hell by Jesus is meant to show that the Patriarchs should not be regarded as evil, nor should the writings of the Old Testament be entirely rejected. However, assigning Satan as the mouthpiece of the Jewish doctrine that Jesus is not the Son of God underscores the early Church's total condemnation of such a view.

The gospel account begins at the scene of Christ's crucifixion on the cross. As Jesus was hanging on the cross, Bartholomew looked up and saw that Jesus had suddenly vanished. Then, he heard Jesus' voice coming up from the underworld. Bartholomew asked the risen Jesus to explain what had happened. Jesus explains that after he vanished from the cross, he was asked by Michael the archangel to journey down into the underworld and retrieve Adam and several other Biblical patriarchs including Abraham, Isaac and Jacob. As Hades announced the arrival of God's son in the underworld, the devil spoke up against Hades, refusing to accept the idea that Jesus was more than a prophet. Then Bartholomew told Jesus that he saw the angels carrying someone out of Hell and wondered who this person was. Jesus replied that it was Adam. Jesus explained that he had descended to Hell to retrieve Adam and bring him back to heaven. Back on earth Jesus' disciples asked him to show them the abyss. Moving the earth to one side, Jesus revealed the underworld lying beneath it. Upon seeing it, the apostles fell on their faces in shock. After the vast chasm was covered up, then Bartholomew asked Jesus to show him the greatest adversary of humanity, namely, the devil. Then, Jesus brought the apostles down from the Mount of Olives into the underworld. Jesus ordered Michael the archangel to sound his trumpet and suddenly the devil appeared. He was bound in fiery chains and held down by six hundred and sixty angels. He was sixteen hundred yards long and forty yards wide. Each of his wings was eighty yards long. His face was fiery red, and his eyes were like sparks. When the apostles saw the devil, they fell to the ground, but Jesus came and raised them up, bestowing upon them the Spirit of God. Jesus told

Bartholomew to put his feet on the devil's neck. Although Bartholomew was afraid, he finally worked up his courage and approached the devil, put his foot on his neck and asked him his name. The devil said that his original name was Satanael, which means "angel of God." After he rejected the image of God, his name was changed to Satan, which means "angel of Hell." Bartholomew asked Satan to describe some of the ways in which the souls of the wicked are punished. Suddenly a wheel and sword flashing with fire and pipes emerged from the abyss. Satan explained that the sword was for the gluttonous. The gluttonous are put into the pipe because in their gluttony they turn to every type of sin. The slanderers are put into the second pipe because they secretly slander their neighbor. The hypocrites are put in the third pipe and the rest are punished by Satan's machinations. Since Satan is unable to leave Hell, he sends out his servants equipped with "many-barbed hooks" to catch souls and bring them back to Hell. They use various things such as drunkenness, laughter and fornication to weaken the souls and entice them. The Gospel concludes with a prayer that asks Jesus to save the sinners of the world.

Another description of the underworld is provided in the 4th century CE apocryphal Gospel of Nicodemus. Once again Jesus rescues the great patriarchs and prophets of the Hebrew Bible from the clutches of Hell. Further details concerning the fate of the souls who died prior to the coming of Jesus is given in this apocryphal Gospel. Many members of the early Church wondered about the fate of those souls who had died prior to the time of Jesus' appearance in the world. Was salvation available to these souls? The Gospel of Nicodemus addresses this issue by describing Jesus' rescue mission. In the past, when the Hebrew patriarchs and others died, their souls descended into Hell where they waited during the interim period for the coming of Jesus Christ into the world. Besides bringing salvation to those living in the present, Jesus saved these souls of those who died in the past by coming down to Hell and bringing them back to heaven.

The Gospel of Peter and The Apocalypse of Paul

The non-canonical Gospel of Peter was discovered in the 19th century in Egypt. Most scholars believe it was written in the 2nd century CE sometime after the four canonical gospels of the New Testament. Like other

Journeys to the Underworld and Heavenly Realm

Jewish and Christian apocalypses, elaborate otherworldly punishments and rewards are described set in the context of the eschatological future. In the future a time will come when a general resurrection of the dead will take place. Then, all the souls of the damned in Hell would finally come before God to receive their final Judgement. According to this text, the bodies of the dead will rise from the ground just like seeds planted in the earth that grow up into harvested wheat. For those who have lost their faith, great cataracts of fire will burst forth and a great darkness will descend upon the earth. On the final Day of Judgement, all the oceans of the earth will change into fiery coals and everything in them will burn. In the sky, the stars will melt and everywhere on earth the people will flee in fear. There will be no escape from God's wrath because a great flame will engulf sinners. In a section of Hell called Akhmim many souls will hang by their tongues.

Other horrifying punishments were shown to Peter. In the final judgment, murderers will be thrown into a great gorge full of poisonous snakes and awful worms. The souls of the murdered will watch them writhing in torment. Slanderers and deceivers will be forced to chew on their tongues. Those who were implicated in the death of the martyrs will have their lips cut off and have their mouths burned with fire. Those who had failed to give any money to the poor will be forced to wear rags and roll their bodies upon hot, sharp pebbles. Money lenders will be made to stand in a great lake filled with feces and blood. Others will be coerced into going up and down a high hill and given no rest. After seeing these frightful things, Peter was taken to a heavenly garden filled with gleaming sunlight located far away from the dark, nightmarish world of Hell. The scent of flowers filled the air. This was the place where those who had lived a righteous life on earth were given the gift of immortal bliss in the presence of God and his angels.

Another noteworthy Christian apocalypse is the 4th century CE Apocalypse of Paul. In the introductory passage, it states that during the consulate of Theodosius Augustus the Younger and Cynegius a certain person was living in Tarsus in a house that once belonged to the apostle Paul. At night, an angel appeared to him and told him that a marble box containing Paul's revelation was buried in the foundation of the house. At first the man thought that this angelic vision was a delusion and so he refused to

Seven. The Journey to Moral Awareness

look for the marble box. However, when the angel reappeared to the man, he was convinced that the vision was real and so he decided to dig up the foundation in search of the box. When he found the box, he opened it up and there inside was the revelation of St. Paul.

At the beginning of the narrative St. Paul states that on one occasion he saw some angels who were leading souls upward to heaven to stand before God for their judgment. Paul noticed that he was surrounded by bright light. Paul was taken to the edge of a river where there were some fruit trees. When Paul asked why each tree produced so much fruit, the angel said that in his generosity God gives many gifts to the worthy. Paul was taken by an angel to Lake Acherusia located near the city of Christ. Only the righteous could enter the city since it was on the road to God. Fornicators and sinners could enter the city only if they decided to repent and be baptized by Michael the archangel in the waters of the lake. With thousands of angels singing in the background, Paul climbed aboard a golden boat and floated across the lake to the city of Christ. Upon his arrival, he was greeted by the city's inhabitants. The city was made of gold and had twelve walls around it. Whenever anyone came through the gate to enter the city, the men standing by the trees outside the gates began to weep because many of them were not allowed to enter. The trees bowed and swayed in sympathy for those sinners who could not enter the city. The angel led Paul to a river of honey where he saw the prophet Ezekiel, Amos, Micah and Zechariah. Then, Paul was led to the river of milk where he saw all the infants that Herod had killed. Michael the archangel told Paul that everyone who is chaste and pure in their life will be taken to the city of Christ to receive the promise of God. Then he was taken to the north part of the city where all those who showed hospitality to strangers received God's gifts. There he saw the patriarchs of the Bible including Abraham, Isaac and Lot. In the east part of the city Paul was taken to a river of oil where all those who dedicated themselves to God resided. In the middle of the city there stood a great altar. Standing next to the altar was King David holding a harp in his hand. As he began to sing, his voice rang out loudly and shook the very foundations of the city. The angel told Paul that since it is not proper to offer a sacrifice to God without David, therefore David must sing psalms at the time that Christ's body and blood are offered in heaven.

Journeys to the Underworld and Heavenly Realm

This chapter focused upon the experience of moral obligation as it is expressed various ancient Judeo-Christian and pagan otherworldly journey narratives. Portions of the *Egyptian Book of the Dead* were examined as well as a Zoroastrian text entitled *the Menok* and several other Judeo-Christian documents. Judgment of the dead in the afterlife functions as the central theme of many of these narratives. *The Egyptian Book of the Dead* describes the deceased soul's journey to *Tuat* and the "weighing of the heart" in the Hall of Judgement. The outcome of the judgment determined the fate of the soul and whether it would join Osiris in the land of the blessed or be sent into the fires of oblivion. The Zoroastrian text entitled *the Menok* states that when a person dies, then their soul goes upon a journey across a great cosmic bridge leading to the hereafter. While traveling across the bridge, the soul is judged by a mysterious figure called the "Requiter." If the soul is judged to be worthy, then it can cross the bridge to enter the land of the blessed. Otherwise, it is condemned to the fires of Hell. In several ancient Judeo-Christian texts certain noteworthy Biblical figures such as Enoch or Paul participate in visionary journeys in which they learn about what awaits the just and unjust upon death in the next life. In these narratives it is revealed that sometime in the indeterminant future, a final judgment will take place for all of humanity. At that point, a general resurrection of the dead will take place; God will usher in His glorious kingdom and all the sinners who have violated God's moral edicts will receive their punishment in the fires of Hell. On the other hand, those who have remained steadfast and true to God's law will be given their well-deserved reward of everlasting life in heaven.

Conclusion

In this book, attention has been focused upon a group of ancient and early medieval narratives describing journeys to the underworld and heavenly realm. It was shown that the subject-matter of these otherworldly journey narratives is primarily religious in nature since they speak about topics such as the sacred cosmos, the relationship between the gods and mortals as well as a variety of supernatural events. Since these narratives deal with material of a spiritual nature, this book has sought to identify the underlying sources of religious inspiration expressed in these texts as well as to situate them in their proper historic context. Otherworldly journey narratives underwent a significant process of change and development in ancient and medieval times involving the expression of various types of spirituality. In analyzing these narratives six categories of religious experience have been detected: numinous experience, mystical experience, spiritual transformation, courage in the face of death, the intellectual apprehension of the divine and the experience of moral judgment. Otherworldly journey narratives have been selected from the ancient Near East, the Greco-Roman world and early medieval Europe that manifest each of the six modes of religious experience. It has been suggested that rather than appearing in the world as a single phenomenon, awareness of the sacred takes shape in different ways, depending upon the historical context. In ancient Mesopotamia, a certain set of factors exert influence whereas in the Greco-Roman or medieval world a different set of circumstances prevail. Given the fact that otherworldly narratives were a popular form of literary expression in ancient and medieval times, it is not surprising that different kinds of spirituality became interwoven into these stories. These narratives appear in a variety of cultural settings including

Conclusion

the ancient Near East, Greco-Roman society and pagan Europe spanning many centuries of history. Although many different literary styles and genres have been utilized to tell stories of otherworldly journeys, it is important to remember that a substratum of religious awareness lurks beneath the surface of many of these texts. Addressing this underlying subtext has been the main preoccupation of this book.

After a preliminary discussion of definitions and objectives in the Introduction, Chapter One focused upon the ancient cosmological outlook which appears in the background of many of these otherworldly journey stories. Several ancient Near Eastern and Greco-Roman creation myths were examined. First, the Babylonian creation myth (*Enuma Elish*) was discussed, followed by the Genesis creation story and the story of the birth of the gods in Hesiod's *Theogony*. By means of a comparative analysis, important thematic similarities and differences between the cosmological outlook of the ancient Mesopotamians, the ancient Hebrews, the Greeks and Romans were noted. Although the ancient cosmological outlook undergoes change and development in Hellenistic times due to Ptolemy's astronomical research, it continues to thrive during the early Medieval period, as exemplified by Norse mythology. In archaic stories of the creation, the birth of the cosmos occurs either under violent or peaceful circumstances. One example of a "violent creation" appears in the ancient Babylonian creation myth (*Enuma Elish*) where the formation of the cosmos takes place as a byproduct of a brutal clash between the gods. Another violent creation story appears in Hesiod's *Theogony*. Like other ancient creation myths, Hesiod states that in the beginning there was only an undifferentiated chaotic mass out of which Earth (*Gaia*) mysteriously emerged into being as a cosmic emanation. Then, Earth gave birth to Sky (*Ouranos*). When *Gaia* and *Ouranos* conjoined together all the other gods of the universe came into existence. Gaia's children, the Titans did not get very well along with Zeus and his offspring and so a great cosmic war ensues. Zeus triumphantly wins the battle and the Titans are locked away at the bottom of the dark underworld chasm. Other more peaceful creation stories appear in ancient Egyptian lore as well as in the Hebrew Bible. During the Middle Kingdom of ancient Egyptian history, the Heliopolis creation myth tells the story of the creator-god Atum who comes forth out of the watery chaos and climbs to the top of a great hill.

Conclusion

In a series of non-violent, creative acts, Atum fashions all the other gods of the cosmos, including the god Shu (Air) and Telnut (Moisture). Shu separates the sky from the earth. In the Hebrew Bible, Yahweh, the supreme god of the universe creates the world in seven days. Earth was described as a "formless mass" and after separating the light from the darkness, God created the sky by creating an expanse away from the watery chaos. Then he created the land by ordering the water under the sky to be gathered in a single place. In Norse mythology, the creation of the cosmos is the byproduct of a series of peaceful actions of the gods. In the early Middle Ages, the three-fold view of the universe is clearly reflected in the mythic narratives of the *Prose* and *Poetic Eddas*.

Chapter Two addressed the subject of numinous experience as it is conveyed in various archaic underworld journey narratives. Whereas many archaic creation myths speak about a watery chaos as the first cause of everything including the earth and the heavens, ancient underworld journey narratives describe a shadowy world where the souls of the dead live. Numinous experience involves the encounter with divine beings living in a transcendent, supernatural realm. Usually, these types of meetings are shrouded in mystery and produce feelings of wonder and awe in those experiencing them. Examples of numinous experiences are prolific throughout the history of religion. Reference to numinous experience is well testified in various ancient underworld narratives such as in Book XI of *The Odyssey* and Book Vi of the *Aeneid*. The Greek oracles such as the Delphic oracle and the Oracle of Trophonius provide ritual reenactments of the mythic underworld journey (*katabasis*). In some sense, the mythic descent of heroes such as Odysseus or Aeneus to the realm of the dead is comparable to the ordeal of the shaman of pre-literate society. These narratives in *The Odyssey* and *Aeneid* provide detailed descriptions of encounters with the souls of the dead living in the remote lower regions of the underworld. Life in the netherworld is mostly an unfortunate and unhappy experience for the souls dwelling there. Even though Odysseus has little trouble recognizing the identity of various souls he encounters in Erebus, nevertheless their souls appear to him in the form of ghostly shadows devoid of any real vitality or life. Those undertaking numinous journeys to the underworld usually are required to follow special instructions and procedures to successfully enter since one is traveling to a place that is

Conclusion

"wholly other" from the profane world. Various divine helpers such as the witch Circe, Sibyl, the prophetess and Charon, the ferryman provide necessary assistance to Odysseus and Aeneus in finding their way through the shadowy world below.

Chapter Three focused upon stories of heavenly ascents and mystical journeys circulating in the ancient world. Whereas numinous experience involves encounters with supernatural beings existing outside of oneself, mystical experience takes place entirely within oneself. Sometimes making the distinction between these two forms of religiosity can be difficult. Frequently this difficulty rests in the fact that the recipients of the mystical experience often believe they have encountered supernatural beings existing outside of themselves instead of within their own psyche. The term "mysticism" is used to include a wide variety of paranormal and telepathic experiences such as out-of-the-body experiences and dream visions. Mystical states of consciousness are described and doctrinally understood in various ways in the religious traditions of the world. In classical Greek times, examples of mystical religious experience can be identified in the context of Orphism and the cult of Dionysus. Later, in Hellenistic-Roman times, a few individuals such as the pagan sophist Aelius Aristides and the Christian martyr St. Perpetua of Carthage describe fascinating first-person accounts of visionary experience. Likewise, some fantastic visionary writings appear in the Hebrew Bible. For example, in the Book of Daniel a series of strange apocalyptic dream-visions are described. Although it could be argued that some of these texts may be the product of literary invention, some authentic psychological experience may be at least vaguely reflected in these accounts.

Chapter Four examined a third kind of religious experience referred to as spiritual transformation. Often the experience of spiritual transformation can be understood metaphorically as a journey. Hence, several ancient and medieval narratives were examined which portrayed spiritual transformation metaphorically in terms of a journey. Becoming aware of the sacred can produce a variety of powerful psychological effects upon one's life and can also bring about an abrupt change in an individual's self-perception. Sometimes this change in perspective can lead to an individual's religious conversion; a spiritual awakening of this type can take several different forms. In the case of Greco-Roman paganism, an individual

Conclusion

could adopt several different religious affiliations at once. Although religious exclusivism has always been an important feature of the great monotheistic traditions of the western world, it was not a characteristic of the ancient polytheistic faiths. Ample details about pagan spiritual transformation are provided by the Hellenistic-Roman author Apuleius in his semi-autobiographical novel entitled the *Metamorphoses*. Furthermore, spiritual transformation functions as the central theme of a variety of other ancient myths that speak about" the dying and rising gods." In these stories, a god or goddess usually undergoes some type ordeal involving a descent to the world below. After suffering a period of loss or grief, the god or goddess is subsequently allowed to journey back to the world above. Usually some kind of bargain is struck for the god to be released back to the world above. Stories of the "dying and rising gods" functioned as a popular way of expressing the idea of spiritual transformation. Originally these kinds of stories probably were connected to the agricultural cycle, but eventually they served an important role in the mystery-religions. Chapter Five concluded with an examination of the Scandinavian tale of Baldr's journey to the underworld. Unlike the other dying and rising gods of the ancient Mediterranean world, once the Norse god Baldr travels into the world below, he is never able to go back to the world above again.

Chapter Five examined two iconic underworld journeys narratives in terms of a fourth type of religious experience labeled as "Courage in the Face of Death." One important function of religious institutions is to assist human beings in coming to terms with suffering and death. In mythology, the topic of death is frequently explored in terms of an explanation of its origins. The subject of death is a primary concern of two mythological epics, namely, *The Epic of Gilgamesh* and medieval tale entitled *Beowulf*. Both Beowulf and Gilgamesh achieve their heroic status by courageously confronting death in the underworld. In distinction those who believe in the existence of the immortal soul, both Gilgamesh and Beowulf come to realize that death is final and there is no life beyond this world. In *The Epic of Gilgamesh*, the turning point in the story comes when a snake comes up from a river and plucks away the flower of immortality. As a result, Gilgamesh achieves his heroic status by accepting his own mortality. He knows that only the gods have immortality. Toward the end of the medieval tale of *Beowulf*, Beowulf realizes that he is likely to

Conclusion

die at the hands of the horrific monster of the deep. Believing that there is no life beyond the grave, he accepts his tragic fate. He consoles himself by knowing that his acts of courage will always be remembered forever once he passes away.

Apprehending the holy through one's intellectual faculties represents the fifth category of religious experience examined in Chapter Six. In this chapter, becoming intellectually aware of the divine was explored in terms of an examination of two documents, namely, Plato's *Myth of Er* and Cicero's *Dream of Scipio*. Each story describes an individual's journey to the heights of heaven where spiritual wisdom is attained. Plato's *Myth of Er* discusses what happens to the soul of a young warrior named Er after he is slain in battle. The *Dream of Scipio* is the Latin counterpart to *The Myth of Er*. Although in many ways Cicero is much more of a skeptic than Plato, the *Dream of Scipio* is similar in terms of style and content to *The Myth of Er*. Both Plato and Cicero believe that philosophy holds the key for attaining everlasting bliss in the hereafter. However, the message of Cicero's *Dream of Scipio* is somewhat different than what Plato is trying to point out in *The Myth of Er*. For Plato, philosophy leads to spiritual enlightenment by providing a person with knowledge of the forms. Knowledge of the forms leads to a cessation to the endless cycle of births and rebirths and the attainment of eternal bliss in the world of pure Being. Cicero believes that it is only by selflessly devoting oneself to civic activities for the sake of the state that one will ever taste the eternal fruits of spiritual happiness in the hereafter. In addition to philosophic reflection, Cicero believes that practical action is also an important ingredient for the attainment of spiritual happiness.

Chapter Seven examined a variety of ancient pagan and Judeo-Christian stories describing the journey of the soul in the next life and the fate awaiting it. A sixth category of religious experience relates to the journey to moral awareness. Once a person becomes conscious of the presence of the sacred in his or her life, frequently that person subsequently realizes that certain changes in their behavior need to be made. In short, contact with "Ultimate Reality" usually leads to the realization of one's moral obligations to those around them. In antiquity, stories of underworld and heavenly journeys frequently encouraged moral behavior in this life by showing the fate of the soul in the next life. In the ancient Near East, many

Conclusion

tales of underworld journeys and heavenly excursions incorporated the theme of ethical obligations into their narrative structure. In ancient Egyptian lore, realizing one's ethical obligations in this life was encouraged by describing the judgment of the soul in the hereafter. Upon death, it was believed that the soul of the deceased would travel to the Land of the Dead (*Tuat*) to be judged by the gods of the dead. Based upon a review of one's actions while alive on earth, a soul was judged to be either good or evil. If the outcome was positive, then the soul would be allowed to join Osiris in his kingdom. On the other hand, if a soul was judged to be evil, then that soul would be thrown into a great fire and be destroyed. Similar kinds of ideas are outlined in Zoroastrianism, Hellenistic Judaism and Christianity. The Zoroastrian document entitled t*he Menok* describes the soul's judgment in the next world. A similar emphasis on the judgment of the soul is found in several Hellenistic Jewish and early Christian documents such as the Book of Enoch and the Gospel of Peter. Many Judeo-Christian narratives portray the fate of the individual upon death in stark terms. On the one hand, those who have committed sins in their life on earth will be punished and tortured forever in Hell. On the other hand, eternal happiness in heaven will be awarded to those who have remained faithful to God's laws during their life on earth.

The popularity of stories of underworld and heavenly journeys eventually spilled over into the Renaissance and the modern world where they continued to be told and re-told. These charming tales of magic and wonder have captivated the imagination of many millions of believers and non-believers alike. This book has sought to demonstrate how these imaginative tales articulated some of the ways in which people experienced the sacred. The fact that the various forms of spiritual awareness find expression in these narratives provides an important reason why these stories have resonated so deeply in the hearts and minds of many people throughout history.

Chapter Notes

Preface

1. See Ian Barbour's discussion of religious stories and his typology of religious experience in his *Religion and Science: Historical and Contemporary Issues*, Harper Collins Publishers, New York, 1997, p. 113–115. Our typology of the six categories of religious experience is largely based on Barbour's typology. An excellent historical overview of western concepts of the afterlife are discussed in Alan Segal's *Life After Death: A History of the Afterlife in Western Religion*, Doubleday, New York, 2010.
2. John Stephens, *The Dreams and Visions of Aelius Aristides*, Gorgias Press, New Jersey, 2013. *Ancient Mediterranean Religions: Myth, Ritual and Religious Experience*, Cambridge Scholars Press, UK, 2016.

Introduction

1. John Hinnelis, ed., *The Routledge Companion to Study the Study of Religion*, Routledge, New York, 2009; see especially Chapter 1, "Why Study Religions."
2. See the discussion of prehistoric religion in Willard Oxtoby, Amir Hussain and Roy Amore, ed., *World Religions: Western Traditions*, Oxford University Press, Ontario, Canada, 2014, p. 5–9.
3. Willard Oxtoby, Amir Hussain and Roy Amore, ed., *World Religions: Western Traditions*, p. 5–6.
4. *Ibid.*, p. 7–8.
5. For more of the relationship between myth and religion see Chapter Three, "Myth and Religion" in Robert Segal's *Myth: A Very Short Introduction*, 2nd Edition, Oxford University Press, Oxford, United Kingdom, 2015.
6. Sir James Frazer, *The Golden Bough*, Macmillan Paperback Edition, Macmillan Publishing, New York, 1963.
7. Sigmund Freud, *Totem and Taboo*, A.A. Brill trans., Moffat Yard and Co., New York, 1918.
8. Emile Durkheim, *The Elementary Forms of the Religious Life*, Carol Cosman, trans., Oxford University Press, World Classics Edition, Oxford, 2008.
9. Rudolf Otto, *The Idea of the Holy*, Oxford University Press, Paperback Edition, London, 1959.
10. James explains why he does not believe that distinct religious emotion exists in *The Varieties of Religious Experience*, Chapter Two, "Circumscription of the Topic," New York, 1961, p. 39–58.
11. Ludwig Wittgenstein, *Philosophical Investigations*, Section 43.
12. Clifford Geertz, "Religion as a Cultural System," in M. Banton, ed., *Anthropological Approaches to the Study of Religion*, London, Tavistock Publications, 1965, p. 5.

Chapter Notes—One

13. Peter Berger, *The Sacred Canopy*, Doubleday, New York, 1967, p. 26. Many of Berger's ideas on the sociological function of religion are applicable to the formation of worldviews.

14. Mircea Eliade, *The Sacred and the Profane*, trans., W. Trask, Harcourt, New York, 1959, p. 17–18.

15. Ninian Smart, *The Religious Experience*, Prentice Hall, New Jersey, 1996, p. 3–8.

16. W. Richard Comstock, *The Study of Religion and Primitive Religions*, Harper and Row, New York, 1972. p. 31.

17. Mircea Eliade, *Myth and Reality*, trans. W. Trask, Harper and Row, New York, 1963, p. 5–6.

18. Gerald J. Larson," The Study of Mythology and Comparative Mythology"; cf., *Myth in Indo-European Antiquity*, ed. by Gerald James Larson, C. Scott Littleton and Jaan Puhvel, University of California Press, Berkeley, 1974, p. 1.

19. *Ibid.*

20. Koran, Surah 17.1: "Glory to (God) Who did take His servant for a journey by night from the Sacred Mosque to the Farthest Mosque whose precincts We did bless —in order that we might show him some of our signs for He is the One Who heareth and seeth all things..."

Chapter One

1. Mircea Eliade, *The Sacred and the Profane*, p. 37.

2. Ancient Mesopotamian cosmology is discussed in W.G. Lambert's *Ancient Mesopotamian Religion and Mythology*, ed. A.R. George, and T.M. Oshima, Mohr Siebeck Publishers, Tübingen, Germany, 2016; see especially chapter 3. See also Thorkild Jacobsen, *The Treasury of Darkness: A History of Mesopotamian Religion*, Yale University Press, New Haven, 1976.

3. Stephanie Dalley, *Myths from Mesopotamia: Creation, The Flood Gilgamesh and Others*, Oxford University Press, Revised Paperback Edition, 2000, p. 233. Dalley's translation updates the James Pritchard's translation appearing in *Near Eastern Texts*, Princeton, New Jersey, 1950, p. 60–72, which is reprinted in *Essential Sacred Writings from Around the World*, p. 98–108.

4. *Ibid.*

5. *Ibid.*, p. 254.

6. *Ibid.*, p. 260.

7. Cf., Geoffrey Parrinder, ed., *World Religions: From Ancient History to the Present*, Facts on File Publications, New York, 1971; see especially Chapter Nine on ancient Egyptian religion, p. 135–145.

8. Ps. 17.

9. Exodus 19.16. The New International English translation of the Bible has been used, co-published by Zondervan Publishers and Tyndale House Publishers, Grand Rapids, 1998.

10. Ex. 19.18.

11. Gen. 9.13.

12. Gen. 1.1–2.

13. Gen. 1.6–8.

14. Luther Martin discusses the threefold cosmology of the Greeks and Romans in his *Hellenistic Religions: An Introduction*, Oxford University Press, Oxford, 1987, p. 6–10.

15. It should be noted that the female divine principle of "wisdom" aptly named Sophia appears in several sources including the Hebrew Bible, ancient Gnostic writings and the Apocryphal Gospels. In the Book of Proverbs 8.23–30, this female principle described as being brought forth as the first of God's creations. "I was appointed from eternity, from the beginning, before the world began. When there were no oceans, I was given birth, when there were no springs abounding with water; before the mountains were settled in place, before the hills, I was given birth, before he made the earth or the fields or any of the dust of the world. I was there when he set the heavens in place, when he marked out the horizon on the face of the deep.... Then I was the craftsman at his side."

16. Hesiod, *Theogony*, line 126 ff.
17. *Ibid.*, line 621–628.
18. *Ibid.*, line 737–744.
19. *Ibid.*, line 749–755.
20. See Barbour's discussion on the differences between the world view of Ptolemy and Copernicus in his *Religion and Science*, p. 6–23.
21. Mircea Eliade, ed., *Essential Sacred Texts from Around the World*, p. 119.
22. Snorri Sturluson, *The Prose Edda*, Jesse L. Byock, trans., Penguin Books, London, 2005 cf., "The Sibyl's Prophecy," p. 12.
23. *Ibid.*, p. 27–28.
24. For a discussion of the concept of the *axis mundi* see Mircea Eliade, *The Sacred and the Profane*, p. 35–37. Closely related to Eliade's sacred/profane distinction is another concept that has relevance for the study of otherworldly narratives. Throughout his books Eliade frequently mentions the concept of the "center of the world" that is represented in the form of the *axis mundi*. Whenever a manifestation of the sacred occurs in this world, an opening or breakthrough of the divine world into the profane world has taken place. This opening of the sacred originates either in the upper or lower world. The net result of such an opening is that the three cosmic levels, earth, heaven and the underworld have been put in communication. Perhaps the clearest example of the axis mundi in its pure form can be found in traditional societies. For example, the symbolism of the cosmic pillar appears in the myths and rituals of the traditional tribe known as the Arhilpa. In mythical times, the high god Numbakula consecrated the territory by creating a sacred pole from out of a tree trunk. After blessing it with blood and blessing the territory, the god disappeared into the upper realm by climbing up into the heavens. Eliade discusses the persistence of the archaic world view as well as ancient Germanic and Norse religion in volume 2 of his *A History of Religious Ideas*, University of Chicago Press, Chicago, 1982, p. 172–179. For more on Eliade's general views on myth and religion see Douglass Allen's *Myth and Religion in Mircea Eliade*, Routledge, New York 2002.
25. Snorri Sturluson, *The Prose Edda*, trans., Jesse Byock, p. 12.
26. *Ibid.*

Chapter Two

1. Steven Katz, ed., *Mysticism and Philosophical Analysis*, Steven Katz, "Language, Epistemology, and Mysticism," Oxford University Press, New York, 1978, p. 26.
2. See Ian Barbour's typology of religious experience that appears in his *Religion and Science: Historical and Contemporary Issues*, HarperCollins, San Francisco, 1997, p. 110–114. Barbour's typology of religious experience is largely based upon Frederick Streng's theories; cf., Frederick Streng, *Understanding Religious Life*, Dickenson Publishing Company, Encino, CA, 1976, p. 66–125.
3. Ex, 3, 5–6.
4. Frederick Streng, *Understanding Religious Life*, p. 73.
5. For an introduction to the thought of Rudolf Otto see Todd A. Gooch, *The Numinous and Modernity: An Interpretation of Rudolf Otto's Philosophy of Religion*, Walter de Gruyter, Berlin, 2010; see especially Ch. 4 entitled "Otto's Investigation of the Holy," pp104–131.
6. Mircea Eliade, *Patterns in Comparative Religion*, trans. Rosemary Sheed, Signet, New York, 1963, p. 1.
7. Mircea Eliade, *The Sacred and the Profane*, p. 21.
8. For more on the Greek oracles see Pausanius, *Description of Greece*, vol. 1, trans., Peter Levi, Penguin Books, London, 1971; cf., John Stephens, *Ancient Mediterranean Religions: Myth, Ritual and Religious Experience*, p. 102–104.
9. Pausanius, *Description of Greece* 9.39.4.
10. In the latter part of the twelfth century, *The Vision of Tundale* tells the story of

a wealthy man named Tundale whose soul was taken on a journey to purgatory where he has a series of numinous encounters with horrifying creatures of the underworld, angels and a collection of tortured souls who are being punished in various ways. At one point, Tundale meets the devil who is described as having two large black wings, and claws of iron and steel on his hands and feet.

11. John Stephens, *Ancient Mediterranean Religions: Myth, Ritual and Religious Experience*, p. 118f. cf., L.R. Farnell, *Greek Hero Cults*, Oxford University Press, London, 1921.

12. Martin Nilsson, *A History of Greek Religion*, Oxford at the Clarendon Press, London, 1949, p. 103.

13. See Erwin Rodhe's comments of the Homeric conception of the psyche or soul in Psyche: *The Cult of the Souls and the Belief in Immortality among the Greeks*, trans. W.B. Hillis, Routledge, Abington, Great Britain, 1925, p. 6. Rodhe describes the Homeric conception of the soul as "the body's shadow-image "or "a feebler double of man."

14. Homer, *Iliad*, 23, 122–123, Robert Fagles, trans., Penguin Classics, New York, 1991, p. 56–563.

15. Job 7.9.

16. Job 10.20–22.

17. Homer, *The Odyssey of Homer*, 10.508–516; I have used Richmond Lattimore's translation, Perennial Edition, Harper and Row, New York, p. 165.

18. Od. XI.390–394.

19. Here Sir James Frazer's multi-volume work on magic and religion entitled *The Golden Bough* should be mentioned. Rather than conducting his own ethnographical research, Frazer relied upon the research of a multitude of missionaries and travelers. Frazer observed that in many myths a common pattern existed that involved deities labeled as the" dying and rising gods"; in many myths, a dying male god and a female deity of vegetation and the harvest are closely linked together. The death and re-birth of the male god symbolized the annual cycle of nature in which plant life comes to an end in the wintertime only to be reborn in the spring. Osiris, the god of the dead functions as the consort of the Great Mother, the goddess Isis in Egyptian mythology; similarly, Attis is linked Cybele, the Great Mother Goddess of Asia Minor. In the *Golden Bough* Frazer also purposed his evolutionary theory regarding humanity's social development. In the early stages of human history, people saw the world primarily in terms of magic. Eventually religion evolved out of magic and then science emerged out of religion. According to Frazer, mythology and folklore are remnants of a by-gone era where humanity tried to explain the world in a misguided childlike way. Like Müller, Frazer sought a simple solution to the mystery of the origins of myth and religion. Unfortunately, simple solutions do not work for complex, multifaceted phenomena such as the mythology of the world.

20. Virgil, *The Aeneid*, VI.343–349; I have used Allen Mandelbaum's translation of *The Aeneid*, Bantam Classic Edition, New York, 1981. For commentary on the Aeneid see Christine G, Perkell, ed., *Reading Vergil's Aeneid: An Interpretive Guide*, University of Oklahoma Press, Norman, 1999; see also Nicholas Horsfall, *Virgil, Aeneid 6: A Commentary: Introduction, Text and Translation*, De Gruyter, Berlin, 2013.

21. *Aeneid*, VI.428–429.

22. *Ibid.*, VI.434.

23. *Ibid.*, VI. 515.

24. *Ibid.*, VI.847–857.

25. *Ibid.*, VI.919–927.

26. See Chapter Seven.

27. *Aeneid*, VI,1158–1161.

28. Apollodorus, *Library*, II.2.5.12.

29. J.H. Breasted, trans., *Development of Religion and Thought in Ancient Egypt*, Chicago, 1912; cf., Mircea Eliade, ed., *Sacred Texts from Around the World*, p. 353; For an excellent overview of ancient Egyptian religion see Emily Teeter, *Religion and Ritual in Ancient Egypt*, Cambridge University Press, New York, 2011.

30. For a discussion of the *ba*, the *ka* and the *akh* mentioned in *The Egyptian Book of the Dead*, see John Stephens, *Ancient Mediterranean Religions: Myth, Ritual and Religious Experience*, p. 45–47.

31. An English translation of *The Story of Adapa* is provided by Stephanie Dalley in *Myths from Mesopotamia: Creation, the Flood, Gilgamesh and Others*, Oxford University Press, revised paperback edition, 2000, New York, 182–188. An English translation of the story of Etana's ascent to heaven appears in S. Dalley's, *Myths from Mesopotamia: Creation, the Flood Gilgamesh and Others*, p. 189f. An earlier translation of *The Story of Adapa* also is included in *Ancient Near Eastern Texts*, James B. Pritchard, ed., Princeton University Press, Princeton, New Jersey, 1958, vol. 1, p. 76–80. For commentary on the story see Seth L. Sanders, *From Adapa to Enoch: Scribal Culture and Religious Vision in Judea and Babylonia*, Mohr Siebeck, Tübingen, Germany, 2017.

32. Stephanie Dalley, trans., *Myths from Mesopotamia: Creation, the Flood, Gilgamesh and Others*, p. 187.

Chapter Three

1. See Frederick Streng's discussion of mysticism in his *Understanding Religious Life*, p. 113–125.

2. Katha Upanishad, II.3.5; cf., S. Radhakrishnan, trans., *The Principle Upanishads*, Harper and Row, New York, 1953, p. 630–632.

3. Ninian Smart, *World Views: Cross-Cultural Explorations of Human Beliefs*, Prentice Hall, New York, p. 67–70.

4. R.C. Zaehner, *Concordant Discord: The Interdependence of Faiths*, Oxford University Press, London, 1970.

5. *Ibid.*, p. 195.

6. See Peter Katz's article entitled "Mystical Experience, Mystical Doctrine, Mystical Technique," in Mysticism and Philosophical Analysis, ed. Steven Katz, Oxford University Press, New York, 1978.

7. William James, *The Varieties of Religious Experience*, p. 299.

8. Ninian Smart, *World Views: Cross-Cultural Explorations of Human Beliefs*, p. 68.

9. Mircea Eliade, *A History of Religious Ideas*, University of Chicago Press, Chicago, 1978 vol. 2., p. 180.

10. Ovid, *Metamorphoses*, trans., Rolfe Humphries, Indiana University Press, Bloomington, 1983. It is worth noting that in the thirteenth century the classical Orpheus myth is once again re-told in a revised form the Middle English poem entitled *Sir Orfeo*.

11. Pausanius, *Description of Greece*, II.31.2.

12. Plato, *The Republic of Plato*, II.6–7.363C–365A, trans., B. Jowett, Random House, Anchor Book Edition, New York, 1973, cf., Pausanias, *Description of Greece*, 6:2, 26.1–2; excerpted in Marvin Meyer, ed., *The Ancient Mysteries: A Sourcebook of Sacred Texts*, University of Pennsylvania Press, Philadelphia, 1987, p. 99–100.

13. W.C.K. Guthrie, *Orpheus and Greek Religion*, Princeton University Press, New Jersey, 1935, p. 172–173; cf., Mircea Eliade, ed., *Essential Sacred Texts from Around the World*, p. 358–359.

14. Diodorus Siculus, *Library of History*, 3.66.1–2.

15. Marvin Meyer, ed., *The Ancient Mysteries: A Sourcebook of Sacred Texts*, p. 94; cf., Pausanias, *Description of Greece*, 6:2, 26.1–2.

16. Apostolos Athanassakis, trans., *The Orphic Hymns*, Scholars Press, Missoula Montana, 1977, 4, 1–4.

17. Luther Martin, *Hellenistic Religions*, Oxford University Press, London, 1987, p. 93.

18. Gen. 28.13–15.

19. Gen. 28.18–21.

20. Marvin Meyer, ed., *The Nag Hammadi Scriptures*," Allogenes the Stranger," trans, John Turner, Harper Collins, New York, 2007, p. 695.

21. *Ibid.*, p. 697.
22. On the origins of Gnosticism see Birger Pearson, *Ancient Gnosticism: Tradition and Literature*, Fortress Press, Minneapolis, 2007.
23. Edgar Hennecke and Wilhelm Schneemelcher, eds., and trans., *New Testament Apocrypha*, vol.2, Westminster Press, Louisville, 1963; cf., Willis Barnstone, ed., *The Other Bible*, Harper One, New York, 2005, p. 524.
24. 2 Cor. 12.1–7.
25. Plotinus, Enneads, V, 3, 17; cf., Bertrand Russell, *History of Western Philosophy*, p. 281. cf., John Stephens, *Ancient Mediterranean Religions: Myth, Ritual and Religious Experience*, p. 250–256.
26. *Ibid.*
27. Porphyry, *Life of Plotinus*, 23, in Frederick Grant, *Hellenistic Religions*, Bobbs and Merrill, New York, 1953, p. 169.
28. Herodotus, *The Histories*, G.C. Macaulay, trans., Barnes and Noble Edition, New York, 2004.
29. For an excellent overview of the history of the cult of Asclepius see Emma and Ludwig Edelstein, *Asclepius: A Collection and Interpretation of the Testimonies*, Two vols., Arno Press, New York, 1975. For an English translation of the Sacred Tales of Aelius Aristides see C.A. Behr, *Aelius Aristides and the Sacred Tales*, A.M. Hakkert, Amsterdam, 1968. For more on Aelius Aristides see my article entitled "The Dreams of Aelius Aristides," *International Journal of Dream Research*, vol. 5, no. 1, April 2012, p. 76–86; *The Dreams and Visions of Aelius Aristides*, Gorgias Press, Piscataway, New Jersey, 2013, and *Ancient Mediterranean Religions: Myth, Ritual and Religious Experience*, Cambridge Scholars Press, UK, 2016, p. 238–265.
30. A.D. Nock, *Conversion: The Old and the New in Religion from Alexander the Great to Augustine of Hippo*, Oxford University Press, Oxford England, 1952, p. 110. Nock claims that the type of religious quest described in Thessalos' letter "was often no doubt a real experience." Other scholars such as A.J. Festugiere and E.R. Dodds are convinced that individuals like Thessalos or Aristides all believed that they were the recipients of religious visions from the gods.
31. "The Visions of Zosimus," appears in C.G. Jung's *Alchemical Studies*, Bollingen Series XX, Princeton University, Princeton, 1967, 59–109.
32. A.D. Nock "A Vision of Mandulis Aion," *Harvard Theological Review*, vol. 27, 1934, p. 64.
33. Willis Barnstone, ed., *The Other Bible*, p. 171–181; cf., John Stephens, "The Dreams of Perpetua: An Historical Application of the Continuity Hypothesis," *International Journal of Dream Research*, vol. 6, no. 2 Oct. 2013, p. 71–78; cf., *Ancient Mediterranean Religions: Myth, Ritual and Religious Experience*, p. 243–244.

Chapter Four

1. Frendrick Streng, *Understanding Religious Life*, p. 99–109.
2. William James, *The Varieties of Religious Experience*, p. 160.
3. Lucian, "The Death of Peregrine," in *The Selected Satires of Lucian*, ed., and trans., Lionel Casson, W.W. Norton, New York, p. 364–381, 1968.
4. Regarding the differences between Christian conversion and pagan adhesion see A.D. Nock's classic study entitled, *Conversion: The Old and New in Religion from Alexander the Great to Augustine of Hippo*, p. 14f.
5. Ian Barbour, *Religion and Science*, p. 112.
6. For more on the mystery religions see Walter Burkett, *Ancient Mystery Cults*, Harvard University Press, Cambridge, Mass., 1989.
7. An English translation of *Inanna's Descent to the Underworld* can be found in T. Jacobsen's *The Harps That Once*, Yale University Press, New Haven, Ct., 1987. A much older translation appears in Samuel

Chapter Notes—Five

Kramer, *The Sumerians: Their History, Culture and Character*, University of Chicago Press, Chicago, 1963 p. 153–155. An excellent commentary on the text is given by Charles Penglase in his *Greek Myths and Mesopotamia: Parallels and Influence in the Homeric Hymns and Hesiod*, Routledge, London, 1994; see especially Ch. 2, p. 13 f.

8. For more background on Sumerian religious literature see Jeremy Black. Graham Cunningham, Eleanor Robson and Gabor Zolyomi, trans., *The Literature of Sumer*, Oxford University Press, New York, 2004; see also Samuel Kramer's, *The Sumerians: Their History, Culture and Character:*

9. We have used Stephanie Dalley's translation of *The Descent of Ishtar to the Underworld* which appears in her *Myths from Mesopotamia: Creation, the Flood, Gilgamesh and Others*, p. 154–162, Another recent translation of *The Descent of Ishtar to the Under*world appears in B.R. Foster's *Before the Muses*, CDL Press, Bethesda, Md., 2005. An earlier translation pf the text that is still useful appears in James Pritchard's, *The Ancient Near East: An Anthology of Texts and Pictures*, vol. I, p. 80–85; for more details on the relationship between Inanna and Ishtar see S. Allen, *The Splintered Divine*, de Gruyter Publishers, Berlin, 2015.

10. Stephanie Dalley, trans., *Myths from Mesopotamia: Creation, the Flood, Gilgamesh and Other*, p. 81.

11. Apostolos N. Athanassakis, trans., *The Homeric Hymns: Translation, Introduction and Notes*, Johns Hopkins University Press, Baltimore, 1976, 1–11.

12. Homer, *Hymn to Demeter*, line 18.
13. *Ibid.*, line 248.
14. *Ibid.*, line 305–313.
15. *Ibid.*
16. *Ibid.*, line, 393–404.
17. *Ibid.*, line, 472.
18. *Ibid.*, line 475–482.
19. *Ibid.*
20. Frederick Cole Babbit, trans., *Plutarch's Moralia*, Book V, Loeb Classical Library, Harvard University Press, Cambridge, 1936. See also James Frazer's commentary on the myth of Isis and Osiris in his *The Golden Bough*, p. 420–447.

21. For more on the myths and rituals associated with the god Isis and Osiris see James Frazer, *The Golden Bough*, p. 420–437.
22. *Ibid.*, p. 433–434.
23. See J. Gwyn Griffiths, *The Isis Book*, Brill Publishers, Leiden, 1975, pp1–7; see also John Stephens, *Ancient Mediterranean Religions Myth, Ritual and Religious Experience*, 168–169.
24. Apuleius, *The Golden Ass*, trans., Jack Lindsey, Indiana University Press, Bloomington, 1960, Book XI p. 237–238.
25. *Ibid.*
26. *Ibid.*, p. 239.
27. *Ibid.*, p. 249.
28. Snorri Sturluson, *The Prose Edda*, trans., Jesse Byock, p. 65–70.

Chapter Five

1. For an excellent introduction to the religious beliefs and practices of ancient Mesopotamian religion see Tammi Schneider, *Introduction to Ancient Mesopotamian Religion*, Wm. Eerdmans Publishing, Grand Rapids, Mich., 2011; cf., John Stephens, *Ancient Mediterranean Religions: Myth, Ritual and Religious Experience*, p. 12–29.

2. Stephanie Dalley, *Myths from Mesopotamia: Creation, The Flood, Gilgamesh and Others*, Oxford University Press, revised edition, New York, p. 96, Book IX. Ii, 2000; for additional critical essays on the *Gilgamesh Epic* see John Maier, ed., *Gilgamesh: A Reader*, Bolchazy-Carducci Publishers, Wauconda, Ill. 1997.

3. *Ibid.*, p. 97, IX, iii.
4. *Ibid.*, p. 102, X, ii.
5. *Ibid.*, p. 118, XI, iii.
6. *Ibid.*, p. 119, XI, vi.
7. *Beowulf*, trans., John McNamara, Barnes and Noble Classics Edition, New York New York, 2005, line 1361–1376, p. 46–47. Interesting comments comparing

Gilgamesh and Beowulf appear in Hamda Aliyeva's article entitled The Comparative Typology of the Heroic Figures in the Ancient Sumerian and Anglo-Saxon Epics" *Epistemologia-International Review;* for interpretive insights *on Beowulf see* Scott Gwara, *Heroic Identity in the World of Beowulf*, Brill Publishers, Leiden and Boston, 2008; see also *Interpretations of Beowulf: A Critical Anthology*, ed. R. D. Fulk, Indiana University Press, Bloomington.

    8. *Beowulf*, line 1258–1278.
    9. *Ibid.*, line 1384–1385.
    10. *Ibid.*, line 1386–1387.
    11. *Ibid.*, line 1607–1610.
    12. *Ibid.* line 2511–2537.
    13. *Ibid.*, line 2691–2693.
    14. *Ibid.*, line 2819–2820.
    15. *Ibid.*, line 3180–3182.

Chapter Six

    1. Cf., Frederick Streng, *Understanding Religious Life*, pp. 143–154.
    2. William James, *The Varieties of Religious Experience*, p. 339.
    3. *Ibid.*, p. 338.
    4. Marcus Aurelius, *Meditations*, trans, Robin Hard, Oxford University Press, Oxford, 2011.
    5. J.L. Moles, "The Career and Conversion of Dio Chrysostom," *Journal of Hellenic Studies*, vol. 98, 1978, p. 97.
    6. Philostratus, *Lives of the Sophists*, trans. W. Wright, Loeb Classical Library, Harvard University Press, New York, 1952, vs. 488; cf., J.L. Moles," The Career and Conversion of Dio Chrysostum," p. 97.
    7. For more on the use of mythopoeia by the ancient Greek sophists and philosophers see Fritz Graf's *Greek Mythology: An Introduction*, trans., Thomas Marier, John Hopkins University Press, Baltimore, 1 996, p.,178ff; the influence of Pythagoras' thought upon Plato is discussed by Phillip Sidney Horky in his *Plato and Pythagoreanism*, Oxford, 2013. The relationship between Orphism and Pythagoreanism is discussed by W.K.C. Guthrie in his *Orpheus and Greek Religion*, Princeton University Press, Princeton, New Jersey, 1993.
    8. See Catherin Collobert, Pierre Destree and Francisco A. Gonzalez, eds., *Plato and Myth: Studies on the Use and Status of Platonic Myths*, Brill Publishers, Leiden, Netherlands, 2012.
    9. Plato, *Apol.* 17A–33B.
    10. Plato, *Republic*, 615A, trans. G.M. Grube, revised by C.D.C. Reeve, Hackett Publishing Co., Indianapolis, 1992, p. 286.
    11. Plato, Republic, 617D.
    12. cf., Robert Grant, *Miracle and Natural Law*, North Holland Publishing, Amsterdam, 1952.
    13. Cicero's short narrative entitled *The Dream of Scipio* appears in *On the Republic* VI,9–26 and is included in *Ancient Roman Religion*, edited and translated by Frederick Grant, Liberal Arts Press, New York, 1957, p. 149ff.
    14. Cicero, *On the Republic*, VI, 15.
    15. *Ibid*.
    16. *Ibid.* VI, 16.
    17. *Ibid.*, VI, 25.
    18. *Ibid.*, VI, 26.
    19. *Ibid.*, VI, 29.

Chapter Seven

    1. The ethical ramifications connected to various forms of religious experience are explored by Frederick Streng, in his *Understanding Religious Life*, p. 99–109.
    2. *Ibid.*, p. 103.
    3. Cf., Eva von Dassow, ed., O Goelet and R Faulkner, trans., *The Egyptian Book of the Dead: The Book of Going Forth*, Chronicle Books, San Francisco, 2015.
    4. For more details on ancient Egyptian religion see Emily Teeter, *Religion and Ritual in Ancient Egypt*, Cambridge University Press, New York, 2011; for more on the Egyptian Book of the Dead see *The Egyptian Book of the Dead: The Book of Going Forth by Day*, ed. Eva von Dassow, trans. O Goelet and R Faulkner.

Chapter Notes—Seven

5. Cf., R.C. Zaehner, *The Dawn and Twilight of Zoroastrianism*, Phoenix Press, London, 2003.

6. R. C Zaehner, *The Teachings of the Magi*, Allen and Unwin, London, 1956, p. 133–138; cf., Mircea Eliade, ed., *Sacred Texts from Around the World*, p. 359–363.

7. Mircea Eliade, ed., *Sacred Texts from Around the World*, p. 360–361.

8. *Ibid.*, p. 361.

9. *Ibid.*, p. 361.

10. *Ibid.*, p. 362.

11. *Ibid.*

12. Jeremiah 30, 2–3.

13. John Hick, *Death and Eternal Life*, Harper and Row, New York, 1976 p. 70. For further discussion on the date of the Book of Job see S. Vargon, "Date of Composition of the Book of Job," *JQR*,91 (2001), p. 377–394.

14. *Ibid.*

15. Job 10, 20–22; cf., John Hick, *Death and Eternal Life*, p. 59.

16. Ps. 88:3–5, 10–12.

17. Job 17.14–16.

18. Job 14.11–12.

19. Willis Barnstone, *The Other Bible*, p. 499. Barnstone has English translations of many Hellenistic Jewish and early Christian texts mentioned in this chapter including 1st and 2nd Enoch, Baruch, 4 Ezra, the Gospel of Bartholomew, the Gospel of Nicodemus, the Gospel of Peter and the Apocalypse of Paul. There are several general studies of Judeo-Christian apocalypses; cf., Martha Himmelfarb, *Ascent to Heaven in Jewish and Christian Apocalypses*, Oxford University Press, New York, 2013; Greg Carey, *Ultimate Things: An Introduction to Jewish and Christian Apocalyptic Literature*, Chalice Press, St. Louis, Missouri, 2005. See especially Ch. 1 on I Enoch and the Book of Daniel. There are several excellent scholarly studies of individual Judeo-Christian apocalypses. A collection of scholarly essays on the *Apocalypse of Paul* appears in Jan N. Bremmer's and Istvan Czachesz' *Visio Pauli and the Gnostic Apocalypse of Paul*, Peeters, Leuven, Netherlands, 2007; see also Jan Bremmer and Istvan Czachesz' *The Apocalypse of Peter*, Peeters, Leuven, Netherlands, 2003; see also *4 Ezra and 2 Baruch*, Michael E. Stone and Matthias Henz, trans., intro., and notes, Fortress Press, Minneapolis, 2013.

20. *Ibid.*, p. 499–500.

21. *Ibid.*, p. 517.

22. 1 Cor. 15.35–45.

23. Rev. 1.9–11.

24. *Ibid.*, 12.7–9.

25. *Ibid.*, 21.1–2.

26. *The Shepherd of Hermes*, 1.3, trans. J.B. Lightfoot, internet source www.earlychristianwritings.com.

Bibliography

Allen, Douglass. *Myth and Religion in Mircea Eliade.* Routledge, New York, 2002.
Allen, S. *The Splintered Divine.* de Gruyter Publishers, Berlin, 2015.
Apuleius. *The Golden Ass.* Trans. Jack Lindsey. Indiana University Press, Bloomington, 1960.
Barbour, Ian. *Religion and Science: Historical and Contemporary Issues.* HarperCollins, New York, 1997.
Barnstone, Willis, ed. *The Other Bible.* Harper One, New York, 2005.
Aelius. *Aristides and the Sacred Tales*, ed. and trans. C.A. Behr. A.M. Hakkert, Amsterdam, 1968.
Beowulf. Trans. John McNamara. Barnes and Noble Classics Edition. New York, 2005.
Berger, Peter. *The Sacred Canopy.* Doubleday, New York, 1967.
Black, Jeremy, et al., eds. *The Literature of Sumer.* Oxford University Press, New York, 2004.
Bremmer, Jan, and Istvan Czachesz. *The Apocalypse of Peter.* Peeters Publishers, Leuven, Netherlands, 2003.
_____. *Visio Pauli and the Gnostic Apocalypse of Paul.* Peeters Publishers, Leuven, Netherlands, 2007.
Capps, Walter. *Religious Studies: The Making of a Discipline.* Fortress Press, Minneapolis, 1996.
Carey, Greg. *Ultimate Things: An Introduction to Jewish and Christian Apocalyptic Literature.* Chalice Press, St. Louis, Missouri, 2005.
Collobert, Catherin, Pierre Destree and Francisco, A. Gonzalez, eds. *Plato and Myth: Studies on the Use and Status of Platonic Myths.* Brill Publishers, Leiden, Netherlands, 2012.
Comstock, Richard W. *The Study of Religion and Primitive Religions.* Harper and Row, New York, 1972.
Dalley, Stephenie. *Myths from Mesopotamia: Creation, the Flood, Gilgamesh and Others.* Oxford University Press, 2009.
de Vries, Jan. *The Study of Religion: A Historical Approach.* Trans. Kees Bolle. Harcourt Brace, New York, 1967.
Dodds, E.R. *The Greeks and the Irrational.* University of California Press, Berkeley, 1951.
_____. *Pagan and Christian in an Age of Anxiety.* Cambridge University Press, New York, 1965.

Bibliography

Dronke, Ursala. *The Poetic Eddas: Mythological Poems*. Clarendon Press, London, 1997.
Durkheim, Émile. *The Elementary Forms of the Religious Life*. Trans. Carol Cosman. Oxford University Press, World Classics Edition, Oxford, 2008.
Edelstein, Emma and Ludwig, ed. and trans., *Asclepius: A Collection and Interpretation of the Testimonies*, two vols., Arno Press, New York, 1975.
Eliade, Mircea,. *Essential Sacred Writings from Around the World*. Harper and Row, New York, 1967.
_____. *A History of Religious Ideas*. University of Chicago Press, vol. 2, Chicago, 1978.
_____. *Myth and Reality*. Trans. W. Trask. Harper and Row, New York, 1963.
_____. *Patterns in Comparative Religion*. Trans. Rosemary Sheed. Signet, New York, 1963.
_____. *The Sacred and the Profane*. Trans. W. Trask. Harcourt Brace, New York, 1959.
Festugiere, A.J. *Personal Religion among the Greeks*. University of California Press, Berkeley, 1954.
Foster, B.R. *Before the Muses*. CDL Press, Bethesda Maryland, 2005.
Frazer, James. *The Golden Bough*. Macmillan Paperback Edition, Macmillan Publishing, New York, 1963.
Freud, Sigmund. *Totem and Taboo*. Trans. A.A. Brill. Moffat Yard and Co., New York, 1918.
Fulk, R.D., ed. *Interpretations of Beowulf: A Critical Anthology*. Indiana University Press, Bloomington, 1991.
Graf, Fritz, *Greek Mythology: An Introduction*. Trans. Thomas Marier. Johns Hopkins University Press, Baltimore, 1996.
Grant, Frederick, ed. and trans. *Ancient Roman Religion*. Liberal Arts Press, New York, 1957.
_____, ed. and trans. *Hellenistic Religions*. Bobbs and Merrill, New York, 1953.
Grant, Robert, *Miracle and Natural Law*. North Holland Publishing, Amsterdam, 1952.
Griffiths, J. Gwyn, ed. and trans. *The Isis Book*. Brill Publishers, Leiden, 1975.
Gwara, Scott. *Heroic Identity in the World of Beowulf*. Brill Publishers, Leiden and Boston, 2008.
Hennecke, Edgar, and Schneemelcher, Wilhelm, eds., and trans. *New Testament Apocrypha*, vol. 2. Westminster Press, Louisville and London, 1963.
Herodotus. *The Histories*. Trans. G.C. Macaulay. Barnes and Noble Edition, New York, 2004.
Hesiod. *Theogony and Works and Days*. Trans. M.L. West. Oxford University Press, Oxford, 2008.
Hick, John. *Death and Eternal Life*. Harper and Row, New York, 1976.
Himmelfarb, Martha. *Ascent to Heaven in Jewish and Christian Apocalypses*. Oxford University Press, New York, 2013;
Hinnelis, John, ed. *The Routledge Companion to the Study of Religion*. Routledge, New York and London, 1999.
Homer. *The Iliad*. Trans. Robert Fagles. Penguin Classics, New York, 1991.
_____. *The Odyssey of Homer*. Trans. Richmond Lattimore. Perennial Edition, Harper and Row, New York, 1999.
The Homeric Hymns: Translation, Introduction and Notes. Trans. Apostolos Athanassakis. Johns Hopkins Press, Baltimore, 1976.

Bibliography

Horky, Phillip S. *Plato and Pythagoreanism*. Oxford University Press, Oxford, 2013.

Horsfall, Nicholas. *Virgil, Aeneid 6: A Commentary: Introduction, Text and Translation*. De Gruyter, Berlin, 2013.

Jacobsen, Thorkild. *The Harps That Once*. Yale University Press, New Haven, 1987.

_____. *The Treasury of Darkness: A History of Mesopotamian Religion*. Yale University Press, New Haven, 1976.

James, William. *The Varieties of Religious Experience*. Macmillan Publishers, New York, 1961.

Katz, Steven, ed. *Mysticism and Philosophical Analysis*. Oxford University Press, New York, 1978.

Kramer, Samuel. *The Sumerians: Their History, Culture and Character*. University of Chicago Press, Chicago, 1963.

Lambert, W.G. *Ancient Mesopotamian Religion and Mythology*. Ed. A.R. George and T.M. Oshima. Mohr Siebeck Publishers, Tubingen Germany, 2016.

Larson, Gerald, Scott C. Littleton and Jaan Puhvel, eds. *Myth in Indo-European Antiquity*. University of California Press, Berkeley, 1974.

Lucian. *The Selected Satires of Lucian*. Ed. and trans., Lionel Casson. W.W. Norton, New York, 1968.

Maier, John, ed. *Gilgamesh: A Reader*. Bolchazy-Carducci Publishers, Wauconda, Ill., 1997.

Martin, Craig, and Russell T. McCutcheon, eds. *Religious Experience: A Reader*. Routledge, London, 2014.

Martin, Luther. *Hellenistic Religions: An Introduction*. Oxford University Press, Oxford, 1987.

Meyer, Marvin, ed. *The Ancient Mysteries: A Sourcebook of Sacred Texts*. University of Pennsylvania Press, Philadelphia, 1987.

_____. *The Nag Hammadi Scriptures*. HarperCollins, New York, 2007.

Moreman, Christopher, M. *Beyond the Threshold: Afterlife Beliefs and Experiences in World Religions*. Rowman and Littlefield, Lanham, Md., 2008.

Nilsson, Martin. *A History of Greek Religion*. Oxford at the Clarendon Press, London, 1949.

Nock, A.D. *Conversion: The Old and the New in Religion from Alexander the Great to Augustine of Hippo*. Oxford University Press, Oxford, 1952.

The Orphic Hymns. Trans. Apostolos Athanassakis. Scholars Press, Missoula Montana, 1977.

Otto, Rudolf. *The Idea of the Holy*. Oxford University Press, Paperback Edition, London, 1959.

Ovid. *Metamorphoses*. Trans. Rolfe Humphries. Indiana University Press, Bloomington, 1983.

Parrinder, Geoffrey, ed. *World Religions: From Ancient History to the Present.*, Facts on File Publications, New York, 1971.

Pausanius. *Description of Greece*, 2 vols. Trans. Peter Levi. Penguin Books, London, 1971.

Pearson, Birger. *Ancient Gnosticism: Tradition and Literature*. Fortress Press, Minneapolis, 2007.

Bibliography

Penglase, Charles. *Greek Myths and Mesopotamia: Parallels and Influence in the Homeric Hymns and Hesiod.* Routledge, London, 1994.
Perkell, Christine, G., ed. *Reading Vergil's Aeneid: An Interpretive Guide.* University of Oklahoma Press, Norman, 1999.
Plato. *The Republic of Plato.* Trans. B. Jowett. Random House, Anchor Book Edition, New York, 1973.
Plutarch's Moralia, Book V. Trans. Frederick Cole Babbit. Loeb Classical Library, Harvard University Press, Cambridge, Mass., 1936.
Pritchard, James, ed. *Ancient Near Eastern Texts,* 2 vols. Princeton University Press, Princeton, New Jersey, 1950.
Rupke, Jorg. *On Roman Religion: Lived Religion and the Individual in Ancient Rome.* Cornell University Press, Ithaca, N.Y., 2016.
Russell, Bertrand. *The History of Western Philosophy.* Simon & Schuster, New York, 1946.
Sanders, Seth. *From Adapa to Enoch.* Mohr Siebeck Publications, Tübingen, 2017.
Schaumberg, Michael, ed. *Contemporary Theories of Religion: A Critical Companion.* Routledge, New York, 2009.
Schneider, Tammi. *An Introduction to Ancient Mesopotamian Religion.* Wm. B. Eerdmans Publishing, Grand Rapids, Mich., 2011.
Segal, Alan. *Life After Death: A History of the Afterlife in Western Religion.* Doubleday, New York, 2010.
Segal, Robert. *Myth: A Very Short Introduction,* 2nd edition. Oxford University Press, Oxford, 2015.
Smart, Ninian. *Dimensions of the Sacred: An Anatomy of the World's Beliefs.* University of California Press, Berkeley, 1999.
_____. *The Religious Experience.* Prentice Hall, New Jersey, 1996.
_____. *World Views: Cross-Cultural Explorations of Human Beliefs.* Prentice Hall, New York, 2000.
Stephens, John. *Ancient Mediterranean Religions: Myth, Ritual and Religious Experience.* Cambridge Scholars Press, Newcastle upon Tyne, UK, 2016.
_____. *The Dreams, and Visions of Aelius Aristides.* Gorgias Press, Piscataway, N.J., 2013.
Streng, Frederick, *Understanding Religious Life,* 2nd edition. Dickenson Publishing Co., Encino, California, 1976.
Sturluson, Snorri. *The Prose Edda.* Trans. Jesse L. Byock. Penguin Books, London, 2005.
Virgil. *The Aeneid.* Trans. Allen Mandelbaum. Bantam Classic Edition, New York, 1981.
von Dassow, Eva, ed.. *The Egyptian Book of the Dead: The Book of Going Forth by Day.* Trans. O. Goelet, and R. Faulkner. Chronicle Books, San Francisco, 2008.
Wach, Joaquin. *The Comparative Study of Religion.* Columbia Paperback Edition, New York, 1958.
Zaehner, R.C. *Concordant Discord: The Interdependence of Faiths.* Oxford University Press, London, 1970.
_____. *The Dawn and Twilight of Zoroastrianism.* Phoenix Press, London, 2003.
_____. *The Teachings of the Magi.* Allen and Unwin, London, 1956.

Index

abyss 19, 105, 141, 144
Adam 135, 144
Adapa 44–46, 165
Aelius Aristides 2, 65, 67, 157, 162; *see also* Sacred Tales
Aeneid 14, 31, 33, 36–42, 93, 117–118, 138, 151, 160; *see also* Virgil
Aeneus 30, 31, 36–41, 118, 120, 151, 152; *see also Aeneid*; Virgil
Aesir 90–91
Alexander the Great 162
All-Father 26; *see also* Norse mythology
Allah 124; *see also* Islam
Amun 20
Anchises 40–41
anthropomorphism 13
Anu 45–46
Apocalypse of Paul 145–146, 165
Apollonius of Tyana 110
Apuleius 16, 72, 85–86, 91, 153, 163; *see also Metamorphoses*
Arius 109
Artemis 54, 64
Aruru 94, 96
Ascension of Isaiah 61
asceticism 48, 54, 56, 63–64, 105
Asclepius 65–66, 162
Asgard 25–26, 90–91
astrology 118; *see also* divination
Athanasian Creed 107
Athena 54, 72
Athens 71–72, 113
Attis 6, 160; *see also* Cybele
Atum 19, 151
Augustine 162
Axis Mundi 25, 97, 159; *see also* Cosmic Tree

Babylonian Exile 20, 130, 132

Bacchanalia 57; *see also* Dionysius
Baldr's Descent to the Underworld 89–91
Barbour, Ian 28, 71, 157, 162
Baruch 134–135
Beowulf 20, 93–95, 99–105, 153, 163–164
Berger, Peter 9–10, 158
Bridge of the Requiter 128–129; *see also* Zoroastrianism
Buddha and Buddhism 10, 12, 49–50, 93, 109, 124

categories of religious experience 2, 28, 149, 157; *see also* dreams and visions; mysticism; numinous experience; paranormal experience
Cerberus 36, 38–39, 42–43
Charon 33, 38–39, 52–53
Christianity 28, 61, 69–70, 89, 93, 100, 107, 109–110, 124, 129, 137–139, 155; *see also* Gospels
Chung-yung (the mean) 124; *see also* Confucianism
Cicero 16, 106, 118–122, 154, 164; *see also The Dream of Scipio*
Circe 5, 33–34, 152
Claudius Ptolemy 20, 146, 155
Coffin Texts 44; *see also* religion, Egyptian
Comstock, W.R. 12, 158
Confucius and Confucianism 124–125
Constantine (Emperor) 100, 109
conversion, religious 61–62, 68–71, 152, 162
Corpus Hermeticum 59–60
Cosmic tree 25; *see also Axis Mundi*
cosmology: Biblical 20–21; Egyptian 19–20; Greco-Roman 22–23, 158; Mesopotamian 17–19; Norse 24–26; Orphic 53–55
Council of Nicaea 109
Cratylus 111; *see also* Plato

Index

creation myths 17, 19, 22, 151–152; Babylonian 18, 20, 26, 150; Ennead of Heliopolis 19; Genesis 21–23
Cult of Asclepius 65, 162; see also Aelius Aristides; incubation; Sacred Tales
Cybele 6, 160; see also Attis

daemon 56, 113, 116–117
Dalley, Stephanie 158, 161, 163
Daniel 59, 67, 152, 165
Dante 15
death and re-birth 160
De Divinatione 118; see also Cicero
Demeter 16, 43, 72–73, 76, 78–83, 91, 118, 163; see also mysteries
Descent of Ishtar to the Netherworld 76, 77, 163
Dharma (the Way) 125
Diodorus of Siculus 83, 161
Dio of Prusa 110
Dionysius (cult)54, 56–57, 152; see also entheos; omophagia
divination 34, 65, 118; see also astrology
Dodds, E.R 162
Domitian (Emperor) 110–111
The Dream of Scipio 16, 117–119, 154, 164
dreams and visions 3–4, 65–67, 90, 105, 157, 162; see also Aelius Aristides; Paul, the Apostle; Perpetua; Thessalos of Tralles
dukka (suffering) 93; see also Buddha and Buddhism
Durkheim, Emile 7, 157
Dumuzi 45, 75–76
dying and rising gods 6, 71–73, 89–91, 153, 160; see also Attis; Cybele; Isis; Osiris

Eleusis 42, 71–72, 78; see also Demeter; mysteries
Eliade, Mircea 9–10, 25, 29, 158–161, 165
Elijah and Elisha 46–47
Empedocles 54
Enkidu 94–97
Ennead of Heliopolis 19
Enoch 16, 59, 130, 132–134, 137, 148, 155, 165
entheos (the divine within) 56–57; see also Dionysius
Enuma Elish 15, 17, 23, 26, 150
Epic of Gilgamesh 13, 16, 93–99, 153; see also Gilgamesh
Epicureanism 119
Erebus 15, 31, 39, 118, 151
Erishkigal 74
Euphemerus 11
Eurydice 52–53; see also Orpheus

exclusivism, religious 69–70
Exodus 20, 28–29, 158
expression, religious 7, 57–58, 64
Ezekiel 147
4 Ezra 135–136, 165

Fates 25, 37
Fields of Gladness 41
Frazer, James 6–7, 157, 160, 163; see also Golden Bough
Freud, Sigmund 7, 157, 164
Furies 39–40, 53

Gates of Horn and Ivory 42
Gateway to the Underworld 37, 76–77, 125
Geertz, Clifford 9–10, 157
Genesis 15, 20–22, 58, 132, 150
Gilgamesh 13, 16, 94–99, 102, 105, 153; see also Epic of Gilgamesh
Ginnungagap 24, 26
Golden Apples of Hesperides 42
Golden Bough 6, 37–38, 40, 157, 160, 163; see also Frazer, James
Gospels: Bartholomew 143–145, 165; Luke 140; Mark 140; Nicodemus 136, 143, 145; Peter 20, 59, 136–137, 145–147, 155, 165
Greco-Roman philosophy 109–110, 119
Greek Sophists 112, 164
Grendel 94, 99–103; see also Beowulf

Hades 33, 34, 36, 43, 52, 54, 55, 79, 80, 83, 140, 144
Heliopolis Creation Myth 19–20, 150
Heraclitus 54
Hercules 32, 36–43, 70, 112
Hermes 42, 80, 83, 142–143, 165
Hermod the Bold 90
hero cults 32, 160
Herodotus 64, 85, 162
Hesiod 22–24, 26, 113, 150, 159, 163; see also Theogony
Hinduism 49–50, 109, 124–125
Homer 12–17, 31, 56, 72, 75, 78, 112, 117–118, 126, 131, 138, 160, 163; see also Iliad; Odyssey
Homeric Hymn to Demeter 16, 76, 78, 81–83, 91, 119; see also Homer; Iliad; Odyssey
Horus 19, 81, 84
Hrothgar 100–102
Huwana 96

Iliad 11, 33, 160; see also Homer; Homeric Hymn to Demeter and Odyssey
immortality 13, 38, 42, 44, 54, 55, 58, 71, 73, 79, 83, 94, 99, 105, 109, 119, 122, 126, 130, 136, 138, 139, 153, 160

Index

Inanna's Descent to the Underworld 74, 76, 91, 162
incubation 65
ineffability 51, 63
initiation 72, 78, 86–89
Isaac 28, 59, 144
Ishtar 76–78, 80, 91, 96–97
Isis 6, 16, 64, 69–73, 83–87, 91, 161, 163; see also Myth of Isis and Osiris; Osiris
Islam 15, 70, 107, 109, 124

Jacob 28, 58–59, 144
James, William 28, 68, 108, 161–162, 164
Jeremiah 130, 134, 165
Jesus' Descent to Hell 61–62, 109, 139–140, 143–145
Jewish apocalyptic literature 132, 136–137
Jewish Pseudepigrapha 132
Job 33, 130–131, 160, 165

katabasis (journey downward) 30, 151
Katz, Steven 27–28, 159, 161
Kramer, S. 163
Kronos 23, 78

Labors of Hercules 32
Larson, Gerald 12, 158
Laws of Manu 125
Loki 90–91
Lucian 69, 162; see also Peregrinus
Lucius 85–89; see also Metamorphoses

mana 29, 32
Mandulis 66, 162
Marcus Aurelius (Emperor) 110, 164; see also Meditations
Marduk 18–19, 21, 76
Martyrdom of St. Perpetua and Felicitas 66
meditation 49
Meditations 164; see also Marcus Aurelius
Medusa 42
Mencius 125; see also Confucius and Confucianism
Meno (Plato) 111; see also Plato
Menok 16, 127, 148, 155; see also Zoroastrianism
Metamorphoses (Apuleius) 52, 72, 85–91, 153; see also mystery religions
Michael the archangel 144, 147
Midgard (Earth) 25
miracles 56
Mithra 72
Modgud the gatekeeper 90
monotheism 68, 70, 153
Mosaic Covenant 16

Moses 28
Mt. Sinai 20, 28
Muhammad 15; see also Islam
Muller, Max 6, 160
mysterium fascinans and mysterium tremendum 8; see also Otto, Rudolf
mystery religions 55, 57–58, 71–72, 81, 85, 91, 93, 110; see also Demeter; Story of Isis and Osiris
mystes (initiates) 72, 161–162; see also mystery religions
mysticism 27–28, 48–51, 62, 67, 152, 159, 161; see also dreams and visions; paranormal experience
The Myth of Er (Plato) 16, 41, 112–118, 121, 154; see also The Dream of Scipio
The Myth of Isis and Osiris (Plutarch) 16, 71, 81–85, 91; see also Isis; Osiris

Nag Hammadi 60, 161
negative theology 61, 64; see also Plotinus
netherworld 30, 34, 37, 76, 151
New Testament 59, 61, 132, 137, 140, 145; see also Gospels
Nifhel (Dark World) 26
Nifl-heim (Underworld) 25–26
Nilsson, Martin 32, 150
Ninshubur 71, 73
Nirvana 93
non-duality 49–51, 63
Norns (fates) 25
Norse mythology 33, 89, 150–151
numinous experience 2, 15–16, 27–31, 43, 46–51, 62, 67, 91, 108, 149–151; see also categories of religious experience

Odin 24–25, 90; see also Baldr's Descent to the Underworld; Norse mythology
Odysseus 15, 31–41, 102, 111, 117, 121–122, 151–152; see also Homer; Odyssey
Odyssey 11, 13, 15, 31–36, 39, 93, 117, 138, 151, 160; see also Homer; Homeric Hymn to Demeter and Iliad; Odysseus
Omophagia 57; see also Dionysus
On the Nature of the Gods (Cicero) 118, 151, 159; see also The Dream of Scipio
oracles 30; Delphic 95, 110; Trophonius 31, 151
Orpheus 30, 52–55, 116, 118, 161, 164; see also The Story of Orpheus and Eurydice
Orphism 51–57, 67, 111, 152, 161, 164
Osiris 6, 16, 19, 73, 81–85, 88–91, 126, 148, 155, 160, 163; see also Isis; The Myth of Isis and Osiris
Ouranos 22–23, 57, 150
Ovid 52–53, 118

Index

paganism 12, 70–73, 152
Palestinian Judaism 137
Parable of Sheep and Goats 140
paranormal experience 48–51, 59; *see also* dreams and visions; mysticism
Patanjali 49
Paul, the Apostle 61–62, 136–139, 145–148, 165
Paulus 119–120
Pausanias 31, 54, 159, 161
Peregrinus 69–70, 88
Pergamum 65, 140; *see also* Asclepius; Cult of Asclepius
Perpetua 66, 152, 162
Phaedo (Plato) 111, 113; *see also* Plato
Pharisees 130, 132
pilgrimage 64–65, 124
Plain of Forgetfulness 117; *see also Aeneid*; Virgil
Plato 16, 41, 55, 58, 106, 109–119, 121, 132, 154, 161, 164; *see also The Dream of Scipio*; *Meno*; *Phaedo*; *Republic*; *Symposium*; *Timeaus*
Plotinus 61, 63–64, 67, 162; *see also* mysticism; negative theology
Plutarch 71, 81, 84, 91, 163; *see also The Myth of Isis and Osiris*
Poetic and Prose Eddas 15, 24, 26, 151; *see also* Norse mythology
Poimandres 60
polytheism 100, 153
Porphyry 63, 162
Pre-Socratics 11, 54–55, 112
Pritchard, James 158, 161, 163
Prodicus 55, 112
prophecy 34–35, 137
Protagoras 11, 55
Psalms 47, 131
Pyramid Texts 15, 44; *see also* religion, Egyptian
Pythagoreanism 111, 164

Ragnarok 24, 91; *see also* Norse mythology
reincarnation 41, 111
religion: archaic 34; definition 8–10; Egyptian 19–20, 44, 126; Greek 23, 32, 71; Mesopotamian 96, 126; origin and essence 5–8; Roman 11, 71, 118
Republic 55, 112–114, 118, 161, 164; *see also* Plato
resurrection of the dead 129–132, 137, 139–142, 146, 148
Revelation of John 59
Rig Vedas 125
River Gjoll 90
River Lethe 40–41

River Styx 33, 37–38, 52–53, 98
Road to Hel 90

Sacred Tales 65, 162; *see also* Aelius Aristides
Satan 18, 62, 100, 141, 143–145
Scipio Africanus 119–121
scorpion men 97
shamanism 4, 30–32, 52–53
Shamash 97–98
Sheol 33, 131, 133, 135, 138
Shepherd of Hermes 142–143, 165
Sibyl of Cumae 37
Sibyl's Prophecy 24, 159
Sisyphus 39, 53
skepticism 54, 119
Smart, Ninian 10, 49, 51, 52, 158, 161
Socrates 69, 111, 113; *see also* Plato
soma-sema doctrine 55; *see also* dualism
stoicism 110, 119
The Story of Orpheus and Eurydice (Ovid) 52–53
Streng, Frederick 159, 161, 161–162, 164
sun-worship 19–20
Symposium 113; *see also* Plato

Tammuz 46, 76–77
Tartarus 15, 23, 37, 39–43, 115
teleological argument 108
theism 48, 51, 61, 124
Theogony 15, 22–23, 150, 155; *see also* Hesiod
Theseus 15, 43
Thessalos of Tralles 65–67, 162
Thor 6, 25
Thurii, South Italy 56
Timaeus 113; *see also* Plato
Tisiphone 39; *see also* Furies
Titans 23, 40, 54, 150; *see also* Hesiod; *Theogony*
Torah 20–21, 128
Totem and Taboo 7, 157; *see also* Freud, Sigmund
transmigration of the soul 111
Tuat 126, 148, 155; *see* religion, Egyptian
Typhon 81–83; *see also* Isis and Osiris

Upanishads 49, 161
Urshanabi (boatman) 29
Uruk 94–95; *see also Epic of Gilgamesh*; Gilgamesh
Utnapishtim 98

Valhalla 26, 90
vegetarianism 51, 56; *see also* asceticism
Virgil 31, 36, 39, 41, 47, 138, 160; *see also Aeneid*

Index

Vision of Tundale 159–160
Void 22, 24

Wach, Joachim 170
Waters of Death 98
Wiglaf 94, 104–105
Wittgenstein, Ludwig 9, 157

Xenophanes 11–12; *see also* Pre-Socratics; stoicism

Yahweh 20–22, 151
Yggdrasil (Ash Tree) 24–25; *see also Axis Mundi*; Cosmic Tree
Yoga Sutras{e49

Zechariah 147
Zeus 22–23, 32, 40, 54, 70, 79–83, 118; *see also* religion, Greek
Zoroastrianism 127, 130, 155, 165
Zosimus of Panapolis 66 162